# The Family Business

## Its Governance for Sustainability

Fred Neubauer
and
Alden G. Lank

Foreword by Professor John L. Ward

First published 1998 by
MACMILLAN PRESS LTD
Houndmills, Basingstoke, Hampshire RG21 6XS
and London
Companies and representatives
throughout the world

ISBN 0–333–69299–3

A catalogue record for this book is available
from the British Library.

10   9   8   7   6   5   4   3
07   06   05   04   03   02   01

Copy-edited and typeset by Povey–Edmondson
Tavistock and Rochdale, England

Printed and bound in Great Britain by
Creative Print & Design (Wales), Ebbw Vale

*To our wives*
**Magda and Connie**

*and*

*To* **Frank Tilley**
*the Canadian owner-manager who launched the Family Business Area at IMD and without whose urging this book might never have been written*

# Contents

**Part VI   Putting Governance Insights into Practical Use**

# Foreword

For the family-owned business, good governance makes all the difference. Family firms with effective governance practices are more likely to do strategic planning and to do succession planning. On average, they grow faster and live longer. Moreover, they are more likely to develop the important formal policies addressing critical family business issues such as redemption, family employment, dividends, etc.

Then why do so few business-owning families have effective boards and regular family meetings? For example, in North America we find fewer than 15 per cent of all mid- to large-sized family firms have either an independent board or family meetings. Many, many fewer have a formal family governance system as proposed by Fred Neubauer and Alden Lank in this book.

My experience is that the primary reasons so few business-owning families avail themselves of the benefits of effective governance are that they do not imagine the possibilities and they do not know how to do it. Simply put, they do not have good models and helpful instructors to guide the way.

This book, *The Family Business: Its Governance for Sustainability*, does just that. It provides excellent and motivating real examples from businesses and families all over the world. The authors, Fred Neubauer and Alden Lank, also provide clear guidance on how to organise and manage the governance systems. Between them, they have studied the governance systems of more business-owning families than anyone I know.

Families who do have independent boards and regular family meetings will also benefit from this book. Neubauer and Lank provide new and powerful ways to use the business board effectively. They keep the focus of the board on the most appropriate and most valuable tasks. Too often boards bog down in operational details and uncertain direction.

The authors also help families clarify the often confusing language of family governance. They provide clear definitions and roles for the family, the family assembly, and the family council. Most helpfully, they show how the business board and the family's governance system interrelate. It is one thing to have the benefit of effective business and family governance systems. It is even better to harness the synergy of the two together.

The importance of family business governance is just now being appreciated. The early pioneering work of Dr Léon Danco opened the door. Now university-sponsored educational programmes for business-owning families, such as the outstanding international programme at the International Institute for Management Development in Lausanne, Switzerland, are convincing business-owning families that they are not alone and that they can take concrete steps to better secure their future and their dream of family continuity.

Through these programmes, which have now reached more than 10 000 successful family firms, more and more are learning the special value of effective governance. They have heard those who do have independent boards and family meetings praise their contributions. They have begun to imagine the strength good governance offers employees, the family's shareholders, and the other critical constituents of the firm. Perhaps they even sense a moral responsibility of accountability to others.

Now, with this book by Neubauer and Lank, families in business can better understand the rich power of effective governance. They can also learn how to make it work for them.

JOHN L. WARD
*Ralph Marotta Professor of Private Enterprise*
*Loyola University, Chicago*

# Acknowledgements

There are many people to whom we owe thanks for helping us to give birth to this book. In the first place, we would like to express our gratitude to Dr Peter Lorange, President of the International Institute for Management Development (IMD), Lausanne; ever faithful to his philosophy that teaching at IMD should be research-based, he has been totally supportive of the project, both the research underlying this book as well as the writing.

Others to whom we owe a heartfelt word of thanks for their contributions, directly and indirectly, to this book are our colleagues at IMD. They were all too willing to give us access to some of their research and to offer advice generously. In particular we would like to mention Professor Stewart Hamilton and Industry Professor Joachim Schwass. Furthermore each of IMD's Executives-in-Residence, Family Business Area – Frank Tilley, George Raymond, Dr Gerald Stempler, Richard Owens and Jonathan Pellegrin have influenced our thinking on many of the subjects treated in this book.

Three other persons deserve special mention, namely those on the original faculty of IMD's Leading the Family Business (LFB) educational programme, which has been offered twice annually since December 1988. The original team comprised Dr John Davis, Dr Ivan Lansberg and Professor John L. Ward. While only John Ward remains on the current LFB team, all three have continued to share with the authors their deep knowledge and experience about family business throughout the intervening years. Our thanks, friends.

We also wish to acknowledge the very special contributions of the CEO of 'Bergman' AB and the Chairman of the 'Bergman' Family Council (the family name has been changed). They have kindly allowed us to quote extensively from the Bergman Values and Policy statement. The authors have had the pleasure of working with the Bergman family and its enterprise over several years to help them in developing a new governance system. This, in no small measure, has heightened our awareness and deepened our knowledge of the challenges faced by venerable family firms in the 'cousins' confederation' stage of development. In a similar vein, we thank the Wild Family Council for permitting us to cite their unique 'Constitution Committee' in Chapter 4.

We are also very grateful to Gordon Adler, Senior Writer at IMD, for his patience in editing our manuscript. Furthermore we gladly acknowledge the substantial contribution that two of IMD's Research Associates – Dr Monica Wagen and Denise Kenyon-Rouvinez – have made to the book. We are particularly indebted to them for drafting the majority of the different mini-cases used throughout the book to illustrate our conceptual schemes.

Our secretaries Anne-Marie Tassi and Juliet Greco played a vital role in producing the typescript. They never lost their patience and good humour as they worked their way through the different drafts of the manuscript. Without such a solid 'back office' our lives as authors would have been much more difficult, particularly towards the end of the project.

The never-failing support of Nicole Vautier and Christiane Schelling of IMD's documentation department should also be recognised here; no effort to assist us was too much for these gracious ladies.

Last, but by no means least, a particular word of thanks to the many family business 'practitioners' (for us this word means those in family businesses) who helped us to shape and test our ideas. Many of them are alumni of IMD's Leading the Family Business programme; others we met during consulting assignments. Without them, this book would have lost much of its practical relevance.

Despite all this generous support, we as authors do, of course, accept all responsibility for the content of this work. We hope the reader will find it stimulating, provocative and ultimately useful.

FRED NEUBAUER
ALDEN G. LANK

The authors and publishers wish to thank the following for permission to use copyright material: Alfred A. Knopf, Inc. for Figure 2.1 from Levinson *et al.*, *The Seasons of a Man's Life*, 1978; American Management Association for Figure 2,2 from Adizes, 'Organizational Passages: Diagnosing and Treating Lifecycle Problems of Organizations' *Organization Dynamics*, Summer 1979; Business Owner Resources for Tables 2.1, 2.2 and 2.3 from Ward, *Keeping the Family Business Healthy: How to Plan for Continuing Growth, Profitability and Family Leadership*; *Financial Times* for the article, 'Campari Publishes Accounts for the First Time'; Harvard Business School for Figure 2.3 from Greiner, 'Evolution and Revolution as Organizations Grow', *Harvard Business Review*, July–August 1972, and Figure 7.2 from Collins and Porras, 'Building your Company's Vision', *Harvard Business Review*, September–October 1996; Johnson & Johnson for permission to use their Credo in Chapter 7; NetMarquee Inc. for Figure 1.3. Every effort has been made to trace all the copyright-holders, but if any have been inadvertently overlooked the publishers will be pleased to make the necessary arrangement at the first opportunity.

# Prologue:
# What this Book is About

Through gale or calm, now swift, now slack, yet steadily careering;
Type of the modern – *emblem of motion and power* – pulse of the continent
(Walt Whitman, 1819–1892, 'To a Locomotive in Winter').

A century and half ago in Berlin, on 1 October 1847, Werner von Siemens and his partner Johann Georg Halske formed the Telegraphenbauanstalt Siemens & Halske, the forebear of today's vast Siemens empire, a group of firms that for all practical purposes is still largely influenced by the Siemens family. In those early days, Werner's cousin Georg Friedrich Siemens contributed the starting capital of 6842 thaler, truly a family affair.

## POWER AND PRESTIGE

'I have always dreamt from my early youth on of the creation of a business with global reach . . . which would not only bestow on myself but also on my descendants power and prestige throughout the world', Werner von Siemens wrote to another relative in 1887.[1]

His vision came true. The original partnership had only ten employees, today it employs almost 400 000 people, generates a turnover of DM94 billion (1995–96) and after-tax profits of DM2.5 billion. During its evolution Siemens not only bestowed 'power and prestige' on the founder and his descendants; being one of the pioneers in its field, it also helped to drive the industrialisation process in almost two hundred countries all over the globe.

Siemens is only one example of a telling observation: throughout our economic history no institution has driven economic development the way the family-based enterprise has. This observation prompted us to start this Prologue with a line from the poem 'To a Locomotive in Winter' by the American poet Walt Whitman: . . . emblem of motion and power . . .' It seems to us that these words capture beautifully the role of family-controlled enterprises and their significance in our economies: they have been and still are true locomotives. And this role dates back to the beginning of Western civilisation. Found among the writings of Aristotle was a short document on economic activities during the Hellenic Age, which states that during the Hellenic period, private individuals (with the support of armies of slaves) dominated three sectors of the economy: agriculture, banking (accepting deposits and granting credits), and the production, transportation and sale of manufactured goods.[2]

The Greek government preserved for itself a monopoly only in the areas of collecting taxes – at least in principle – and the exploitation of natural resources. The economic activities of private individuals of that period were household-based, that is, family-controlled. This situation did not change greatly during the time of the Roman Empire and the subsequent Middle Ages, remaining more or less the same until well after the discovery of the New World.

Even during early phases of the era of industrialisation, family-controlled enterprises drove the economic development process. Ample evidence for this is provided by the huge family fortunes that were amassed as the result of pioneering economic activities in the early days of the United States, for instance. Land-based fortunes (such as that of the Astor family), the great fortunes built on railroad construction (for example that of the Vanderbilt family), on banking (J. P. Morgan) and on industry (Rockefeller, Carnegie and Ford are just three of many examples) were all controlled by strong personalities who in turn were firmly rooted in their respective family clans.[3]

Even after the separation of capital and management in the nineteenth century, the owning families continued to 'call the shots' when it came to directing the enterprises at the highest levels. And even in this day and age, when many of the better known corporations are owned by large numbers of dispersed, anonymous shareholders (that is, they have lost their family business character), family-controlled enterprises still generate between 45 per cent and 70 per cent of the GNP of their respective countries, as we will show in Chapter 1.

The far-reaching influence of family-controlled enterprises has become quite visible again in recent decades. On both sides of the North Atlantic during the recessions of the 1980s and 1990s, family enterprises were among the most effective 'locomotives' of the economies in which they were located: they created jobs; they were among the few enterprises that were successful enough to pay taxes; and they displayed the agility and flexibility necessary to manoeuvre successfully in the troubled economic waters of their national economies. The situation has been similar in other parts of the world. In Asia, for instance, family-controlled enterprises, with all their vitality, elasticity and tenacity, have driven the (at least until late 1997) much-admired, thriving economies of that part of the world.

How these 'locomotives' of our economies are directed and controlled at the highest level is the subject of this book, that is, *this is a book on the governance of family businesses.* Governance and family-controlled enterprises are relatively new topics in the management literature and research, we believe they have been undeservedly overlooked.

*Corporate governance* – in family businesses as well as in public corporations – has been studied systematically and on a broad scale for only a couple of decades. In the United States the discussion of the issue has led to a large-scale 'soul-searching' process in major companies, resulting in self-imposed guidelines on how boards should conduct their affairs and leading to the spectacular firing of some high-profile chief executives in companies such as General Motors, IBM and Digital, to name but a few – events that would have been unthinkable only a decade ago. In Europe it culminated, for example, in the publication and partial implementation of the Cadbury Report in the UK – an effort by UK industry and capital markets to get their 'governance house' in order before legislators stepped in with a statutory solution. The Cadbury Report has been widely discussed throughout the industrialised world, and several countries (for example France, South Africa and the Netherlands) have issued their own version of it.

*Family businesses,* the second of the two neglected topics, have been of interest to management researchers and writers in the United States for quite some time; in Europe, in stark contrast with their economic significance in the different countries (think of the *Mittelstand* in Germany and the *Piccoli Forte* in Italy, for instance) as a topic for scholarly inquiry, they have been largely ignored until the last decade. A good indication is the fact that there are only three academic chairs of family business in existence in Europe: one at IESE in Barcelona, one at INSEAD in Fontainebleau and one at IMD in Lausanne. Correspondingly, the literature on family-controlled enterprises is not as voluminous as in other areas of management and, more importantly, there are significant white spots on the map of discovery. Particularly scarce are research and writings in the area of governance in family enterprises.

This is one of the voids this book tries to fill. It is the outgrowth of a rather fortuitous constellation at one of the European management schools – IMD in Lausanne, Switzerland. For historical reasons, at that institute both academic fields – research and teaching in the area of family businesses and of corporate governance – have been cultivated for a number of years. It was therefore quite natural that a representative of each stream at IMD banded together to look into the issue of corporate governance in family-controlled enterprises. And whatever strength this book has, it probably rests on the fact that the two authors' combined insights into the two disciplines serve as roots for this book. During the last decade Fred Neubauer has been researching and teaching at IMD in the area of corporate boards and corporate governance. Alden G. Lank is the holder of the Stephan Schmidheiny Chair of Family Enterprises at IMD and Director of the Leading the Family Business programme (also at IMD); he is also well represented in the literature of his field.

## THE FOUNDATIONS OF THIS BOOK

This book draws on three main sources:

- Our extensive teaching and consulting experience with family enterprises in general.
- Our research in the area of corporate governance in family-controlled enterprises (to be discussed in more detail below).
- Our literature research. We gladly acknowledge that we have made extensive use of the insights derived from other research (undertaken especially in the United States in the area of corporate governance in family enterprises. In this context the work of John L. Ward of Loyola University in Chicago stands out).

In addition we have had access to data from the Family Business Network (FBN), which is headquartered at IMD (although independent), and data collected over the years from the participants of IMD's Leading the Family Business programme. Lastly, we have been able to draw on a major consulting assignment outlined in the following box.

## THE TARGET AUDIENCE OF THE BOOK

The book has been written for those practising managers – family members and non-family members alike – who are involved in directing and controlling relatively large, family-controlled enterprises. Small family businesses are thus not the prime target audience of this book (although their managers will find a considerable number of suggestions that will help them to improve the way they run their firms). Consultants, academics and researchers in the field will also find many useful insights.

How do we define a family business? We devote a good proportion of the first chapter to this difficult question, but to sum up, for us a family enterprise is a proprietorship, partnership, corporation or any form of business association where the voting control is in the hands of a particular family. It does not help the discussion if one defines issues of control through the family too formalistically. In this book, what we typically mean by a family-controlled company is a firm where the family has the voting majority. There are, however, borderline cases where a family may not dominate a company formally and legally, but their *de facto* influence – because of the company's name and traditions their indirect influence via third parties and the fact that all shares other than the ones held by the family are widely dispersed – is nevertheless comparable to formal and legal domination. Strictly speaking such companies are not family controlled, but strongly family influenced. A good case in point is Siemens, which was mentioned at the beginning of this Prologue. The Siemens family controls only about 10 per cent of the voting rights of the company, the other 90 per cent being spread among roughly 607 000 individual, non-family shareholders. This arrangement (together with the role of the banks in the German corporate system) means that the influence of the Siemens family is still very far-reaching.

Although this book concentrates on companies where families have the legal voting majority, we will occasionally refer to 'family-influenced companies' (as described above) – excluding all companies in this twilight zone would ignore the reality that there are rarely hard and fast lines of separation, but rather differing shades of grey in transition zones. We experienced this phenomenon in the case of degrees of control in family businesses.

The book also presents an *international perspective* on the governance of family businesses. There are several reasons for this. First, family businesses are being increasingly forced to move their activities beyond their national markets into the international arena. Second, giving the book an international thrust substantially enriches the discussion as well as allowing comparisons to be made. One could ask whether it is really possible to look at family businesses across national boundaries. We believe it is, for two reasons.

## The Bergman Project

The Bergman family – now in the fourth and fifth generations – owns a broadly based, multinational company whose sales are the equivalent of US$4 billion. The family is large, and as a consequence there are more than 200 family shareholders. There are no outside shareowners, and the stock has not yet been floated on the stock exchange. None of the existing shareholders owns a dominant portion of the capital. In the process of shifting from the fourth to the fifth generation, the family felt a need to restructure the existing, relatively informal governance system of its firm. In order to get some external input into the process, the family turned to the two authors. The project was carried out between 1993 and 1996.

It was clear from the outset that the task of creating a new governance structure had to be achieved in a way that would preserve certain aspects of the particular culture and values of the corporation as well as of the founding family, while at the same time ensuring that the various businesses of the group remained forceful entities in their respective industries. Following logically from this situation, the objectives for the project were:

- To create a governance system suited to the issues at hand.
- To gain the support of the family members for the new governance system.
- To assist the family, the board and the CEO to implement the new system.

Our task was to identify key factors that typically shape a corporate governance system in a family-controlled company and to find out how they relate to each other. Using the model of a political constitution as a starting point helped us to focus our efforts. The model provided us with guidance on which elements of a political constitutional system might make sense in a business setting (and which would not!) While parallels between the political and the corporate system could not be made literally, they sharpened our view of what to look for.

*Developing a Governance Data Base*

As corporate governance is a very young, scholarly discipline, we could not fall back on some ready-made tool kit to handle the problem at hand. Instead, we had to identify the key elements through research.

As a starting point we conducted a review of the literature on the approaches of other family businesses to corporate governance. We had to cast our net relatively widely to include articles, monographs and corporate histories. We found a large number of accounts that addressed the issue, although they differed markedly in depth and completeness. In isolation, many of them were obviously incomplete; taken together, however, they provided a rich picture of how different family businesses have tried to handle their respective governance problems. We found about a dozen interesting examples, which we wrote up as mini case studies. These included firms such as L'Oréal (France), Beretta (Italy), Vorwerk (Germany) and Schlumberger (France).

The second phase of our research was a series of interviews with owner-managers. The abovementioned case studies – in addition to the insights gained by analysing the general data base – helped us to frame the questions we asked during in-depth interviews with representatives of seven large family-controlled companies in Sweden, Finland, Germany, Switzerland, and the United States. Each of these interviews lasted two to three hours and they produced a wealth of data and ideas. To ensure frankness in the interviews, we promised confidentiality.

*Pattern Detection*

Next, we conducted a thorough content analysis of our data bases – general materials, cases, minutes of the interviews – in order to identify the key elements these companies had used to construct their governance systems. This effort produced several literary works, including a monograph, *Appraising and Redesigning a Governance Structure for a Family Business*, which was published as Supplement 8 (September 1996) to the *Directors' Manual* (Hemel Hempstead: Director Books). As we have already published the material elsewhere, in this book we have made only indirect use of our findings.

Of extreme importance for this book were the lessons we learned from applying our insights to the family company that had commissioned the study. The company became an extensive laboratory for trying out and applying the insights we had gained from our research.

First, bringing family businesses from different parts of the world together in IMD's Leading the Family Business programme has turned out to be very meaningful for the participants: the cross-fertilisation of ideas engendered by that gathering has been remarkable indeed. The same is true of the lively cooperation among family-controlled companies from different national settings in the Family Business Network.

Second, rather than looking into different legal prescriptions for family businesses in different national settings, the book puts the *actual behaviour* of family businesses at the centre of the discussion. As the research of one of the authors in the area of corporate boards shows, this is a very fruitful (and legitimate) approach.[4] This research demonstrated not only that there are similar behaviour patterns in corporate governance across countries (as one observer put it, 'Intelligent people all over the world seem to solve their problems in similar ways'), but also that, due to the increasing globalisation of firms, their practices seem to be converging ever more closely. Do not misunderstand: there are obvious differences between family businesses and their governance processes in different countries; but what they have in common outweighs their differences. This is our justification for adopting an international perspective.

One of the consequences of stressing the international features of family businesses (in contrast to stressing national peculiarities) is that there are no chapters in this book on topics such as tax optimisation, estate planning and country-specific legal structures for family businesses. In addition to being country-specific, these issues are highly technical in nature, and when dealing with them, families need the advice of specialists in the national rules pertaining to these issues.

## REFERENCE POINTS: REAL LIFE EXAMPLES

Throughout the book we will develop concepts that relate to the different aspects of governance in the family business. Concepts and managers sometimes do not seem to go well together; we have found that managers prefer as many practical examples as possible. They do not mind following a conceptual discussion if they have had practical experience of the concept. We will therefore take heed of this fact by illustrating the concepts with examples chosen from two categories of companies. First, we will discuss *large, privately held enterprises*, as owners of family businesses look instinctively towards them as role models. However, as the saying goes, he who steps only into the footsteps of others never leaves an imprint, and this is one of the reasons why we will also use *large, publicly owned companies* as reference points. Frequently, these are the secret models of family enterprises, and, they have the further illustrative advantage that they are forced to function under the rather rigorous regime of the capital markets (which is not necessarily true for family-controlled enterprises): the frequently merciless eye of the highly mobile and detached investor in the general capital market forces on publicly owned companies a healthy discipline in different areas that makes them a rich source of ideas on how to run a private company.

In addition, mini-cases have been specifically written to illustrate points made in the text. These mini-cases (which are presented in boxes in the text) discuss real companies, but the names of some have been disguised. In order to serve their purpose they have to be succinct, and they therefore have the character of vignettes rather than full case studies.

## THE STRUCTURE OF THE BOOK

The book is divided into six parts, moving step by step from relatively general concepts and approaches to more specific ones that sharpen the focus of the discussion.

### Part I: The World of Family Business

In order to discuss the issues of corporate governance in the family business setting, we first need to prepare the ground. This is done in Chapters 1 and 2.

In Chapter 1 we define the term family business and show the significance of family businesses in our economies. In Chapter 2 we show how family businesses typically evolve and what stages of development they typically go through. This is important because the stage of development of a family enterprise impacts on the governance structure chosen. The emphasis of the book will be on one rather advanced stage of development, namely the stage where the firm has become a 'cousins' confederation' (where ownership is in the hands of the extended family and the business has become relatively large). Several considerations prompted us to make this choice. The most important one is that the limited research conducted so far in the area of family-controlled firms has concentrated largely on family businesses in the early stages of their development – the stage of the founders and the subsequent stage of sibling partnerships. The stage of the family dynasty (or cousins' confederation) has been looked into much less by researchers and writers alike. This situation is particularly unsatisfactory if one considers the fact that family businesses in the cousins' confederation stage are typically the best known, largest and most influential family enterprises, despite the fact that they are less numerous than the army of firms in the earlier stages of development.

## Part II: The Concept of Corporate Governance and a Classical Governance Structure in a Family Business

In Part II we narrow the discussion and look at one key aspect of family business: its governance (Chapter 3). We define the concept of corporate governance as 'a system of processes and structures to direct, control and account for the business at the highest level'. *Directing* in this context means being involved in decisions that are truly strategic in nature. *Controlling* means oversight of management performance and monitoring the achievement of objectives. *Accounting for* means reporting to those making legitimate demands for accountability on the part of the firm (for example shareholders, employees, the public at large and other stakeholders). Controlling and accounting for are different activities; they can nevertheless be seen as two sides of the same coin and will therefore be discussed together.

In Chapter 3 we also outline a classical governance structure in a family business at an advanced stage of development ('cousins' confederation'), focusing on:

- The family (as the ultimate source of power) and its institutions.
- The board of directors.
- Top management.

## Part III: Family Institutions and the Board of Directors

In accordance with our policy of moving from the general to the more specific, in this part we single out two elements of a classical governance structure – the family and the board of directors – and take a closer look at them. We devote Chapter 4 to the family and its institutions (for example, the family council and others). In Chapter 5 we present our understanding of a board, its role, how it is composed and so on. In this context, we stress that boards typically play a key role in corporate governance. We also point out, however, that a board can only fulfil its governance duty in close cooperation with the other elements of the governance structure, mainly the family and top management.

How does the board spearhead the discharging of the typical governance tasks – directing, controlling, accounting for? This abstract list of tasks has to be translated into a set of practical measures that a board (in cooperation with the other elements of a governance system) can take in order to discharge its governance tasks. To this end we will look at the measures taken by the board of a large South African insurance company – Sanlam. From this list we will select four that are of particular importance to us:

- The appointment of the CEO.
- Establishing a vision and strategy for the firm.
- Securing the resources to satisfy the financial needs of the company and the family.
- Controlling the firm at the highest level.

The first three of these governance measures form part of the directing task of corporate governance (Part IV) and the last represents the controlling/reporting aspect (Part V).

## Part IV: The Directing Task of Corporate Governance: Key Measures

In Part IV we take a closer look at the first three of the governance measures identified in Part III as the ways and means of discharging the directing task. We devote one chapter to each, each time showing that the board typically spearheads the handling of the measure, but does so in close cooperation with the family and top management. In Chapter 6 we look into CEO succession, first from within the family and then from outside. In Chapter 7 we look into the ways and means used by the board to get the family (and top management) involved in establishing a vision and a strategy for the firm. In Chapter 8 we look into aspects of financial strategy: ways of securing the financial resources needed by the firm and the family in order to function well. Questions such as whether or not to go public play a major role here.

## Part V: Handling the Controlling Task of Corporate Governance

In Chapter 9 we discuss what is necessary to allow the different elements of a governance structure – the board, the family, top management – to control the firm effectively and efficiently. In this context we will also briefly look at ways of accounting for the activities of the firm (reporting *vis-à-vis* third parties with a legitimate interest in the information).

Together, Parts IV and V acquaint the reader with a large array of ways and means of handling the four key corporate governance measures.

**Part VI: Putting Governance Insights into Practical Use**

Part VI attempts to help the reader apply some or all of the tools and concepts covered in the previous five parts to his or her own family enterprise. Chapter 10 focuses on developing a corporate governance structure. It draws heavily on the board research undertaken at IMD and applied successfully by a number of corporations.

The Epilogue tries to answer the following question: what does it mean to be an enlightened and responsible owner of a large family business in the cousins' confederation stage, assuming the family want to retain full control of the business? The suggested propositions are derived from the authors' work with numerous families grappling with this vital issue.

An additional word on Part VI is appropriate. While the authors wish to offer the reader some help in improving the governance structure of his or her company, we try to avoid giving overly normative advice. As Max Weber, the towering German sociologist, put it: 'An empirical science is not suited to teach anybody what he ought to do, but only what he can do – under certain circumstances, what he might want to do.'[5] The best we can offer is a reasoned argument for our points of view.

CONCLUSION

Family businesses are the backbone of our economies. In many respects our free enterprise system is built on them. We have to keep them healthy and well-governed, as the well-being of our society depends on them to a large degree. For that contribution they ought to be applauded. As Jonathan Swift (1667–1745) put it in *Gulliver's Travels*, 'whoever could make two ears of corn or two blades of grass to grow upon a spot of ground where only one grew before, would deserve better of mankind, and do more essential service to his country than the whole race of politicians put together.'

# NOTES

1. D. H. Lamparter, 'Von Menschen und Märkten', *Die Zeit*, 13 June 1997, p. 27.
2. G. Mann and A. Heuss (eds), *Propyläen Weltgeschichte*, Berlin-Frankfurt: Propyläen Verlag, 1962, p. 535.
3. G. Myers, *History of the Great American Fortunes*, New York: The Modern Library, 1936.
4. See A. Demb and F. F. Neubauer, *The Corporate Board: Confronting the Paradoxes*, New York: Oxford University Press, 1992.
5. *Neue Zürcher Zeitung*, 1 December 1985.

# Part I
# The World of Family Business

# INTRODUCTION

In order to discuss the issues of corporate governance in the family business setting, we first need to prepare the ground; this is done in Chapters 1 and 2.

- In Chapter 1 we define the term family business and reveal the significance of family businesses in our economies.
- In Chapter 2 we show how family businesses typically evolve and what stages of development they typically go through. This chapter is particularly important, as the stage of development in which a family enterprise finds itself impacts on the governance structure to be chosen.

# 1 Nature and Significance of Family Business

> You are a King by your own Fireside,
> as much as any Monarch on his Throne.
> (Miguel de Cervantes, Don Quixote de la Mancha, 1547–1616)

## DEFINING FAMILY ENTERPRISES

One of the first tasks to confront the serious student of family business, or as some prefer it, 'family enterprise', as a field of scholarly inquiry, is to determine what is meant by the term. Researchers from academia and consulting organisations are not the only ones grappling with the definition. Based on the authors' numerous conversations with journalists pursuing some hot story involving conflict between members of a family who are in business together, the question is often posed: 'Tell me, what is a family business *really*?' Turning to owning families for help, unfortunately, is not particularly fruitful. The authors have served for several years on the faculty of the International Institute for Management Development's Leading the Family Business (LFB) programme. The marketing of LFB makes it quite clear that the workshop is only intended (with very few exceptions) for those who presently lead (or own) or who will lead (or own) their own family's enterprise. The opening question at LFB has traditionally been: 'What does the term 'family business or enterprise' mean to you?' The range of responses is large and idiosyncratic to the point that some participants wonder whether or not their newly met colleagues are unwelcome interlopers!

That there is no consensus on the definition of family enterprise in the research/teaching and consulting communities, among journalists (and hence the public) and even among those running a family business is simultaneously frustrating and understandable. After all, as a distinct field of study it has existed for only about 30 years in the United States and for a decade or so in Europe. The US Family Firm Institute, the premier professional association for consultants, academics and research-ers, is barely ten years old. The Family Business Network, the Lausanne-based, world-wide association that primarily groups business owners and their families, was founded only in 1990. Thus, as in any young field, it should not be surprising that there is little consensus on a definition.

However there are additional explanations. Family enterprises are notoriously secretive and usually do not welcome into their firms for research purposes even well-intentioned outsiders who are prepared to guarantee confidentiality. Even when researchers are allowed in, the samples may be purely a matter of convenience with few participants. The resulting definition of family enterprise may represent the lowest common determinator of the firms in that particular sample. For similar reasons the companies researched by others may require a quite different set of descriptors of the sample even though, in a very general sense, objective observers might agree that the various samples all covered 'family-type' firms.

Furthermore, if one closely examines the published literature on issues that are potentially of considerable concern and utility to those interested in family businesses, one can discern four quite distinct research tradi-tions or sources, as illustrated in Figure 1.1.

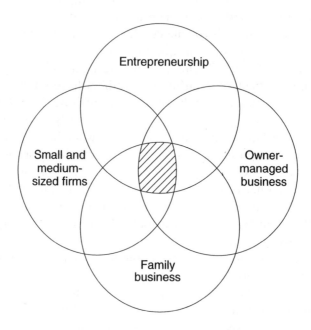

**Figure 1.1**   Related academic fields

Note that while there are several zones of overlap, these add little to the accumulated knowledge and wisdom about family enterprises as such. Researchers have a strong tendency to stay within the boundaries of their own chosen circle and much too rarely establish linkages with those from other traditions. The inevitable result is impoverishment of all four traditions. A further implication is that too little effort is applied to developing a definition of family enterprise that will be commonly accepted by all four traditions, let alone by those of us who identify largely with the bottom circle of Figure 1.1.

One of the most discouraging consequences of this state of affairs is that it is extremely difficult to compare different studies on family business as the probability is extremely high that different definitions have been used of the core subject. Thus too often only the broadest generalisations can be crafted from the existing data base.[1]

## Definitional Elements

A review of the literature has revealed a long list of elements used by various authors to construct their varying definitions. The most important are listed below for two reasons. First, readers can 'cut and paste' to determine which one they prefer. Second, the authors will be able to draw from this and other sources to share their own definition with the reader. In this manner, the reader will be able to understand the underlying construct that has guided the writing of this book. The following are the most common elements of the myriad definitions we found:

- The percentage of share capital (voting or otherwise) owned by a family.
- Employment of owning family in executive or other positions.
- The existence of non-family executives or employees.
- The extent to which the intention is to maintain family involvement in the future.
- The number of generations of the owning family involved in the business.
- The number of families involved in either management and/or ownership.
- Whether a given family accepts that it controls its own enterprise.
- Whether non-family employees accept that it is a family enterprise.

- Whether direct descendants of the founder have management and/or ownership control.
- The size of the enterprise, particularly the number of employees.

This list, of course, is neither exhaustive nor mutually exclusive. Still, most of the key variables used in the literature are noted. Here is an example of one of the earliest and most comprehensive definitions:

> [A] company is considered a family business when it has been closely identified with at least two generations of a family and when this link has had a mutual influence on company policy and on the interests and objectives of the family. Such a relationship is indicated when one or more of the following conditions exist:
>
> - Family relationship is a factor, among others, in determining management succession.
> - Wives or sons of present or former chief executives are on the board of directors.
> - The important institutional values of the firm are identified with a family, either in formal company publications or in the informal traditions of the organization.
> - The actions of a family member reflect on or are thought to reflect on the reputation of the enterprise, regardless of his formal connection to management.
> - The relatives involved feel obligated to hold the company stock for more than purely financial reasons, especially when losses are involved.
> - The position of the family member in the firm influences his standing in the family.
> - A family member must come to terms with his relationship to the enterprise in determining his own career.[2]

For those readers with a thirst to peruse a longer list of definitions, please refer to Appendix 1.1 at the end of this chapter.


OUR SIMPLIFIED MODEL

Reading the list of definitions in Appendix 1.1 leads one to conclude that 'family business', like beauty, tends to be in the eyes of the beholder. Yet there are some commonalties that cut across many, if not all, of the authors' conceptual maps. At the heart of many, implicitly or explicitly, is the idea of family[3] influence or control – generally of two kinds: ownership and management.[4] If one were to try to combine the ownership and management criteria in a two-dimensional figure, it would look something like Figure 1.2.

In position X, all owners and all top management are family (often the case in the early stages of a first-generation family company). In position Y, no employees of the company are family, but 100 per cent of the ownership is in the hands of the family. X could be labelled 'total ownership and management control' while Y could be categorised as anywhere between 'absentee landlord' and 'active landlord', depending on the degree of involvement of the family. An example of the latter would be a family that fills the board of directors exclusively with family members and breathes down the neck of the (non-family) management team. Position Z, which is often found when the family has sold the company but remains as the management team, is arguably still a family

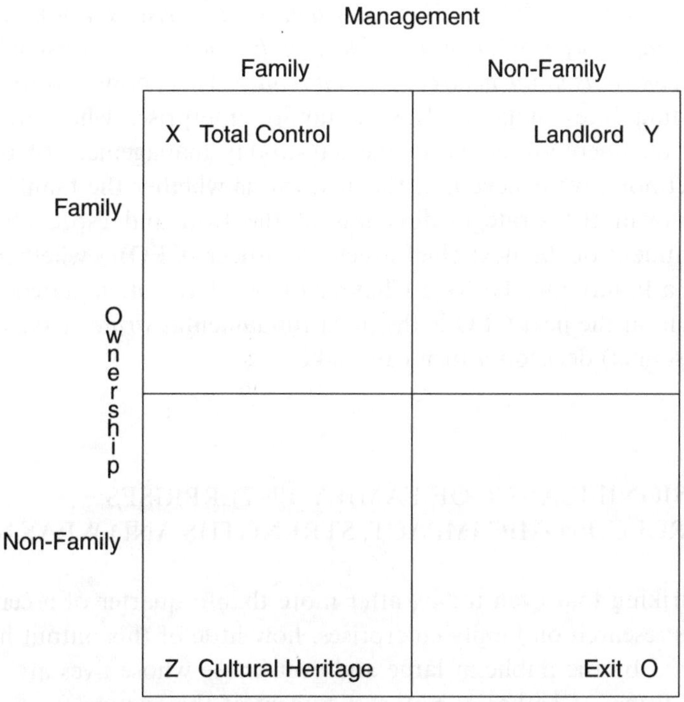

Figure 1.2   The ownership–management matrix

business in the sense that the family's values and management style may still impact significantly on the day-to-day running of the business. Thus the family's cultural heritage may remain in place even after it has lost ownership control. Position O signifies that the business is no longer 'family' as no employees or owners are part of the founding family.

Thus it is probably more reflective of the reality of family business to speak of *the degree to which* an enterprise is family-controlled, as the axes in Figure 1.2 testify. It can be useful to think of family involvement in any given case as a point on a continuum, with total involvement at one extreme (for example position X in Figure 1.2) through partial involvement (positions Y and Z) to no involvement (position O). Of course there is no assumption in this formulation that the points on the continua are necessarily static. The history of family enterprises is filled with examples of families moving back and forth along either continuum, for example from total ownership to none at all, then returning to partial or even total ownership. The case of the Haas family of Levi Strauss in San Francisco is just such an example.

In this book the authors have taken a rather broad position with regard to the definitional debate. For us, *a family enterprise is a proprietorship, partnership, corporation or any form of business association where the voting control is in the hands of a given family*. This permits us to examine interesting cases of governance of family enterprises where no or few family members are active in the day-to-day management of the firm. Furthermore, we believe that the acid test is whether the family has the final say in the strategic direction of the firm and especially in the appointment of the next chief executive officer (CEO) – whether or not this is a family member (see Chapter 6). We have often stated that the decision on the next CEO is the most fundamental *strategic* (as opposed to personnel) decision a firm can make.

## THE SIGNIFICANCE OF FAMILY ENTERPRISES: MACROECONOMIC IMPACT, STRENGTHS AND WEAKNESSES

It is striking that even today, after more than a quarter of a century of serious research on family enterprises, how little of this output has been absorbed by the public at large and even those whose lives are spent in family firms – whether or not as members of the owning family. Those who make their living studying this unique form of organisation generally agree that family firms are the economic motors (Whitman's 'locomotive') of all non-communist economies – a startling and even newsworthy conclusion. However, given the definitional debate outlined in the first part of this chapter, it is extremely difficult, if not impossible, to prove this assertion.

## The Good News

Frustrated by the variety of statistics purporting to describe the impact of US family firms on macroeconomic variables such as percentage of the work force, new job creation and percentage of gross domestic product, Shanker and Astrachan valiantly undertook a study to try to create some order out of this seeming chaos.[5] They concluded that the statistical 'evidence' fell into four categories:

- 'Street lore' (no clear research base or disparate definitions of family enterprise).
- Educated estimates (by experienced and knowledgeable experts).
- Extrapolations (from existing data or from small samples).
- Actual empirical research (using a precise definition, but alas the skimpiest of the four categories).

Shanker and Astrachan, using the best available US information, then developed three definitions of family business that they labelled 'broad', 'middle' and 'narrow'. Their descriptions of each are as follows:

- 'Broad – effective control of strategic direction, intended to remain in family, little direct family involvement.'
- 'Middle – founder/descendant runs company, legal control of voting stock, some family involvement.'
- 'Narrow – multiple generations, family involved in running and owning, more than one member of owners' family having significant management responsibility, a lot of family involvement.'[6]

The power of this typology resides in illustrating the dramatic differences that result in the US macroeconomic data depending on which definition is used (Table 1.1). While our definition has the advantage of including a huge variety of firms – from Ma's corner candy shop to large multinational corporations such as Cargill – the authors' interest and hence experience has been mostly with medium-sized to large multinational companies, and it is from these sources that most of this book will draw its examples.

**Table 1.1**   US macroeconomic data

| | |
|---|---:|
| *Broad:* | |
| No. of family firms | 20.3 million |
| Percentage of GDP | 49 |
| Percentage of workforce | 59 |
| Percentage of new jobs created | 78 |
| | |
| *Middle:* | |
| No. of family firms | 12.2 million |
| Percentage of GDP | 30 |
| Percentage of workforce | 37 |
| Percentage of new jobs created | 48 |
| | |
| *Narrow:* | |
| No. of family firms | 4.1 million |
| Percentage of GDP | 12 |
| Percentage of workforce | 15 |
| Percentage of new jobs created | 19 |

**Source**:   Shanker and Astrachan (1996).[7]

We are not aware of any equivalent study with this degree of rigour. However we have gathered from colleagues what Shanker and Astrachan would describe as 'educated estimates', using their broad definition, and the results bear a striking resemblance. Table 1.2 shows a few examples in terms of the estimated percentage of all registered businesses that are thought to be family enterprises.[8]

Estimates of contribution to GDP as well as employment vary from 45 per cent to 70 per cent throughout the non-communist world. And every observer with whom we talked claimed that the majority of new jobs created in the last decade can be attributed to family firms, broadly defined. The reasons are not difficult to determine. There are of course many huge, multinational, family-controlled firms that are household

**Table 1.2**   Family enterprises as an estimated percentage of registered companies

| | *Per cent* |
|---|---:|
| Portugal | 70 |
| United Kingdom | 75 |
| Spain | 80 |
| Switzerland | 85 |
| Sweden | > 90 |
| Italy | > 95 |
| Middle East | > 95 |

names,[9] including Ford, Bechtel, Mars, Estée Lauder and Levi Strauss (USA); Tetra Laval, the Wallenberg group and, H&M (Sweden); Hermès, Michelin, Bic, Marie Brizard and L'Oréal (France); Tata (India); Kuok group (Honk Kong); Seagram and Bata (Canada); Fiat, Ferrero, Barillo, Beretta and Benetton (Italy); Lego (Denmark); Caran d'Ache, SGS and André (Switzerland); C&A (Netherlands); Bahlsen (Germany); Kikkoman (Japan); Claroen Pokphmd (Thailand); and the Rothschild banking family. Yet the overwhelming majority are small (even micro) and medium-sized firms. It is the latter that have created the new jobs and not the behemoths – whether or not family managed and/or owned. The largest companies have become synonymous with 'downsizing' or its equivalent euphemism 'right-sizing'.

While transnational research (using equivalent definitions) on the macroeconomic impact of family enterprises is badly needed, there is no indication that this will be undertaken in the near future. This said, it is our hypothesis that family firms are among the most important (if not *the* most important) contributors to wealth and employment in virtually every country. Hence more care should be taken by public policy makers everywhere to ensure their health, prosperity and longevity. Spain and the United Kingdom are shining but very rare exceptions.

There is other good news about family firms, this time on the financial front. Certain studies have indicated that family enterprises outperform their non-family counterparts in several aspects. Leach and Leahy[10] examined 325 very large UK industrial firms in the 1980s and concluded that ownership control implied:

- Higher valuation ratios.
- Greater profit margins.
- Higher returns on shareholders' capital.
- Higher growth rates of sales.
- Higher growth rates of net assets.

A study published in *Forbes*[11] indicated that, of the biggest 800 publicly traded firms, the 31 where a member of the founding family held the post of CEO were, on average, 15 per cent more profitable and 14 per cent faster growing than the industry average and one third more profitable when controlling for size variations.

French family firms, it seems, outperform their non-family counterparts in the Société de Bourse Française (SBF) 250 companies. Over the period 31 December 1989 to 6 May 1996 the capitalisations of the SBF 250 increased by 8.8 per cent on average, while the ODDO Family

Business Index, comprising the 76 family companies in the SBF 250, increased by 73.3 per cent.[12]

Figure 1.3 shows the performance of 210 of the largest family firms in the United States (the Family Business Stock Index, FBSI) compared with the S&P 500. It is clear from the data that from 1976 to 1996 the FBSI stocks consistently outperformed those of the S&P 500.[13]

The Pitcairn family (US founders of Pittsburgh Plate Glass) compared the performance of 205 quoted 'family heritage' companies with that of 1800 publicly owned companies ('family heritage' companies are those with a minimum capitalisation of US$200 million and the owning family holds at least 10 per cent of the stock). The results showed that each US dollar invested in the early 1970s in the family heritage companies would have increased by an average of almost 22 per cent per annum by the early 1990s, while on average a dollar invested in the control group would have increased by 14.5 per cent per annum. Their conclusion: family heritage companies are better investments.[14]

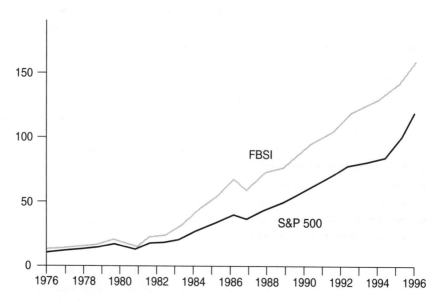

The indexes are calculated to include reinvested dividends. The S&P is adjusted to equal 10 in 1976 so the indexes can be compared on the same scale.

**Source**: *Family Business*, Summer 1996.

**Figure 1.3**   The Family Business Stock Index (FBSI) versus the S&P 500, 1976–96

Thus it seems evident that family enterprises – small, medium and large – are often very significant actors on the world-wide macroeconomic and financial scene, producing better than average results for stockholders, family or otherwise. In addition, our numerous interviews with participants in IMD's Leading the Family Business programme strongly suggest that successful[15] family firms manifest characteristics that are often lacking in large publicly-owned companies. As a senior executive (taking part in another programme) of a troubled, multibillion dollar, publicly traded (non-family) company once avowed to one of the authors, 'We are studying what the best family firms are doing to see what we can emulate. I am sure they are doing many things better than we are!'

To what do these owning families attribute their success? Here are the most common responses:

- Introducing excellent management development systems, at least for family and often for non-family employees also.
- Training family members in ownership rights and responsibilities – for example the norm of stewardship and creating wealth for future generations.[16]
- Treating employees fairly and with loyalty that is usually reciprocated; many non-family employees may be third and subsequent generation employees of the firm.
- Having a strong sense of responsibility to society – local, regional, national or transnational – which is often reflected in the contribution of time and money to worthwhile community projects.
- Emphasising value for money and quality, as the family's good name depends on the product or service.
- Taking decisions quickly as everybody knows where the locus of power is.
- Taking a long-term strategic perspective not bound by next quarter's earnings and working to maximise shareholder wealth even a generation hence.
- Remaining innovative and entrepreneurial, the keys to future success.

The above list is part of a longer one but the general thrust is evident. Our respondents believe deeply that these characteristics differentiate them from their non-family-company counterparts. To the extent that this assertion is true (again, further research is needed), they represent competitive advantages and can be a cause for optimism about the future of family firms.

**The Bad News**

It would be seriously misleading to convey the impression that all is well in the world of family business. Unfortunately there is plenty of bad news too. At the top of the list, family enterprises are notoriously short-lived. Studies on the longevity of family companies in several countries have all come to the same conclusion. While it is impossible to make exact national comparisons, the general tendency is clear: between two thirds and three quarters of family businesses either collapse or are sold by the founding family during the first generation's tenure. Only 5–15 per cent continue into the third generation in the hands of the descendants of the founder. These figures compare unfavourably with the staying power of equivalent non-family-controlled companies. Because family enterprises are a – if not the – chief contributor to the economic and social well-being of all capitalist societies, this fragility is a cause for concern. What factors can explain the lack of longevity?

First of all, there can be little doubt that family enterprises are the most complex form of business organisation. At first sight, this statement may seem preposterous. However reflect on Figure 1.4, which depicts a highly simplified model of a typical (all but the smallest) corporation.

The CEO who holds a role in position 7 is faced with managing all seven sets of roles in a synergistic manner in pursuit of the

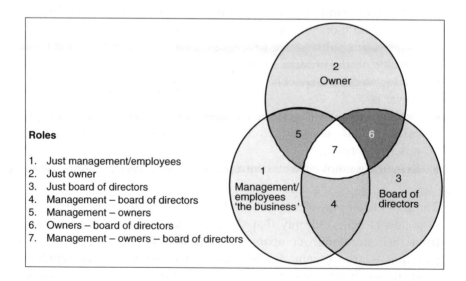

**Roles**

1.  Just management/employees
2.  Just owner
3.  Just board of directors
4.  Management – board of directors
5.  Management – owners
6.  Owners – board of directors
7.  Management – owners – board of directors

**Figure 1.4**   A typical corporation

business's mission and objectives – no sinecure under the best of circumstances.

Figure 1.5 (which we call the 'three circle and tie' model) adds but one dimension: family. By so doing, the number of roles to be managed by the CEO in position 15 more than doubles – a significant increase in complexity.

This conception of the family-controlled corporation begins to explain some of the negative dynamics commonly associated with such organisations.[17] Popular television series such as 'Dynasty' and 'Dallas', for example, delight in highlighting the squabbles between and within generations. These conflicts are often attributed to 'personality differences'. Yet an analysis of Figure 1.5 shows that the basis of the differences may be related more to role or perspective than personality. A good example is the important, frequently emotionally charged, decision concerning the dividend payout ratio. A person in role 15, acting, say, as chairman of the board/CEO/owner/family, quite logically may have a very different opinion from the younger sister or brother in role 5, with no seat on the board and no employment in the family's enterprise. In the former's case, one could expect a strong desire to maximise the reinvestment of profits in the business while the sibling might like to see a bigger and more frequent dividend cheque.

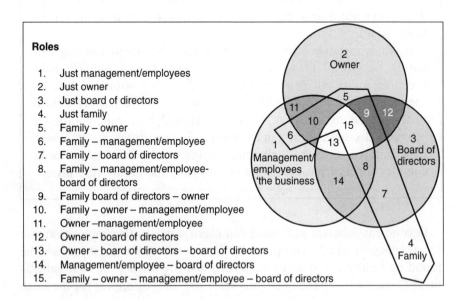

**Roles**

1. Just management/employees
2. Just owner
3. Just board of directors
4. Just family
5. Family – owner
6. Family – management/employee
7. Family – board of directors
8. Family – management/employee-
   board of directors
9. Family board of directors – owner
10. Family – owner – management/employee
11. Owner –management/employee
12. Owner – board of directors
13. Owner – board of directors – board of directors
14. Management/employee – board of directors
15. Family – owner – management/employee – board of directors

**Figure 1.5** A typical family corporation

The inevitable overlapping of family with the three circles in Figure 1.5 leads to challenges that no totally publicly held corporation has to face. The mini-case in the following box illustrates an all too common scenario taken from a real (but disguised) family enterprise in Switzerland.

---

**Dunand S.A.**

Georges, 64, third generation, is CEO, sole owner and member of the board. His son, Jean, 31, a bachelor, is vice president of manufacturing and technology and likewise a member of the board. Daughter Marie, 34, is married with one son, Marcel, 12, and holds the post of vice president of sales and marketing. She too is a board member.

Marie and Jean thoroughly detest each other and have been in sibling conflict since early childhood. Marie (as well as Jean) expects to be nominated as CEO and take voting control when Georges decides to retire. Marcel, her son, is an outstanding student and has displayed entrepreneurial skills and an interest in the business, even at such a young age. In his mother's mind there is no doubt that he will replace her as head of the family enterprise when she decides to step down. There is a board meeting scheduled for next Friday to decide on certain strategic investments that will start to impact in 10 years' time.

It is not farfetched to suppose that the next board meeting will hardly be typical of what one would expect in a publicly held corporation. In all probability, the family's emotional dynamics (developed over its whole life span) will covertly or overtly dictate their discussions on what, in theory, should be a purely rational business decision. Yes, family businesses are different. It is not hyperbole to state that, all things being equal, there is no more complex form of business organisation than the family enterprise.

---

Beyond the inherent enhanced complexity, what other factors explain the fragility of family companies? What causes them to slip from the founding family's grip or go bankrupt, usually during the first generation? There are two parts to the answer. First, they disappear for the same reasons as any corporation, whatever its ownership or management structure, including:

- The opportunity to sell at an attractive price (in a capitalist economy this provokes no automatic opprobrium).
- An inability to anticipate or adjust to changes in the market place.
- Insufficient investment in R&D.
- Inadequate control of costs.
- Lack of access to affordable capital.
- Other poor management practices.

Second, and not surprisingly, family enterprises also face certain specific challenges unique to themselves, such as:

- Failure to find capital for growth without diluting the family's equity (total ownership control being a sacrosanct principle for many families).
- An inability to balance optimally the family's need for liquidity and the business's need for cash.
- Poor estate planning and the inability of the next generation to pay inheritance taxes.
- Unwillingness on the part of the older generation to 'let go' of ownership and management power at an appropriate moment.
- An inability to attract and retain competent and motivated family successors.
- Unchecked sibling rivalry with no consensus on the chosen successor.
- An inability to attract and retain competent senior non-family managers.
- Unmanaged conflict between the cultures of the family, the board and the business and an inability to develop appropriate governance structures that assign optimal roles to each of the governance institutions or bodies.

The above list is striking because of the predominance of factors related to managing the process of ownership and management succession – the single most important reason for the fragility of family enterprises. This subject, particularly the management dimension, will be examined in depth in Chapter 6.

There is further dismaying news, at least from the European perspective. As stated earlier, most family businesses are small and medium-sized, with commensurate levels of gross sales and employment. While there are very few transnational studies comparing family and non-family enterprises of this size, one of the most ambitious was undertaken by

Aerts and Donckels.[18] They looked at eight countries: Austria, Belgium, Finland Great Britain, Netherlands, Norway, Sweden and Switzerland. They compared the experiences of a matched sample (1132 companies) of family versus non-family firms. The definition of family enterprises used by the researchers was that at least 50 per cent of the capital was held by one family. The companies employed fewer than 500 persons. The results paint a rather dismal picture:

- Fewer family businesses (FBs) than non-family businesses (NFBs) import.
- Fewer FBs than non-FBs export.
- Fewer FBs than non-FBs derive more than 25 per cent of their turnover from exports.
- Fewer FBs than NFBs derive more than 50 per cent of their turnover from exports.
- Fewer FBs than non-FBs take licences from foreign companies.
- Fewer FBs than non-FBs give licences to foreign companies.
- Fewer FBs than non-FBs have a branch abroad.
- Fewer FBs than non-FBs have a production plant abroad.

If one believes that firms of whatever size must learn to internationalise in the brave new world of huge trading blocs, these data augur ill for small and medium-sized European family firms, many of which have been able to survive precisely because they have been pampered players in protected national markets. For most, those days are over.[19]

## AN OPTIMISTIC FUTURE

It would be inappropriate to end this chapter on such a negative note. The authors remain enthusiastically optimistic about the ability of family enterprises to continue to be the economic locomotives of the free world. There will inevitably be many casualties, and shakeouts will occur in all countries. Yet our prediction is that family enterprises will continue to be in the majority and will remain significant contributors to GNP, employ-ment and new job creation. Why?

Firstly, in most economies a huge generational shift is taking place as the post Second World War business leaders step down from their positions. The members of the incoming generation are better educated (many with business degrees), often multilingual, less chauvinistic and have travelled the world more extensively than their parents. There is no *a priori* evidence that they are less entrepreneurial or innovative than those they are replacing.

Secondly, the new generation will have access to more research and knowledge about the strengths and weaknesses of family businesses. They will be able to build on this knowledge to increase the longevity of their firms.

Thirdly, there have never been more opportunities for new leaders to learn from each other. In the United States alone there are some 100 university-based forums for family businesses and over 1000 programmes that focus on entrepreneurship. Many MBA programmes now offer electives on family business. The Family Business Network also provides venues where family business owners and their families can learn best practices from each other.

Fourthly, there is an increasing awareness in the consulting community that family enterprises are not just like any other form of business.[20] The best of them are educating themselves about the generic challenges faced by family firms, thereby enhancing their ability to be helpful to this special breed of clients. And there is evidence that family firms are starting to be less resistant to this kind of help.

Finally, the massive geopolitical changes that have taken place since the fall of the Berlin Wall give ample reason for optimism about the future of family enterprises. Communism has been an abysmal failure, and while the various forms of capitalism have not been unmitigated successes, they have provided more wealth to more people than any other system so far devised. The countries of the former Soviet Union and their Warsaw Pact neighbours have a massive reconstruction job before them. Undoubtedly foreign aid and investment will play an important role as they strive to become First-World economies. This is a necessary but insufficient condition. To rebuild these economies, there is no option but to return to the very roots of capitalism: the family-owned firm and the family industrial or service business. This trend is already evident on a massive scale in all of the former communist world.

In our view family enterprises are here to stay. And they will continue to have an important role to play, as eloquently stated by King Juan Carlos I of Spain in his address to the 300 delegates attending the 6th Annual World Conference of the Family Business Network, held at El Escorial in October 1995 (see the box overleaf for an excerpt).

---

### King Juan Carlos Speaks on Family Business

'I would like to reflect for a moment on the role of a family business in the future of our economies and, consequently, in a society concerned about conflicts whose only solution lies in the system of globalized relationships in which we move. There are, in this respect, a series of possibilities which, if properly directed, will provide the economic system with elements of reconciliation and progress.

Firstly, family firms are in a position to provide an important element of balance in the business tissue of each country. This tissue is made up of many cells of differing sizes and densities, and only a suitable proportion of each type guarantees the optimum performance of the whole.

Family business also involves a series of interpersonal relationships and a leader or leaders who, although subject to the variables affecting any kind of behaviour, must have the ability to combine tradition and experience with the intuitition and good sense needed to establish short term objectives that are feasible in human terms, will stimulate responsible participation, and that endeavour to resolve differences by way of consensual solutions rather than through confrontation.

Finally, your companies are more easily able to adapt to the changes and innovations demanded by the ever more complex and changeable economic conjuncture. The principles that inspire family firms, their very structure and the particular way they are managed all facilitate a non-traumatic rationalisation, when this becomes necessary, and can even open the door to new formulas for growth. This is an important asset in these difficult times, when it is essential to use a number of different solutions.'

---

Katherine Graham, famed head of the Washington Post Company, strikes a similar, positive note based on her experience with her own family enterprise:

I think that family-owned companies bring special qualities to the table and that family members can bring singular attributes to a business enterprise. Possibly, quality may be nourished most easily by a family, whose perspective extends beyond the immediate horizon. There are exceptions, to be sure, but family members can provide stability and continuity, and family ownership can prevent takeovers, which is important to smooth operations in this period of disruptive and often ill-considered mergers and acquisitions.[21]

## CONCLUSION

This chapter has confronted the challenge of trying to define 'family business' or 'family enterprise'. The many definitions provided (see especially Appendix 1.1) clearly show the lack of consensus among the various students of the field. We have chosen to describe a family enterprise simply as 'a proprietorship, partnership, corporation or any form of business association where voting control is in the hands of a given family'.

Any form of business organisation has strengths and weaknesses. Family-controlled firms, however, have their own distinctive qualities – both positive and negative in terms of their ability to survive. We conclude, however, that despite certain important fragilities, family businesses are here to stay and will remain the 'locomotive' of our economies throughout the non-communist world.

## APPENDIX 1.1

The following are examples of how various authors have defined the term 'family business', ranging from the deceptively simple to the fairly complex:

- 'The . . . family-controlled enterprise . . . refers to a firm in which the founders and their heirs have recruited salaried managers but continued to be influential shareholders, held executive managerial positions, and exercised decisive influence on company policy' (Church).[22]
- 'a family business [is] one in which both ownership and policy making are dominated by members of an "emotional kinship group"' (Carsrud).[23]
- '[A] family firm [is] an enterprise that, in practice, is controlled by the members of a single family' (Barry).[24]
- 'a business in which the members of a family have legal control over ownership' (Lansberg, Perrow and Rogolsky).[25]
- 'Controlling ownership [is] vested in the hands of an individual or of the members of a single family' (Barnes and Hershon).[26]
- 'A business where a single family owns the majority of stock and has total control. Family members also form part of the management and make the most important decisions concerning the business' (Gallo and Sveen).[27]
- 'firms in which one family holds the majority of the shares and controls management' (Donckels and Fröhlich).[28]

- '[A business] owned and run by members of one or two families' (Stern).[29]
- 'Most simply stated, a family firm is one that includes two or more members of a family that has financial control of the company' (Ward and Aronoff).[30]
- 'We define a family business as one that will be passed on for the family's next generation to manage or control' (Ward).[31]
- 'What is usually meant by 'family business' is either the occurrence or the anticipation that a younger family member has or will assume control of the business from an elder' (Churchill and Hatten).[32]
- 'A family business is any business where more than one member of a family takes on management or active ownership responsibility. You have a family business if you work with someone in your family in a business you both own or which you may someday own. The essence of a family business is that blood, work and business ownership are held in common' (Jaffee).[33]
- 'Strictly speaking, a family business is one that has been started by a family member and has been passed on, or is expected to be passed, to succeeding generations of the family, sometimes through marriage. Descendants of the original founder(s) will own and control the business. Also, members of the family work, participate in, and benefit from the enterprise' (Bork).[34]
- 'We define a family business in which majority ownership or control lies within a single family and in which two or more family members are or at some time were directly involved in the business' (Rosenblatt, de Mik, Anderson and Johnson).[35]
- 'A family business is defined here as an organization whose major operating decisions and plans for leadership succession are influenced by family members in management or serving on the board' (Handler).[36]
- 'A business firm may be considered a family business to the extent that its ownership and management are concentrated within a family unit, and to the extent its members strive to achieve, maintain, and/or increase intraorganisational family-based relations' (Litz).[37]

## NOTES

1. The discussion on the difficulties of arriving at a consensual definition of 'family business' or 'family enterprise' should not detract from the many excellent research papers that have contributed significantly to our knowledge of family business within the framework of each author's definition. The reader is simply reminded to check for comparability of definitions before generalising across studies of family business. The best source of cutting-edge research on the subject is the Family Business Review published by the *Family Firm Institute*, Brookline, MA, USA.
2. R. G. Donnelly, 'The Family Business', *Harvard Business Review*, vol. 42, No. 4, (July–August 1964), p. 94.
3. We shall not debate in this book the complex issue of defining what is a 'family'. Suffice it to say that there are significant cultural differences in delimiting the boundaries of family just as within a given culture different people will differ in their definitions. A good example in many Western

cultures is whether or not in-laws are family and whether or not they can hold shares in the enterprise.

4. Once again, there is little consensus on the meaning of 'ownership control' let alone 'management control'. The former is usually couched in terms of the percentage held of the voting stock. More than 50 per cent is usually a safe bet but well below that figure can still mean ownership control if the remaining equity is broadly held.

5. M.C. Shanker and J.H. Astrachan, 'Myths and Realities: Family Businesses' Contribution to the US Economy – A Framework for Assessing Family Business Statistics', *Family Business Review*, vol. 9, no. 2 (Summer 1996), pp. 107–24.

6. Ibid, p. 109.

7. Ibid, p. 116. Net new jobs data covered the 1976–90 period.

8. The figure used by Shanker and Astrachan for the total number of US business enterprises (including sole proprietorships, partnerships and corporations) is 23.4 million. Hence the comparable percentage figures for the US are: broad, 90.6 per cent; middle, 54.5 per cent; narrow, 18.3 per cent.

9. It is estimated that 13 per cent of the FTSE largest 100 companies and 35 per cent of the Fortune 500 list would fall within the broad definition.

10. D. Leach and J. Leahy, 'Ownership Structures, Control and the Performance of Large British Companies', *Economic Journal*, vol. 101 (1991), p. 1435.

11. *Forbes*, 22 May 1995.

12. *ODDO Génération*, June 1996, p. 2.

13. *Family Business*, Summer, 1996, p. 19.

14. D. Junge, 'The Pitcairns', Proceedings of the 5th FBN Conference Family Businss Network, Lausanne, 1995, p. 171.

15. 'Successful' in this context means firms that have remained in the control of the founding family for two or more generations and which remain financially sound.

16. Management development and education on the meaning of responsible ownership often starts before the children have reached their teenage years. It typically takes place around the dining table as the parents talk about the events of the day at the family's firm. Subsequently the children's socialisation into the business may be deepened by working in the business during evenings, weekends and school/university holidays.

17. In anticipation of Chapter 3, this model has other advantages in that it allows a visualisation of how a family enterprise may change over time. The size and the degree of overlap of the business, ownership, board and family circles and tie will probably change. For example, a newly married couple in their early twenties launch their local enterprise in the late 1940s selling 45 and $33\frac{1}{3}$ rpm vinyl records. They are the co-owners, only employees and sole members of this family unit. Assume they meet monthly as an informal board of directors to discuss the strategic development of their firm. At this early stage the four components of the model lie almost on top of each other. If the business succeeds and some 25 years later two of their three children, who do not yet own shares, enter the firm, additional employees

have been hired and a trusted and experienced independent director added who has bought 10 per cent of the voting shares, not only have each of the circles and the tie become larger but the component parts no longer lie upon each other and are separated in space. By the time the company is sold to outsiders and no family members hold shares or are in the business, the firm has mutated to something much closer to Figure 1.4.

18. A. J. Haahti (ed.), *Interstratos (Internationalization of Strategic Orientations of European Small and Medium Enterprises)*, Brussels: European Institute for Advanced Studies in Management, 1994.
19. Happily there is also evidence that a restricted number of mostly medium-size companies have been able to dominate particular market niches on a world-wide basis. See H. Simon, *Hidden Champions: Lessons from 500 of the World's Best Unknown Companies*, Boston: Harvard Business School Press, 1996, for a fascinating series of success stories.
20. The Family Firm Institute is investing heavily in defining the body of knowledge necessary to master the intricacies of consulting with family enterprises.
21. K. Graham, *Personal History*, New York: Alfred A. Knopf, 1997, p. 619.
22. R. Church, 'The Family Firm in Industrial Capitalism: International Perspectives on Hypotheses and History', in C. E. Aronoff, J. H. Astrachan and J. L. Ward (eds), *Family Business Sourcebook II*, Marietta, Georgia: Business Owner Resources, 1996, p. 559.
23. Cited in M. H. Morris, R. W. Williams and D. Nel, 'Factors Influencing Family Business Succession', *International Journal of Entrepreneurial Behaviour & Research*, vol. 2, no. 3 (1996), p. 68. Using 'emotional kinship group' as the key descriptor points out the pitfalls of trying to be too exhaustive. Such a designation would include elite military units such as the US Marine Corps, which most students of the field find a bit removed from the concept of a family enterprise.
24. B. Barry, 'The Development of Organization Structure in the Family Firm', *Family Business Review*, vol. II, no. 3 (Fall 1989), p. 257.
25. I. Lansberg, E. L. Perrow and S. Rogolski, 'Family Business as an Emerging Field', *Family Business Review*, vol. I, no. 1 (Spring 1988), p. 2.
26. Cited in W. C. Handler, 'Methodological Issues and Considerations in Studying Family Businesses', *Family Business Review*, vol. II, no. 3 (Fall 1989), p. 257.
27. M. A. Gallo and J. Sveen, 'Internationalizing the Family Business: Facilitating and Restraining Forces', *Family Business Review*, vol. IV, no. 2 (Summer 1991), p. 181. As is not uncommon, in subsequent research Gallo (with M. J. Estapé) changed the definition to encompass one or two families if they hold more than 10 per cent of the shares and if the joint share of the three next largest shareholders is no greater than one third of the shares held by the one or two dominating families. This definition is unique.
28. R. Donckels and E. Fröhlich, 'Are Family Businesses Really Different? European Experiences from STRATOS', *Family Business Review*, vol. IV, no. 2 (Summer 1991), p. 149.
29. Cited in Handler, 'Methodological Issues', op. cit., p. 280.

30. J. L. Ward and C. E. Aronoff, 'Just What Is A Family Business', in Aronoff *et al.*, *Family Business Sourcebook II*, op.cit., p. 2.

31. Cited in Handler, 'Methodological Issues', op.cit., p. 259.

32. Cited in ibid., p. 260.

33. D. T. Jaffee, *'Working with the Ones You Love'*, Emeryville, CA: Conari Press 1991 p. 27.

34. D. Bork, *Family Business, Risky Business,* New York: Amacon, 1986, p. 24.

35. P. C. Rosenblatt, L. de Mik, R. M. Anderson and P. A. Johnson, *The Family in Business: Understanding and Dealing with the Challenges Entrepreneurial Families Face*, San Francisco: Jossey-Bass, 1985, pp. 4–5.

36. Handler, 'Methodological Issues', op. cit., p. 262.

37. R. A. Litz, 'The Family Business: Toward Definitional Clarity', *Family Business Review*, vol. VIII, no. 2 (Summer 1995), p. 78. Note that as the last part of his definition relates to intentions, a simple four-cell matrix is established; PNFB, potential non-family business; FB, family business; NFB, non-family business; PFB, potential family business.

# 2    Stages of Evolution of Family Enterprises

It is indeed a desirable thing to be well descended, but the glory belongs to our ancestors

(Plutarch, Greek philosopher and historian, ca 125–50 BC)

Part of the task of Chapter 1 was to grapple with the thorny issue of defining the subject of this book: the family enterprise. When reading the many definitions cited, one is struck by how many seem to convey a static, non-dynamic picture of the family firm. Yet both intuitively and experientially we know that all enterprises, whether or not they are family managed and/or owned, are anything but static. They change, transform, mutate and evolve over time. In other words they are dynamic. They share this vital characteristic with all organisms, plant or animal but most especially, in our context human.

The challenge, and it is a significant one, is to find ways of clearly describing the complex evolutionary patterns of human organisations in general and specifically family enterprises in particular. Not surprisingly, many authors have tried to do so and we will draw on a handful in this chapter. We do so because it is clear that the governance of family enterprises must, of necessity, be guided by the firm's position in the evolutionary life cycle.

The underlying conceptual source of most dynamic models is to be found in the psychological and psychoanalytical literature that traces the development of the individual from (pre-) birth to death. As we will see, extrapolations are made from the life cycle of individuals and applied to the collectivity of individuals that comprises the infrastructure of all organisations. Thus the component parts of organisational life cycles are variously described as 'stages', 'eras', 'phases', 'steps' or 'passages' – most of which are deeply rooted in the human psychological development models created during the twentieth century. Given the fundamentally sequential nature of these models, it is not surprising that considerable emphasis is placed in both the psychological and organisational literature not only on the stages *per se* but also on the transitions between each phase of the life cycle. Let us start with some examples, focusing on the

26

life cycle of the individual. Later in the chapter we shall cite some derivations appearing in the organisational development as well as the family business literature.

## INDIVIDUAL LIFE CYCLES

The simplest psychological models list five basic life cycle stages:

- Birth (sometimes starting with pre-birth)
- Childhood
- Adolescence
- Adulthood
- Death

Levinson and his colleagues[1] undertook the classic, groundbreaking, ten-year study of male adulthood that led to one of the most comprehensive descriptions of the evolution or development of the individual. Their life cycle is split into 'eras', which they define as a time of life with 'its own distinctive and unifying qualities which have to do with the character of living'.[2] Their definition of 'era', tends to go beyond the concept of a typical developmental stage or period. In their descriptions they draw from biology, psychology, social psychology and sociology. As they state, 'The sequence of eras constitutes the macro-structure of the life cycle. It provides a framework within which developmental periods and concrete processes of everyday living take place.'[3] The analogies used for eras are the various acts of a play – the play itself being analogous to the whole life cycle of an individual.

The Levinson *et al.* model has ten eras or seasons:

- Infancy
- Early childhood
- Middle childhood
- Pubescence
- Early adolescence
- Late adolescence
- Early adulthood
- Middle adulthood
- Late adulthood
- Late late adulthood

The age range they assign to the period between infancy and late adolescence is 0–20. Early adulthood belongs to the 17–45 year olds, middle adulthood to the 40–65 year olds, late adulthood to those who are 60+ (note the overlaps). They subsequently add late late adulthood (80+?) but their research sample does not permit generalisations about this very advanced age group. The eras and the cross-era transitions are depicted in Figure 2.1.

Although many more studies could be cited, the above sample is adequate for our purposes. In anticipation of our later discussion of the life cycle of family enterprises, it is important to note here that the many models of individual development share many assumptions that will reappear, albeit with some necessary alterations, when the organisational models are described. All the theorists underline that each individual is unique and that therefore the voyage from the start of life to death

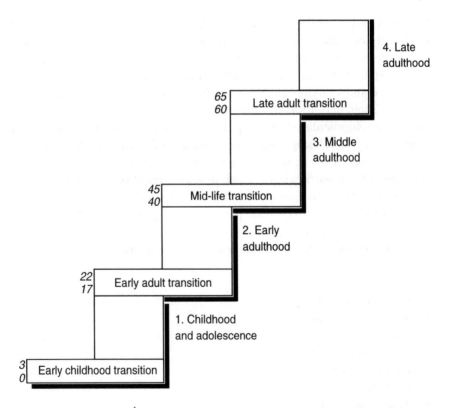

**Source**: Levinson *et al.*[4]

**Figure 2.1** Eras in the human life cycle

is never exactly the same for two or more persons. However the evidence shows that in broad, general terms, individual development seems to pass through various stages (steps, phases, eras and so on) in a fairly predictable pattern. Each stage can be described and has its own inevitable stresses and strains as well as potentially positive outcomes. The goals, priorities, tasks and pitfalls will vary at the different stages and transitions, and hence the way that psychic and physical energy is channelled clearly will not be the same when, say, one is negotiating the early childhood transition and the mid-life transition. At each stage the seeds are sown for the challenges of the forthcoming one, and how well one copes at a given stage predetermines, at least to some degree, how prepared one is to confront the challenges of the next stage. Also predictable is that towards the end of a given stage, the symptoms of a transitional challenge start to appear and these interstage transitions can be enormously stressful and take some years to complete. Note that Figure 2.1 above postulates five-year transitions at the early adult, mid-life and late-adult transitions. Nor is there any guarantee that one will successfully navigate the transition between the various steps. Suicide, premature natural death, self-defeating or self-harming behaviour and social dysfunctionality are all possible outcomes. Still, there is a commonly shared assumption that most individuals, most of the time, will be able to pass relatively successfully through each era and the intermediate transitions. In this process they will continue along the developmental cycle, at varying paces, until biological decline and finally death bring the cycle to its inevitable close.

## ORGANISATIONAL LIFE CYCLES

Before moving to life cycle models that have been developed to illustrate the evolution of family enterprises, let us examine just two models from the literature on organisational development. The first is chosen not only because it is one of the best known but also because it derives directly from the individual development models to which we have referred and has *prima facie* applicability to our understanding of the evolution of family firms. We refer to the work of Adizes, whose seminal article is entitled 'Organizational Passages – Diagnosing and Treating Lifecycle Problems of Organizations'.[5]

Adizes hypothesises that people, products, markets and even societies go through a life cycle composed of four generic stages:

- Birth
- Growth
- Maturity
- Death

As we shall see in a moment, he expands this list to ten stages when he applies it to business organisations. He further declares that to be effective, a well-managed firm must undertake four roles:

> It must *P*roduce the results for which it exists. It must also achieve its results efficiently: It must be *A*dministered, that is, its decisions must be made in the right sequence and with the right timing and right intensity. In the long run, a well-managed organisation must adapt to its external environment. The *E*ntrepreneurial role focuses on adaptive changes, which requires creativity and risk-taking. And to ensure that an organisation can have a lifespan longer than that of its key managers, the fourth role – *I*ntegration – is necessary to build a team effort. Effective and efficient management over the short and long term requires that all four roles – *PAEI* – be performed well.[6]

Adizes then lists and describes in detail the ten 'phases' of his model, the labels of which are evocative (see Figure 2.2). As the firm passes from one stage to the next over time, the four roles – in a descriptive sense – are more or less important. He illustrates this finding through the following shorthand. A capital letter implies that this particular role predominates; lower case implies a lesser role; '-' indicates that the role is largely inoperative. His model is shown graphically in Figure 2.2.

There is no inevitable progression up the curve, as failure can occur at any stage. Adizes labels these causes of exit 'aborted idea' at the courtship stage, 'infant mortality' at the infancy stage, 'the founder's trap' at the go-go stage and 'divorce' at adolescence. The founder's trap is of particular interest to us as it relates directly to many family enterprises in their early stages. Adizes points out that the very behaviour that allowed the organisation to prosper during the go-go stage may, if allowed to continue, prevent its further development:

> What allowed the Infant organisation to survive a hostile environment is the motherlike commitment of its founder. While this commitment is indispensable for the survival of the Infant organisation, it becomes dysfunctional after the Go-Go stages. The loving embrace becomes a

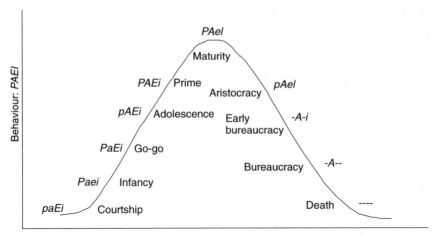

Aging = *f* (mental age, relative market share, functionality of the organizational structure)

**Source**: Adizes (1979)[7]

**Figure 2.2** Organisational passages

stranglehold. The founder refuses to depersonalise policies and institutionalise his leadership, that is, to establish workable systems, procedures, and policies that do not require his personal judgement. To avoid the founder's trap, the *A role* – administrative systems – has to grow in importance.[8]

Adizes' model has most of the earmarks of the previously cited individual development theories. There are describable and predictable stages and transitions, each with its own special characteristics and challenges. There is a starting point (courtship rather than birth or prebirth) and the same end point – death. However there are important differences. While Adizes is very descriptive, he often becomes quite normative and prescriptive.

Knowing the challenges of each stage and transition, he is clear on what should be done to correct the course so as to avoid pitfalls such as the founder's trap. He speaks of two kinds of 'treatment' – preventive and curative. The former applies to the first five stages, which are on the 'momentum' part of his curve. Again, his labels for each of the preventive measures are evocative:

- Courtship: reality testing.
- Infancy: inexpensive support.

- Go-go: directive board.
- Adolescence: rekindle the fire.
- Prime: reorganise and decentralise.

The curative measures apply to the 'inertia' part (post-Maturity) of his curve and again are evocative:

- Aristocracy: A'S/M therapy.[9]
- Early Bureaucracy: surgery.
- Bureaucracy: euthanasia.
- Death: caretakers.

Thus it seems that death may not be inevitable in the organisational passages model – at least if one is intelligent enough to apply Adizes' various treatments in time. With the bureaucracy phase, Adizes implies that it is too late to go back up the curve to a healthier position and euthanasia is probably the only remedy.

From a governance perspective, Adizes' model has several implications. As the family enterprise moves through the various stages, the governance institutions in place – whether family, board, top management or all three – can verify whether or not the appropriate *PAEI* roles are being played. They can look for signs of the various causes for exit and ensure that appropriate preventive and curative treatments are applied in a timely fashion. In a very real sense, Adizes has suggested a most powerful 'early warning system' for the governance institutions of the family firm.

The second model taken from the organisational development literature is Greiner's classic, entitled 'Evolution and Revolution as Organizations Grow'.[10] He claims that to build a model of how organisations develop over time requires an understanding of the interplay and impact of five key variables:

- Age of the organisation
- Size of the organisation
- Stages of evolution
- Stages of revolution and
- Growth rate of the industry.

This conclusion clearly places Greiner in the contingency school of organisation theory, which, simply stated, means in this context that how organisations develop and evolve is dependent or contingent on the interplay of these five variables. Simple cause and effect explanations are thereby excluded.[11] Greiner also belongs to the school of thought that an organisation's future is largely determined by its past. By this conviction he acknowledges that he is influenced by European rather than American schools of psychology.

Greiner's continuum for the age of the organisation goes from young to mature. As shown in Figure 2.3, his version of the life cycle is split into five phases of growth (he has used size of organisation as the *y* or vertical axis). Each development phase has two parts, which he labels 'evolution'[12] and 'revolution'[13] or crisis.

In this model, it is clear that each evolution inevitably creates the conditions for subsequent revolution. For example in 'Growth through

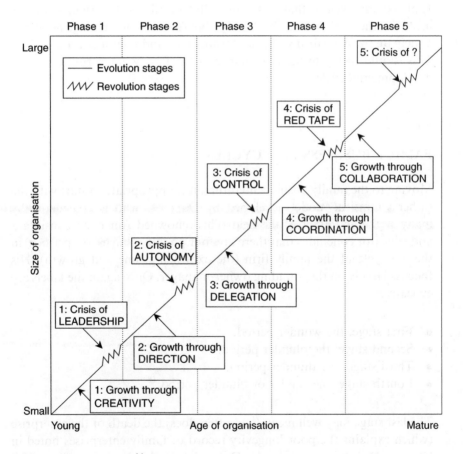

**Source**:   Greiner (1972)[14]

**Figure 2.3**   The five phases of growth

direction' (phase 2) there is a natural tendency to overcentralise power in the hands of the CEO (or owner-manager/founder), which leads to demands (and the need) for greater autonomy (the crisis of phase 2).

How management handles each crisis will directly influence its ability to move the organisation into the next phase. Thus, as in Adizes' model, there is no automatic progression between the phases. Stagnation and death are possible at all points between young and mature. Interestingly, Greiner does not label the crisis in phase 5, but he does guess that that it will be characterised by the ' "psychological saturation" of employees who grow emotionally and physically exhausted by the intensity of teamwork and the heavy pressure for innovative solutions.'[15] Taken to the extreme, this could mean the death of the organisation.[16]

The comments made at the end of the discussion of Adizes' model apply equally well to that of Greiner. By consulting the original sources listed in the end notes, the family, board and top management can anticipate the described stages and transitions and their associated crises. This should facilitate the governance of the family enterprise during its developmental cycle.

## FAMILY BUSINESS LIFE CYCLES

Moving to the family business literature, it is appropriate to start with the rather whimsical model developed by Danco,[17] who is considered by many as the godfather of the field. This renowned American consultant and educator concludes that there are four possible 'stages' or 'periods' in the life cycle of the family firm (the axes being time and growth). His focus is largely on the founding owner-manager. Once again the labels are evocative:

- First stage: the wonder period.
- Second stage: the blunder period.
- Third stage: the thunder period.
- Fourth stage: the sunder or plunder period.[18]

The last stage may well mean (and often does) the death of the enterprise (which explains the poor longevity record of family enterprises noted in Chapter 1), but not necessarily. Danco leaves the door open for a fifth stage, which he labels the 'new wonder':

But there is a third alternative. That is the possibility of investing his successors with his own sense of wonder in the joy of risking and building the business so that they can provide the leadership the business needs to continue to grow, without repeating all the mistakes and hardships of a first generation. This is what I term the rebirth of wonder . . . the real solution to the continuity of the owner managed business.[19]

McGivern[20] uses Kroeger's[21] life cycle model as a basis for insights into how to manage CEO succession in small family firms, thus providing a bridge between the organisation life cycle model and how to manage CEO succession in small family firms. Figure 2.4 depicts the bringing together of the five life-cycle stages (initiation, development, growth, maturity, decline) and the hypothesised managerial roles that are required.

This formulation strongly suggests that the choice of successor (the subject of Chapter 6) should be based on the skills needed for the particular managerial role to be played in the life cycle stage the new CEO will be inheriting. Like Greiner, McGivern works with five contingent variables:

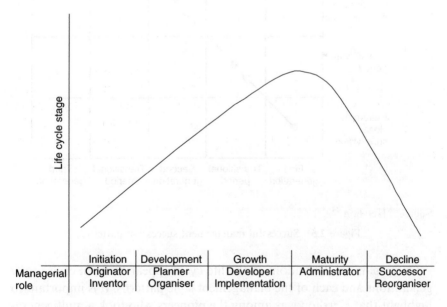

| | Initiation | Development | Growth | Maturity | Decline |
|---|---|---|---|---|---|
| Managerial role | Originator Inventor | Planner Organiser | Developer Implementation | Administrator | Successor Reorganiser |

**Source**: McGivern (1989).[22]

**Figure 2.4**   Managerial development through the life cycle of the small firm

- Stage of business development.
- Motivation of owner-manager.
- Extent of family dominance.
- Organisational climate.
- The business environment.

Hershon[23] creates a two-dimensional graph that explicitly links the progress of a family through three generations (the 'management succession' or *x* axis) and normatively suggests appropriate management styles or 'patterns' (the 'organisation development' or *y* axis) for each stage in the evolution of the family business (Figure 2.5).

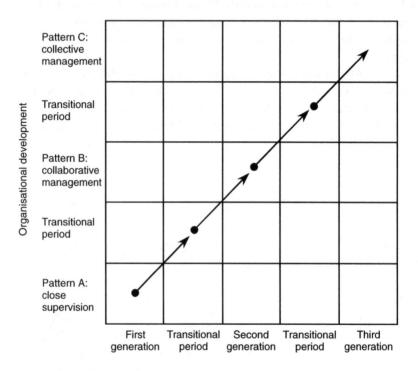

**Source**: Hershon.[24]

**Figure 2.5**   Successful management succession patterns

Once again the transitions in the life cycle appear between each of the generations and each of the management style patterns. It is important to highlight that Hershon was among the pioneers who took a multigenerational perspective rather than just concentrating on what transpires during the tenure of the founder or a single owner–manager.[25]

The next two models to be described were developed by John Ward and represent his thinking at two different points in time: 1988 and 1991. The first conceptualisation comes from his *Keeping the Family Business Healthy*.[26] Ward specifies three different life cycles:

- Business life cycle.
- Organisational life cycle.
- Business owner's life cycle.

As we have seen in the earlier studies cited, Ward[27] also believes that various 'forces' influence the passage of the family firm through various predictable patterns of growth and change. Among these forces are:

- The nature of the business (type of product, its stage in the life cycle, competitive and market conditions, and so on).
- The character of the organisation (size, complexity, speed of change).
- The motivation of the owner–manager (his or her major focus).
- Family financial expectations (the evolution of its needs).
- Family goals (its major focus).

His model has three stages of growth in the life cycle of a family business (Table 2.1). These three stages are labelled as follows:

- Stage I: early.
- Stage II: middle.
- Stage III: late.

Imbedded in his model are parts of the life cycles of the parents or owning generation and their children, thereby anticipating his later ownership framework, which places greater emphasis on the generational perspective. While Ward claims that his approach applies to both entrepreneurial and mature family enterprises, the underlying schema are most applicable, in our opinion, to founder-owned and managed enterprises. However if subsequent generations achieve 'regeneration', it is easily conceivable that the model could repeat itself several times in dynastic families. As we have seen before, the challenges of each stage vary and there are difficult transitions. Individual family firms will stay for varying periods in each stage and many will not continue to exist through the three stages. Management styles[28] and strategy[29], among other things, must change over time if the enterprise is to prosper.

**Table 2.1** Evolutionary stages of a family business

| | Stages | | |
|---|---|---|---|
| | I | II | III |
| Age of business (or business renewal) | 0–5 years | 10–20 years | 20–30 years |
| Age of parents | 25–35 years | 40–50 years | 55–70 years |
| Age of children | 0–10 years | 15–25 years | 30–45 years |
| *Challenges:* | | | |
| Nature of business | Rapidly growing and demanding of time and money | Maturing | Needing strategic 'regeneration' and reinvestment |
| Character of organisation | Small, dynamic | Larger and more complex | Stagnant |
| Owner–Manager motivation | Committed to business success | Desires control and stability | Seeks new interests, or is semiretired; next generation seeks growth and change |
| Family financial expectations | Limited to basic need | More needs, including comfort education | Larger needs, including security and generosity |
| Family goals | Business success | Growth and development of children | Family harmony and unity. |

**Source:** Ward[30]

In his later book, entitled *Creating Effective Boards for Private Enterprises*,[31] Ward looks at the evolution of the family company through two different perspectives: ownership (Table 2.2) and management (Table 2.3).

In Table 2.2 three stages are formulated and the familiar evolutionary step approach is once again highlighted. However in this instance a multigenerational model is presented, with which many long-lived family companies can identify. Dominant shareholder issues are presented for each stage, and as we have seen before, interstage transitions can be extremely difficult. Neither does Ward posit that there is any automatic progression through the stages. Quite apart from the constant danger that the firm may collapse or be sold out of the founding family at any time, family enterprises may stay in the same stage for generations (for example the oldest child may inherit all the shares and behave like a founder). Or a Stage two company may return to being a Stage one company when one sibling buys out another. In this case, the dominant shareholder issues start to look very much like those of a founder stage company. Likewise Stage three companies can cycle back either to Stage two or to Stage one (a process sometimes labelled 'pruning the family tree'). Thus multiple combinations and permutations are possible in the ownership structure over the lives of family enterprises.

**Table 2.2**   Ownership issues in the evolving family business

| Ownership stage | Dominant shareholder issues |
| --- | --- |
| Stage one: the founder(s) | Leadership transition<br>Succession<br>Spouse insurance<br>Estate planning |
| Stage two: the sibling partnership | Maintaining teamwork and harmony<br>Sustaining family ownership<br>Succession |
| Stage three: the family dynasty (also called the cousins' confederation) | Allocation of corporate capital: dividends debt, and profit levels<br>Shareholder liquidity<br>Family tradition and culture<br>Family conflict resolution<br>Family participation and role<br>Family vision and mission<br>Family linkage with the business |

**Source**:   Ward (1991).[32]

Table 2.3 views the life cycle of the family firm through a different lens, namely the evolution of management stages.

This is in fact a hybrid of business approach, management system and organisational form. Dominant management issues vary with each predictable stage, and the transitions can be problematical. Further research is needed on how these two models interact in the real world. One can hypothesise that, depending on which stage of the ownership model coexists with which stage of the management model, they could be mutually supportive or mutually antagonistic, with either beneficial or catastrophic consequences for the family enterprise. With these two models in the foreground, Ward then goes on to describe his experience with the role, structuring and managing of the board of directors of private (mostly family) enterprises.

**Table 2.3**    Management issues in the evolving family business

| *Management stage* | *Dominant management issues* |
|---|---|
| Stage one: entrepreneurship | Survival |
| | Growth |
| Stage two: professionalisation | Adopting professional management systems |
| | Revitalising strategy |
| Stage three: the holding company | Allocation of resources |
| | Overseeing investment portfolio |
| | Corporate culture |
| | Succession and leadership |
| | Performance of investment |
| | Strategy |
| | Shareholder relations |

**Source**:    Ward (1991).[33]

For our final example of life cycle models applied to family firms, we turn to the most recent (and in many ways the most complex) study: 'Generation to Generation: Life Cycles of the Family Business', Gersick *et al.*[34] Basically, the authors have taken a variation of the three circle model described in Chapter 1 and chosen to focus on Family, Ownership and Business and broken each into individual life cycles. The result is a three dimensional matrix they call their 'development model' of the family enterprise.

The 'Family' axis comprises four stages:

- Young business family (older generation at work).
- Entering the business (the next generation is employed in the firm).

- Working together (of two generations).
- Passing the baton (succession).

This has been strongly influenced by the work of Levinson and other individual and family life cycle theorists. The 'ownership' axis is derived directly from Ward (1991) and the three stages are relabelled:

- Controlling owner
- Sibling partnership
- Cousin consortium

The descriptions of each step and the intermediate transitions reflect Ward's fundamental views.

The third axis is the 'business' one, which is also made up of three stages:

- Start-up
- Expansion/formalisation
- Maturity

This is a telescoped version of many of the business life cycle models presented earlier in this chapter. The strength, for us, of this developmental model is that it combines three of the major strands of the life cycle literature. The inevitable downside is the large number of possible combinations deriving from a $4 \times 3 \times 3$ matrix. Furthermore a given family enterprise (particularly a larger and older one) can be at more than one stage on any given axis. Gersick *et al.* are thus forced, to the advantage and relief of the reader, to focus periodically on archetypes such as 'controlling owner', 'young business family' or 'start-up business'. When the spotlight is on succession (as in Chapter 6 below), they can and do roam more widely throughout their model. Their depiction of the three axes is shown in Figure 2.6.

The Ferragamo story (see box below) traces the evolution of a highly successful family firm through the first two stages (founder and sibling partnership) in Ward's model. It clearly depicts a company moving from stage 2 to stage 3 (cousins' confederation) with the third generation starting to come of age. The family has already taken some interesting steps to facilitate the transition between the sibling partnership and cousins' confederation stages.

42

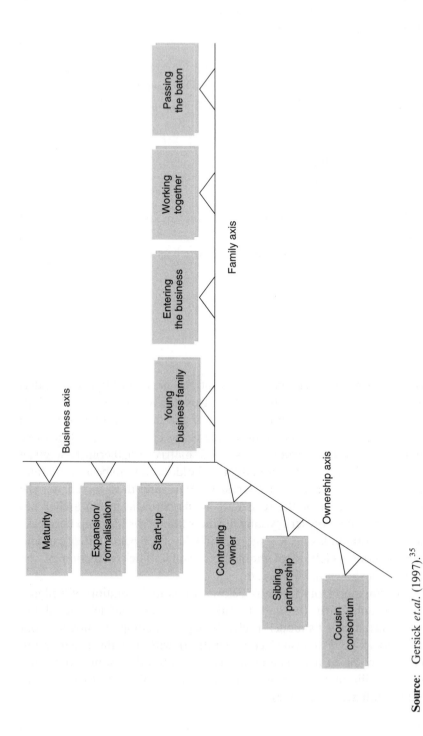

**Source**: Gersick *et.al.* (1997).[35]

**Figure 2.6** The three-dimensional model

### 'Heirs Loom' [36]

'Ferragamo has become a well-regarded player in the luxury-goods big league. Its staff even beat Gucci's in a benefit soccer game here recently. But aggressive expansion is testing the very family-style management on which it has built success.

Already a famed name in shoes, leather goods and scarves, Salvatore Ferragamo SpA has been on a shopping spree in the past 18 months. Starting with the purchase of Emanuel Ungaro couture and perfumes, and acquisitions of a home-fabrics company and three luxury hotels in Florence last year, the company added a fragrance joint venture with Bulgari this past spring.

Such energetic growth would raise financial analysts' eyebrows in the case of a publicly traded firm like Gucci Group NV. But family-owned Ferragamo doesn't need to worry about that: All acquisitions, like everything the company undertakes, were self-financed.

*Financial Health*

"We don't believe in borrowing money. Independence is healthy," says Ferrucio Ferragamo, the firm's chief executive and eldest son of the founder. "Banks offer you money when you don't need it, and then want it back when you don't have any."

In the high-flying, beautiful-people world of luxury goods, Ferragamo's management approach is almost homely in its clinging to family values and the virtues of well-planted nepotism. But it seems to work. Sales have soared this decade (profits aren't disclosed). Harvard Business School assigns the company as a case study in how a family-owned company should be run.

The only problem with this picture is human nature, an unavoidable and sometimes unmanageable thing that has beset family-owned company firms for years. A new Ferragamo generation is coming of age, and the number of family shareholders will nearly quadruple from the current seven. Will they share the same values heading into the 21st century that nurtured a company with its roots in the 19th? And can an evolving family structure survive the pressures of the company's phenomenal growth?

Founder Salvatore Ferragamo, the 11th of 14 children, preached the old-fashioned values of family, faith and value-for-money. He became famous as a shoemaker to the stars, coddling the glamorous arches and imperious insteps of the likes of Eva Peron, Greta Garbo and Audrey Hepburn.

When he died in 1960 at age 62, his widow, Wanda, took the helm until the children, then aged 2 to 17, were old enough to come aboard. Mrs Ferragamo was already thinking of expansion. She wanted to transform "Ferragamo from a shoe company into a real House of Ferragamo," says 52-year-old Ferrucio Ferragamo. "So Mum put one daughter into ready-to-wear, a son in charge of shoes, and so on. Maybe it was unusual, but it worked."

### *All in the Family*

Today, Mrs Ferragamo is company president, her eldest son is chief executive, and each of the five other children runs a division. Together the seven own 100 per cent of Salvatore Ferragamo shares.

What and Where

Ferragamo sales by product and region in 1996, in percent

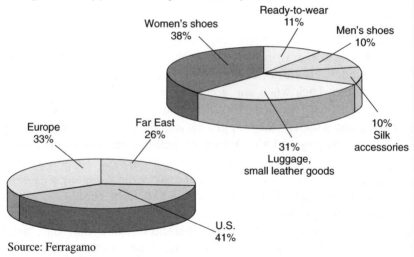

Source: Ferragamo

Andrall Pearson, now an emeritus professor at Harvard University, wrote and taught the first case study of Ferragamo in 1982. "They have family incredibly well-utilised around the business, which you don't usually see in family companies," Prof. Pearson notes. "Each family member has a distinct role that plays to his or her individual strengths. They each have their own playground, and they all succeed.'

Another asset, he says, is the family's willingness to delegate responsibilities to outside talent, which he regards as remarkable for a family company, "where often what you find is a 'family against the rest of the world' mentality."

Prof. Pearson says the scale of Ferragamo's success since he began studying the company has surprised him. "The only things I had doubts about – their ability to grow, to maintain quality, and to delegate where necessary – turned out not to be issues," he says.

Over the past six years, despite weak economies in Europe and Japan, Ferragamo's revenue has grown between 25 per cent and 40 per cent annually, allowing the company to expand at a time when many rivals were tightening their belts. In 1996, sales reached 851 billion lire ($496.5 million), double the level of three years ago.

The company's growth despite unfavorable conditions was partly helped by a strategy to offset currency fluctuations, a key factor given that 80 per cent of Ferragamo's sales come from exports. The company invests some sales from a given market in risk-coverage instruments, such as options or futures, in that market's currency, minimising risk and allowing Ferragamo to keep prices stable.

"Customers appreciate that. You can't keep changing your prices with every currency hiccup," Mr Ferragamo says.

*Private vs Public*

Analysts frequently speculate about when Ferragamo will bow to one trend or another and sell to a larger group or go public – as Gucci, Donna Karan and Ralph Lauren have done, and as Gianni Versage[*] plans to do next year. Mr Ferragamo argues that being a private company offers freedom public companies don't have, especially in difficult times.

"When you're public, you have to think how to make the market and shareholders regard you favorably," says Mr Ferragamo. In addition, "when times are tough, we can still go on the offensive. Rather than trying to save money, we increase advertising, for example. We can afford it," he notes.

The family has agreed not to seek big dividends, but to invest in the company and finance its growth. "It's important that the strategy of the company be a long-term one, and not one of year-to-year profits," Mr Ferragamo says.

Cedric Magnelia, a London-based luxury-sector analyst at Credit Suisse First Boston, acknowledges that Ferragamo's strategy bucks the trend of public offerings from fashion and luxury-goods companies, but says it's one that makes sense.

"It's an excellent brand, and a very solid company. From a financial point of view, there's no need for them to go public. In that, they can be compared to Chanel, another family company with a good cash position and strong external growth," he says.

The big question is whether the current tight-knit family group will succeed in transmitting its values and goals to the next generation. There are already 19 grandchildren, waiting in the wings. Not all will enter the business, but all will inherit shares and a voice in how to dispose of them.

"Once the handover takes place, it's hard to say. There may be some fiscal pressure for them to go public at that point, because of inheritance taxes – that's what pushed Hermès and Clarins in that direction", says Mr Magnelia, referring to two formerly family-owned French groups.

Mr Ferragamo, who himself has five children, admits that the temptation of a flotation may be hard to resist for the next generation. "But I always say to my family, that between the six kids, the mother, and the 19 grandchildren, that makes 26 shareholders. That's quite enough',' he says.

Located in a Renaissance palazzo, Ferragamo's headquarters on Florence's posh Via Tornabuoni include a vast ground-floor boutique, a shoe museum and offices. Amid the formality of vaulted ceilings, frescoes and tapestries, the atmosphere is that of a family house.

Guests wait in what looks like a living room, with an old black-and-white photo in a gilt frame showing Salvatore and Wanda and five of their six children on the steps of a Tuscan villa.

With wavy reddish hair and a wry sense of humor, Mrs Ferragamo, 75, combines the warmth of a gracious hostess with the savvy befitting the president of a global luxury group. Signora Wanda, as employees call her, is determined to keep Ferragamo in the family, and the family in Ferragamo.

One safeguard she developed is a set of rules for grandchildren who want to work for Ferragamo. They must have a university degree and at least one previous professional experience elsewhere, and they must be unanimously accepted by the family.

"We have guidelines so they can come with preparation and humility," Mrs Ferragamo says. One grandchild just got an MBA from New York University; another is studying for a business degree in Milan.

She admits that one reason they decided to buy three Florence hotels, which have little to do with the company's core business, was that "we have to find jobs for 19 grandchildren."

Firmly against going public, Mrs Ferragamo says the shareholders are in the process of drafting a "family pact" to protect the structure in the future by ensuring that even if some family shareholders didn't wish to retain their stake, the shares wouldn't leave the family.

*Quality Control*

It remains to be seen whether the family can also maintain its commitment to quality amid rapid growth. All seven million Ferragamo items sold world-wide each year are still made in Italy, and according to company lore, each is inspected by hand during production before passing through Florence for a final quality check. Salvatore Ferragamo once turned down a $1 million offer for his name because he couldn't guarantee the quality of shoes produced under license . . . .

The next three years, Mr Ferragamo says, will be spent on consolidation and strengthening the brand with high-profile projects like next year's launch of a Ferragamo perfume, one of two involved in the joint venture with Bulgari.

CSFB's Mr Magnelia says Ferragamo needs to rejuvenate its image if it wants to compete with rivals like Gucci and Prada, who've seen explosive growth thanks to their transformations into trendy must-haves for wealthy young urbanites from Beverly Hills to Bangkok.

"The only criticism one could make is that the brand image is a little dusty – their clientele is older than that of, say, Gucci or Prada," he says. The purchase of Ungaro, which has a sexier, trendier image, was an important step in that direction, he says. The launch of a new Ungaro perfume next year in the deal with Bulgari will provide additional exposure.'

(Reprinted with the permission of *Wall Street Journal Europe*.)

* Gianni Versace was murdered soon after the publication of this article.

FOCUS ON COUSINS' CONFEDERATION

Describing the evolution of family enterprises, as we are trying to do in this chapter, reveals not only how complex the subject is but also how many different models (and we have only chosen a few) have been produced to try to explain the phenomenon. One of the simplest and most appealing to us is the stage model, as developed by Ward and Gersick *et al.* (heavily influenced by Ward), which has both ownership and management (among other) implications over the life cycle of family firms. The labels used by the various authors differ, and we prefer those used by Ward:

- Stage 1: founders
- Stage 2: sibling partnership
- Stage 3: cousins' confederation

In the remainder of the book we will generally focus on Stage 3, for two reasons. First, most of the personal experience we have gained as academics and consultants has been with Stage 3 firms. Second, much more research and thinking has gone into Stage 1 and Stage 2 family enterprises than into Stage 3 ones. By emphasising Stage 3, it is our hope that others will pick up the torch and expand our collective knowledge of cousins' confederations.

Stage 3 companies differ in important ways from their predecessors. In Table 2.2 above, Ward has listed seven 'dominant shareholder issues' in Stage 3 (which he labels 'the family dynasty', but which elsewhere he has also referred to as 'cousins' confederation'). They are worth repeating:

- Allocation of corporate capital; dividends and profit levels.
- Shareholder liquidity.
- Family tradition and culture.
- Family conflict resolution.
- Family participation and roles.
- Family vision and mission and.
- Family linkage with the business.[37]

For Gersick *et al.*, there are two key challenges for a Stage 3 company:

- Managing the complexity of the family and the shareholder group.
- Creating a family business capital market.[38]

While each stage has particular challenges, a company in Stage 3 faces significant centrifugal forces that must be thwarted if the firm is to remain family controlled.[39] In the classical Stage 1 firm, both ownership and management tend to be in the hands of the same person, and governance issues are not the major concern. By Stage 2, centrifugal forces may well have started, with only some siblings being both in the business and part-owners. Those external to the firm may have very different views on family and business matters, as suggested in Chapter 1.

With the advent of the cousins' confederation, not only are more (extended) family members involved (with potentially very great age differences) but they will have been brought up by different parents. The norms of the individual nuclear families may be very diverse. The key actors, whether owners or not, will not know each other as well as the siblings of the older generation. If their parents were in conflict, it is not at all unlikely that their tensions will be visited upon the third and even subsequent generations. By now the cousins may be geographically separated and rarely have the chance to get together, making it extremely difficult to keep the family cohesive or enmeshed. Many may be utter strangers to each other.

A further possible complication is that the youngest generation may have few psychological ties to the firm, its products, services and traditions. The majority may never have known the founder and feel no affective link with him or her (which would be unusual in a stage 2 company).

What has typically happened to share ownership by the time third and subsequent generations are in the picture? Unless there has been serious consolidation of shares in the hands of individuals or branches of the family, most shareholders may hold less than 1 per cent. Even though their wealth measured in the value of their shares, may still be significant, these shares may be partially or totally illiquid unless provisions for selling them have been institutionalised. This can lead to considerable frustration, not to mention jealousy, as the non-active family members look at the salaries, benefits and other perks that their siblings and cousins may be receiving from their employment in the family's enterprise.

Furthermore the active family members probably have access to detailed information on the company and its current and future prospects. Information is perceived in this instance (rightfully) as power. Their siblings and cousins, even if they are kept regularly informed, may not have the educational background to understand the data.

Taken together, the above complications are a potentially explosive mixture. This may be a partial explanation of why so few family enterprises are in the cousins' confederation stage.[40]

The Schlumberger story (see box below) provides an example of some of the complexities that can arise in a cousins' confederation. It also illustrates that the inherent challenges can be overcome, in this instance by separating ownership from management and ensuring that the family owners secure wise financial counsel.

---

### Schlumberger: A Complex Cousins' Confederation

In 1919 Paul Schlumberger, then 71 years old, signed a contract with his two sons, Conrad (the scientist) and Marcel (the economist). In exchange for a considerable advance on their inheritance, the sons committed themselves to developing Conrad's scientific research and finding an appropriate industrial application for it. Conrad developed a unique method of analysing underground resources for the petroleum industry. When Conrad died a few years later, Marcel was left to carry out his father's wishes alone. While no profits resulted until 1930, the company soon led its field. Marcel hired his son Pierre to assist him, and placed his two daughters, Conrad's three daughters and their spouses in numerous other jobs. An industrial dynasty was born.

When Marcel died in 1953, Pierre, the only remaining male, seemed the obvious successor. But instead Marcel's daughters, along with their actively involved husbands, claimed priority rights over their father's invention. Furthermore each cousin, empowered as employee and shareholder, tried to gain authority over different business sectors. An organisational chart was officially established. It theoretically divided the business according to various family members' competences. The plan led to an explosive situation that threatened to split the company into several parts. Decreasing profits, the exclusive means of support for six families, created a frightened and uneasy consensus: in order to improve the general financial situation they eventually agreed to a centralised organisational structure headed by Pierre, but not without some reluctance on the part of certain family members.

Diminution of the family conflict allowed Pierre to make several key moves that enhanced his power:

- The company went public (providing liquidity for the family owners)in order to forestall a repeat of the catastrophic family influence.
- He installed a policy prohibiting company employment for any family member, including in-laws.
- He increased the authority of a non-family executive: Jean Riboud, a talented businessman who had helped him with the global reorganisation and later became his right-hand man. Between Pierre and Ribaud, a climate of trust, esteem and efficiency existed. Their complementary skills created a well-balanced and powerful executive team.

As time passed, Pierre slowly withdrew and lost touch with the company. Although the company remained prosperous, dissatisfaction and plotting increased. Under pressure from Pierre's sister (Geneviève Seydoux) and three cousins (Conrad's daughters), M. Lepercq, the family's banker, led the revolt. In May 1965 the family unanimously forced Pierre to leave the company. Riboud was asked by the family to replace Pierre as CEO and chairman of the Schlumberger group.

Riboud gave professionalism priority over family relationships. He enjoyed unrivalled power and used it to stimulate company growth. Family membership of the board was reduced to a minority, and all honorary seats were cancelled.

Four years later Jerôme, Pierre's nephew (one of the 23 cousins of the fourth generation) and a successful banker, wanted to join the board. From the family's point of view he was the next 'crown prince'. But after a few months in the company his arrogance and his attitude towards Riboud created a strained atmosphere. Claiming that there was not enough space for two bosses, Riboud tendered his resignation. The family refused to accept it and Jerôme was forced to leave.

Family unity was maintained through the expulsion from the business of a family member because the female heirs of the third generation wanted to reactivate the rule preventing the employment of family members. In all critical situations they had used their authority to enforce the divorce between management power and ownership. This sense of solidarity among the female cousins, all holders of an impressive fortune, reaffirmed their objective to preserve a healthy company, their mutual cash cow.

Their role of 'goddesses of the temple' was supported by M. Lepercq, a man they trusted. He progressively interceded as the family's banker and financial counsellor. He managed their shares, which at the beginning of the 1990s were estimated to have a value of nearly $10 billion. He kept outside shareholders in check. He represented the family's common interests on the boards of all the various companies in which the Schlumbergers had a stake. He advised the family members on their personal investments, helping them to consolidate their individual patrimony. In all situations he played the role of discreet but efficient intermediary between the owners and the managers.

It was a simple solution in the long-term interests of the shareholders and their heirs – a system that empowered a non-family CEO to run the company and a guardian to look after the patrimony of the family.

The positive oil industry trends accelerated as 1996 progressed, and as a result Schlumberger had an excellent year. Its net income of US$851 million and earnings per share of US$3.47 were 31 per cent and 29 per cent, respectively, above 1995 levels, while operating revenue grew 18 per cent to US$8.96 billion.

The Schlumberger-Seydoux cousins still own about 30 per cent of the family business – enough to maintain control.

CONCLUSION

This chapter has focused on the evolution of family enterprises by drawing from life cycle models developed in the literature on individual psychology, organisation theory and family enterprise development.

Any model, by definition, is a simplification and cannot totally represent the complexity of the phenomena being studied. The advantage, especially for owning family members, of the numerous life cycle models we have quoted is that they can choose which one(s) seem best to depict the history of their family enterprise and its probable future.

The most useful models are those whose stage descriptions further an understanding of the current state of the family, the ownership and the business. Equally important, they should predict both the transitional and the next-stage challenges that have to be faced, thereby providing all the key actors in the governance process with an indication of actions that should be taken to minimise future disruptions. Forewarned means forearmed. The notes at the end of this chapter direct readers to the original sources, where they can delve into the descriptive and normative dimensions of those models that seem most promising.

This is not a book on the life cycles of family enterprises but rather on the *governance* of this most prevalent form of business organisation. Yet it is clear that governance of the family firm is necessarily a function of its position(s) on the various continua we have sampled. Although each of the models has its own strengths and weaknesses, we are attracted to the simple three-stage model outlined in the last section. We have done relatively little work with small, entrepreneurial founder-managed firms in Stage 1. We have had more experience with Stage 2 – sibling partnerships – but this is a field that has been relatively well researched. Thus the material in the forthcoming chapters relies most heavily on what we have learned from our research, consulting and educational efforts with medium-size to very large, multiproduct, multinational family enterprises whose management and/or ownership is controlled by the third or subsequent generations, many of whom are in Stage 3 – cousins' confederation.

## NOTES

1. D. J. Levinson, *The Seasons of a Man's Life*, New York: Ballantine Books, 1978.
2. Ibid., p. 18.
3. Ibid., p. 18.
4. Ibid., p. 20.
5. I. Adizes, 'Organizational Passages: Diagnosing and Treating Lifecycle Problems of Organizations', *Organizational Dynamics*, Summer 1979, pp. 3–25. Adizes acknowledges (on page 3) that the title was borrowed from Gail Sheehy's best-selling book *Passages*, which in turn drew heavily from Levinson op. cit.
6. Ibid., pp. 3–4.
7. Ibid., p. 8.
8. Ibid., pp. 5–6.
9. A'S/M is a consulting intervention especially designed for 'Aristocratic' organisations. It focuses on changing the consciousness of the firm's top management by transforming their expectations and aspirations and developing a teamwork orientation. For a detailed description of all 11 phases of this 'therapy', see ibid, pp. 18–22.
10. L. E. Greiner, 'Evolution and Revolution as Organizations Grow', *Harvard Business Review*, July–August 1972.
11. Greiner is in the mainstream of current thinking about how firms – family or otherwise – evolve. Organisations are seen as highly complex systems whose

development is contingent upon various sets of variables. Authors vary widely on which variables they choose to study, depending on the purpose of their research.

12. 'The term *evolution* is used to describe prolonged periods of growth where no major upheaval occurs in organisation practices', Greiner, 'Evolution and Revolution', op.cit., p. 3.

13. 'The term *revolution* is used to describe those periods of substantial turmoil in organisational life', ibid., p. 3.

14. Ibid., p. 6.

15. Ibid., p. 8.

16. It is important to note that the larger an organisation, the greater the probability that different departments or divisions will be at different stages of the various life cycle models. This enormously complicates the managerial and governance task.

17. L. Danco, *Beyond Survival*, Cleveland: The Center for Family Business, University Press, 1982.

18. For a detailed description of each stage, and their associated myths, see ibid., pp. 21–46.

19. Ibid., p. 46.

20. C. McGivern, 'The Dynamics of Management Succession: A Model of Chief Executive Succession in the Small Family Firm', *Family Business Review*, vol. 2, no. 4 (Winter 1989).

21. The Kroeger model is taken from C. V. Kroeger, 'Managerial Development in the Small Firm', *California Management Review*, 17(1) (1974).

22. McGivern, 'The Dynamics', op.cit, p. 407.

23. Cited in B. S. Hollander and N. S. Elman, 'Family-Owned Businesses: An Emerging Field of Inquiry', *Family Business Review*, vol. 1, no. 2 (Summer 1988), pp. 151–3.

24. Ibid., p. 153.

25. A similar three-stage model was developed by Benson *et al.* in 1990: first generation (starting the business, growth, the plot thickens); second generation; third generation and beyond. The tradition of stage descriptions, challenges and transitions is maintained. B. Benson, with E. T. Crego and R. H. Drucker, *Your Family Business: A Success Guide for Growth and Survival*, Homewood, Ill.: Irwin, 1990.

Several other models of life cycles could be cited before we turn to Gersick *et al.* and Ward (see below). For the reader interested in pursuing the subject further, see L. B. Barnes and S. A. Hershon, 'Transferring power in the family business', *Harvard Business Review*, July-August 1976; Hershon's unpublished dissertation entitled 'The Problems of Management Succession in Family Business', Boston: Harvard Business School, 1975; and W. G. Dyer, Jr, *Cultural Change in Family Firms: Anticipating and Managing Business and Family Transactions*, San Francisco: Jossey-Bass, 1986.

26. J. L. Ward, *Keeping the Family Business Healthy: How to Plan for Continuing Growth, Profitability and Family Leadership*, San Francisco: Jossey-Bass, 1988, p. 20.

27. Professor Ward, of Loyola University, Chicago, has made extremely important contributions to our own understanding and to that of thousands

of other students of the field of family enterprise in his multiple roles as researcher, educator, consultant, editor, publisher and board member.

28. For a synthesis of the necessary changes in managing, see Ward, *Keeping the Family Business Healthy*, p. 30.
29. Ward's rendering of the strategic implications of the business life cycle are given in ibid., pp. 26–27.
30. Ibid., p. 21.
31. J. L. Ward, *Creating Effective Boards for Private Enterprises: Meeting the Challenges of Continuity and Competition*, San Francisco: Jossey-Bass, 1991.
32. Ibid., p. 220.
33. Ibid., p. 221.
34. K. E. Gersick, J.A. Davis, M. McCollon Hampton and I. Lansberg, *Generation to Generation: Life Cycles of the Family Business*, Boston: Harvard Business School Press, 1997.
35. Ibid., p. 17.
36. Amy Barrett, 'Heirs Loom', *Wall Street Journal Europe*, 10 July 1997.
37. Ward, *Creating Effective Boards*, op. cit.
38. Gersick *et al., Generation to Generation*, op. cit., p. 18.
39. See the Epilogue for our views on how to keep the enterprise in the family in the cousins' confederation stage.
40. It has been estimated that in the United States, only 5 per cent of family enterprises are in stage 3 compared to 20 per cent in stage 2 and 75 per cent in stage 1 (Gersick *et al., Generation to Generation*, op.cit., p. 31). We hypothesise, however, that the percentage of stage 3 companies would be higher in Europe, Latin America and the Far East, where the extended family is held in high esteem.

# Part II
# The Concept of Corporate Governance and a Classical Governance Structure in a Family Business

## INTRODUCTION

In this part we look broadly at the key focus of this book: the governance of a family business (Chapter 3). For our purposes, we define the concept of governance as *a system of processes and structures to direct, control and account for the business at the highest level.*

In this context, *directing* means being involved in decisions that are strategic in nature. *Controlling* means oversight of management performance and monitoring the achievement of objectives. *Accounting for* means responsibility towards those making legitimate demands for the firm's accountability (for example shareholders, employees, the public at large and other stakeholders).

Controlling and accounting for are different activities; they can nevertheless be seen as two sides of the same coin. In our later discussion we will therefore discuss them together.

In Chapter 3 we also describe a classical corporate governance structure in a family business at an advanced stage of development ('cousins' confederation'), consisting of:

- The family and its institutions (as the ultimate source of power).
- The board of directors.
- Top management.

# 3 The Concept of Corporate Governance in a Family Business

In the art of governing, one always remains a student.
(Queen Christina of Sweden, 1626–1689)

While family business as a whole was at the centre of attention in Part I, from here onwards, we will concentrate on a specific aspect of running family-controlled enterprises: their governance in broad terms.

## THE GENERAL IDEA OF CORPORATE GOVERNANCE

As already mentioned, corporate governance is a relatively new topic in the field of management theory and practice. A decade ago we had hardly coined the term. And even today, many participants in the management process are put to the test if asked what the term really means. In today's management parlance, corporate governance is an umbrella term that includes specific issues arising from interactions among senior management, shareholders, boards of directors and other corporate stakeholders.

The relative newness of the term does not mean that the phenomena it describes have not always existed; they most certainly have. The recent intensive discussion has mainly been triggered by the spectacular failure of some large companies. In the aftermath of these failures, the question was raised by the public at large, by the shareholders and even by the employees and their unions whether the corporate governance systems should not have prevented this from happening. Earlier efforts to address the issue of how we govern companies at the highest level entered the management discussion under the label 'theory of the firm'.[1] Spreading the concept was hindered by the fact that the term 'corporate governance' does not translate easily into other languages. As a result the English term is increasingly being used even outside the anglophone countries.

59

## DEFINING CORPORATE GOVERNANCE

The word governance comes from the Latin verb *gubernare*, to steer, to direct. Tracing the word 'governance' etymologically makes it easier to understand the definition of corporate governance as it is now used in everyday management practice.

The by now almost legendary 'Cadbury Report' stated that *'Corporate governance is the system by which companies are directed and controlled.'*[2] For our purposes, we shall amend this definition slightly: *Corporate governance is a system of structures and processes to direct and control corporations and to account for them.*[3] Each of the activities mentioned in the definition – directing, controlling, accounting for – requires a brief explanation.

*Directing* an enterprise should not be confused with everyday involvement in management. Rather, this activity means:

- Shaping the strategic direction of the firm in the long term.
- Involvement in decisions that are far-reaching in nature.
- Involvement in the allocation or reallocation of significant financial resources (for example large investment decisions) as well as other resources (for example human resources) such as the appointment of the CEO.
- Involvement in decisions that are precedent setting and/or are difficult to reverse.

In short, directing means being involved in decisions that are strategic in nature.

*Controlling* means oversight of management performance and monitoring the progress towards objectives. As we will see in Chapter 9, the concept of control embraces a large number of elements, both 'hard' and 'soft.'

*Accounting for* means responsibility towards those legitimately demanding accountability on the part of the firm (the stakeholders). As in family-controlled companies the issue of equitable treatment of all family members – those inside the company and those outside – frequently plays a major role, so clear accounting and clear responsibilities for accountability are of pivotal significance. The question of accountability and how it can be guaranteed has gained importance as there has been a tendency to separate the role of the owner from that of the manager. For obvious reasons this separation makes clear accounting particularly important (although one does not have to go quite as far as Adam Smith, who once wrote, 'The directors of joint stock companies being managers rather of other people's money than of their own, it cannot be expected that they should watch over it with the same anxious vigilance with which the partners in a private copartnery frequently watch over their own').[4]

'Controlling' and 'accounting for' are different activities; but they are nevertheless highly complementary and will therefore be discussed together.

While our definition of corporate governance given above is means-oriented (the nature of the key corporate governance tasks), a somewhat different light is shed on the concept if one uses an ends-oriented definition. For example 'Corporate governance is a system of structures and processes to secure the economic viability as well as the legitimacy of the corporation.' The two key terms in this definition are 'viability' and 'legitimacy'. What do they mean?

The term *viability* stems from the French adjective *viable*, 'able to live'. In the case of the family-controlled enterprise, economic viability means securing the long-term sustainable development of the firm.

As for the term *legitimacy*, there exists a huge body of juridical and philosophical insights into the concept. One good example of the rich literature is the volume written and edited by Brenda Sutton,[5] but such publications are of limited significance here as we are interested in the more practical aspects of the concept. For us, the legitimacy of a corporation simply means its acceptance by society. In order to flourish in the long term, a company and its conduct have to be in accord with the norms of the societies surrounding it; otherwise it is doomed. It is a complex concept. As the Brent Spar case taught Shell, one type of corporate conduct – namely deep-sea disposal of an oil platform – may be acceptable in one society (in this case the UK), but not at all in others (for example continental Europe). This means that companies have to proceed with extreme prudence and sensitivity if they want to maintain their legitimacy in an international setting.

The notion of viability/legitimacy is also at the bottom of the definition Demb and Neubauer chose for corporate governance, which they see 'as a process by which corporations are made responsive to the rights and wishes of their stakeholders (that is, all those persons who have 'something at stake' in the company, its shareholders, its providers of funds, its employees, its customers, and the public at large)'.[6]

## FLOATING BORDERLINES: WHOSE TASK?

Whose task is it to make sure that corporate governance issues in a family-controlled enterprise are handled well? In the first phase, this is the responsibility of the owners, the family. Maintaining the legitimacy and economic viability of their firm deserves their full attention. As the family may be too big to be involved in this directly, and as many family members are frequently far removed from the firm, attending to governance is largely the task of the board (which in family businesses is usually dominated by family members).

Another important player in the governance game is, of course, top management. They are usually the driving force behind measures taken by the firm that affect corporate governance. In the context of governance, the relationship between the board and the family on the one hand and the board and top management (or 'executive committee' as it is called in some family businesses) on the other plays a major role. And this relationship is subtle and complex, for two reasons.

First, a substantial proportion of the corporate governance job is shared between the board and top management (although some tasks are also clearly reserved for only one of the two, for example the signing of the annual accounts by the board).

Second, the borderline between the involvement of the board and management typically shifts, as shown in Figure 3.1. The upper part of the figure relates to securing the legitimacy of the corporation as a governance aim (by influencing its conduct).[7]

The lower half relates to the governance task of ensuring economic viability. The tricky thing is that both coordinates can move. The vertical line separates the 'governance turf' of the board from that of management. This line rather frequently moves from the left to the right and *vice versa*. When the sun is shining, economically speaking, the board is typically laid back, leaving a lot of room for management to act. This is shown symbolically in Figure 3.1; in situation 1 the arrow indicates that the vertical axis may move to the right, thus reducing the sphere of influence of the board and simultaneously increasing the 'elbow room' of top management. This situation suggests that the board is relatively passive.

The opposite can happen too: the vertical axis may move to the left, representing increasing activity by and involvement of the board (situation 2 in Figure 3.1). This may occur, for instance, when times are turbulent and the board wants to be sure that they are on top of the situation. Such was the case after the breakdown of the intended merger

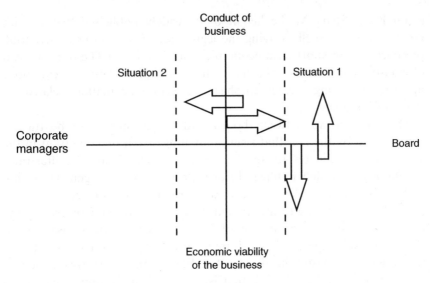

**Source**:   Adapted from Demb and Neubauer (1992).[8]

**Figure 3.1**   The governance portfolio

between Volvo and Renault – the decision to call off the merger forced Volvo's board and management frantically to reorient the company. During the first year after the decision to part ways the Volvo board met almost every week and became deeply involved in shaping the future of the Swedish car maker.

The fact that the sphere of influence between the board and top management cannot be clearly delineated once and for all can be disquieting for some people on both sides. If a manager has the need for firm ground under his or her feet in this respect, he or she may be in the wrong job. In the environment at the top of the corporation, one must be able to 'live with one's feet dangling'. The lack of clear delineation drives home an important point: a key word for the people involved in corporate governance is 'judgement', which can be defined as 'the ability to decide when the board, for instance, should be directly involved in governance matters and when it should stay out.

There is an additional complication: not only can the vertical line move, but so can the horizontal coordinate. This may mean, for example, that conduct/legitimacy issues may at times gain weight relative to economic viability issues. In such a situation, the horizontal coordinate moves downwards, and the increased space above the line symbolises the increased significance of conduct/legitimacy issues. (A typical example is again Brent Spar. At the height of its widely publicised 'battle' with Greenpeace, for Shell, proving the legitimacy of its actions clearly took precedence over short-term economic considerations.) The opposite can obviously take place as well, that is, the horizontal coordinate can move upwards, signaling greater emphasis on economic matters relative to issues of conduct.

The relationship between board and management can be further complicated by the fact that issues may move from one quadrant in the system of coordinates to another. For instance Figure 3.2 illustrates graphically the widely publicised Lopez drama at Volkswagen. The hiring of I. Lopez from General Motors was primarily a management matter (lower left-hand quadrant: an employment contract concerning the economic performance domain of Volkswagen). When accusations of industrial espionage escalated dramatically and Volkswagen was threatened with a lawsuit in the United States, the issue was suddenly catapulted to the board level, that is, it moved to the upper right-hand quadrant (as GM's view of the hiring of Lopez questioned the conduct of Volkswagen). To substantiate this point it can be mentioned that, according to rumours, at the height of the crisis a number of Volkswagen board members made quiet pilgrimages to the United States to soothe ruffled feathers.

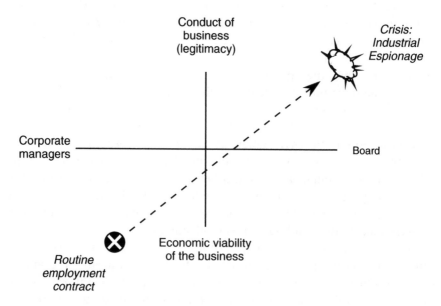

**Source:** Adapted from Demb and Neubauer (1992).[9]

**Figure 3.2**   Movement of tasks from management to board

## CORPORATE GOVERNANCE IN FAMILY-CONTROLLED COMPANIES

The corporate governance function, as defined above, of course also concerns family-controlled companies. So far only a very limited amount of research has been conducted in that area. Among the noteworthy exceptions are the works of Ward[10] and, more recently, Gersick, *et al.*[11]

This does not mean, however, that the corporate governance tasks of directing, controlling and accounting for have not existed in family-controlled enterprises. They have obviously been present all along, although a comprehensive system formally recognising these aspects and assigning explicit corporate governance roles may not have been adopted by many family enterprises. The need for such mechanisms becomes, however, more pronounced when the firm has reached the cousins' confederation stage. At that point, the family may have grown quite distant from the company, so the glue of governance mechanisms becomes of paramount importance.

In their better developed forms, corporate governance systems may well be compared to 'constitutions of states', as we know them from the field of constitutional law. In this context it is worth mentioning that the German word for corporate governance is *Unternehmensverfassung* ('corporate constitution'). The parallels between the frameworks in a family-controlled firm and a political constitution (of, say, a state) are indeed remarkable. Here are a few of the key similarities:

- The constitution of a state, its basic order, can exist in a written or unwritten form. In the first case one would talk about a formal constitution, while the second could be called an actual, *de facto* constitution. A famous example of the latter is the British constitution.
- As in a political constitution, the basic order of a family-controlled company can either be implied in the firm's operating rules, customs, institutions and unwritten 'laws', or it can be embodied in one or more documents; the latter typically bear titles such as 'Statement of Family Principles', 'Family Rules and Regulations', 'Family Values', and, of course, 'Family Constitution'.
- A political constitution identifies the organs of the state, delineates how the state is directed, how the behaviour of the organs is controlled and how these organs account for their actions *vis-à-vis* their constituents. Likewise a corporate governance system (or constitution) in a family enterprise describes the organs of the

business, their tasks, the extent and limits of their power, their internal structure, the composition of their membership and their mode of operating (including their influence on each other). It also delineates the ways in which one enters and leaves those organs and institutions.

### Typical Key Elements of a Family Company Constitution

In our research as well as in our extensive involvement with family-controlled enterprises in an advisory capacity, we discovered that, above a certain size, many of these firms do indeed have a constitution (as we will see in Chapter 4). In some cases it is not explicitly formulated (but is adhered to); in others there are clear, discernible structures that determine the tasks to be handled by the different organs, regulate the distribution of power, the extent and the limitations of that power, the composition of these organs and their relationship to each other as well as the mechanisms to resolve conflicts – all typical characteristics of a constitution.

The shape and make-up of these constitutions differ, of course, in different companies. Nevertheless we have identified a number of common features in the governance systems we have encountered. The typical corporate governance structure in a family business seems to have the following elements:

- The family itself and its institutions, such as family assembly, family council, shareholders' committee.
- The board of directors (where one exists).
- Top management (or the executive committee, as they are sometimes called). Normally they are in charge of the everyday running of the business; but as we saw earlier, they are also involved in certain aspects of corporate governance (see Figures 3.1 and 3.2).[12]

At this point it is necessary to make an important observation (to which we will return repeatedly in the remainder of the book): the different governance tasks can only be handled satisfactorily if the different organs of the corporate governance structure work closely together like a system of communicating vessels.

### CONCLUSION

In this chapter we have identified two major aspects of corporate governance:

- The key corporate governance *tasks*, namely
  - directing,
  - controlling,
  - accounting for/reporting.
- The key elements of a typical corporate governance *structure*, namely
  - the family (and its institutions),
  - the board of directors,
  - top management.

Both lists are rather general and abstract in nature. They have to be fleshed out if they are to be helpful to a practitioner in a family business, and this will be done in Chapters 4–9.

In Chapter 10 we will pull everything together and offer the reader practical advice (in the form of a sequence of steps) on how to go about setting up or redesigning a governance system in a family business and getting it accepted by the owners. That chapter will also look in some depth at the interaction between the elements of a governance structure as well as ways to balance their influence.

## NOTES

1. For more details see B. Tricker, *Pocket Director*, London: Profile Books in association with the *Economist*, 1996 pp. 29–33.
2. The Cadbury Committee was set up in the UK to establish a code of conduct in the corporate governance area, which was to be followed voluntarily by British industry. The report, which was published in 1992, was meant to remove the need for solutions to corporate governance issues. Source of the quote: *Report of the Committee on the Financial Aspects of Corporate Governance*, Gee and Co. Ltd, London, 1992, p. 15.
3. A similar way of seeing corporate governance has been promulgated by Robert I. Tricker (see for instance his book *Corporate Governance*, Hants: Gower, 1984). Tricker's extensive writings on corporate governance have strongly influenced the field. Other important publications by him are *International Corporate Governance* (New York: Prentice Hall, 1994) and *Pocket Director* (London: The Economist Books, 1996).
4. Quoted in S. Wright, 'Ownership and Accountability in Corporate Governance', in S. Saleem and W. Rees (eds), *Corporate Governance & Control*, London: Cavendish Publishing House, 1995, p. 163.
5. B. Sutton (ed.), *The Legitimate Corporation*, Oxford: Basil Blackwell, 1993.
6. A. Demb and F.F. Neubauer, *The Corporate Board: Confronting the Paradoxes*, New York: Oxford University Press, 1992.

7. This way of presenting the complex situation between the board and management was first developed by Ada Demb and Fred Neubauer: see ibid., pp. 61–6.
8. Ibid., p. 62.
9. Ibid., p. 65.
10. J. L. Ward, *Creating Effective Boards for Private Enterprises: Meeting the Challenges of Continuity and Competition*, San Francisco: Jossey-Bass, 1991.
11. K. E. Gersick, J. A. Davis, M. McCollom Hampton and I. Lansberg, *Generation to Generation: Life Cycles of the Family Business*, Boston: Harvard Business School Press, 1997.
12. For additional insights into governing bodies in family-controlled companies, see M. A. Gallo, *Governing Bodies in the Family Company*, Technical Note of the Research Department at IESE, March 1993.

# Part III
# Family Institutions and the
# Board of Directors

## INTRODUCTION

In Part III we take a closer look at two key elements of a classical governance system.

In Chapter 4 we look into the family (as the ultimate source of power) and its institutions (for example the family council). In Chapter 5 we describe what we understand by a board, its role, composition and so on. In this context we stress that boards typically play a key role in corporate governance. We also point out, however, that a board can only perform its corporate governance duty in close cooperation with the other elements of the governance structure, mainly the family and top management. How does the board spearhead the discharging of the typical governance tasks – directing, controlling and accounting for?

The abstract challenges need to be translated into a set of practical measures that a board (in cooperation with the other elements of the governance system) can take to discharge its governance tasks. In order to find a way to make this translation, we first looked at a list of such measures (to carry out the governance tasks) created by the board of Sanlam, a large South African company. From this list we selected four measures that seemed to be of particular importance:

- The appointment of the CEO.
- The establishment of a vision and strategy for the firm.
- Securing the financial means to satisfy the financial needs of the company.
- Controlling the firm at the highest level.

The first three of these governance measures form part of the directing aspect of corporate governance and the last represents the controlling/accounting for aspect.

# 4   Key Elements of a Governance Structure in a Family Business: the Family and its Institutions

Human relationships are vast as deserts: They require boldness. (attributed to Patrick White, Australian writer and Nobel Prize winner, 1973)

The main theme of this book is the governance of family enterprises, corporate governance having been defined in various ways in the previous chapter, including 'systems and structures to direct, control and account for the corporation as well as securing its economic viability and legitimacy'. The focus of this definition is the *company per se,* but in family enterprises one is required to examine the role of the owning family in the governance of its enterprise as it is precisely the family element that differentiates family companies from every other form of enterprise.

A family, like any other organisation, must have a governance structure if it is to continue to function as an entity. How a family in business is governed will have a major impact not only on the family's own health and ability to survive, but also on the success and longevity of its enterprise and how *it* is governed. This chapter's main theme is the family and its institutions.

## NEED FOR A STRONG FAMILY

The authors believe that families who wish to continue as managers and/ or owners of their firm increase the probability of being able to do so if they themselves are strong, cohesive and appropriately 'enmeshed' (as opposed to 'alienated' or 'disengaged'). As Aronoff and Ward have said:

The values, ideals and sense of purpose nurtured by the owning family are potentially a vast source of strength and energy for a business. A healthy owning family with strong values, in fact, may be the greatest resource a business can have.[1]

This sentiment is shared by Whiteside *et al.*: 'A strong cohesive family brings a multitude of potential strengths to a business.'[2]

In his classic, *Anna Karenina*, Tolstoy stated that 'happy families are all alike; every unhappy family is unhappy in its own way'. This conclusion may have been the inspiration for family therapists and family systems specialists to search for the commonalties of strong, cohesive families. Stinnett and De Frain, in their study of 3000 families, came up with the following descriptors:

- Commitment to each other.
- Mutual appreciation.
- Open communication.
- Spending time together.
- Spiritual wellness.
- Ability to cope (with life's challenges).

They added that commitment 'could be considered the foundation on which the other characteristics are built'.[3]

R. Skynner, chairman of the British Institute of Family Therapy, summed up what he had learned over his long career about the characteristics of unusually healthy families by listing six major rubrics:

- Positive attitude to human encounter.
- 'Loose–tight'.
- Efficient communications.
- Control.
- Coalition.
- Preparedness for change.[4]

*Positive attitude to human encounter*. Unusually healthy families tend to be warm and friendly to each other and outsiders. They manifest concern and are kind and supportive in their relations with others. They make good neighbours and voluntarily engage in activities that help the communities in which they live.

*'Loose–tight'*. Unusually healthy families also manifest an interesting paradox. They are extremely intimate and involved with each other and

place great value on long-term fidelity. However they are not so en-meshed that they are incapable of allowing their members independence and their own separate identities. The members can be happy on their own and at the same time look forward with joy to the next time they will meet their relatives.

*Efficient communication.* In line with many other studies of healthy, strong families, Skynner found much evidence of open, clear, direct and frank communication. Healthy families search out opportunities for communication and enjoy dialogue. While discussions can become quite emotional, even heated, the underlying ethic remains one of caring, even when in disagreement.

*Control.* In spite of what may seem to be implied by the above characteristics, Skynner's families are not managed in a *laissez-faire* manner. It is not a case of everyone 'doing his or her own thing'. As the children grow up, parents exercise firm control when needed and explain the reasons for their decisions. However, whenever possible they consult with the children and try to accommodate everyone's needs.

*Coalition.* The families in this sample had a particular view of power sharing. They worked hard to create a coalition between them where power was equally shared. This power sharing was seen as natural and was accomplished with ease and in friendship.

*Preparedness for change.* Healthy families teach their members to consider change as natural and to be expected. Thus the preparedness for change is high and the ability to cope with even the death of a loved one is greater than in most families. That this is possible is due to the strong support systems that have developed over time. The life-long positive relationships in the marriage and the family provide great strength in adversity. These families often have a wide social network where they are valued and from which they can draw support. Lastly, it is common for unusually healthy families have to value systems that transcend self and family, and whose moral and religious codes facilitate the acceptance of change with relative equanimity.

## CONFLICT MANAGEMENT

Our own experience with the cousins' confederation stage prompts us to add one other dimension that we believe is of special importance. It relates to conflict and its management. First, let us define conflict. Here are four ways of looking at it:

- The competitive or opposing actions of incompatibles.
- An antagonistic state or action (as of divergent ideas, interests or persons).
- A hostile encounter: fight, battle, war.
- A type of behaviour that occurs when two or more parties are in opposition or in battle as a result of a perceived deprivation by another or others.

Strong, healthy families, implicitly or explicitly, have accepted and internalised in their own value systems the six following propositions (which we believe to be true):

- Over time, conflict is inevitable within families (and between the family and its business).
- Conflict is not inherently bad; it can be healthy or unhealthy, functional or dysfunctional.
- How conflict is managed is a determinant of the degree to which a family (and its business) remains healthy and strong.
- There are several conflict management strategies; no single one is a panacea.
- Preestablishment of the 'rules of the game' can obviate many family (and family business) conflicts.
- The goal should be to maximise the 'win–win' prospects of all the parties concerned and arrive at the best decision, given the family's (and the family business's) mission, goals and objectives.

It is clear from the way that we have worded these six propositions that we believe they apply equally to intra-family, intra-family business and inter-family and family business conflicts. We hold the same opinion with regard to the conflict-management categories that follow. Figure 4.1 presents the three strategic options that we believe are available to parties in conflict.

### Avoidance

The parties may choose to ignore the conflict. This does not necessarily mean that they do not know it exists. They simply choose to ignore it and carry on as usual, either because they do not have the courage to broach the matter or because they feel it is too unimportant to make an issue of. A typical example of the former is the all-too-real case of management succession, particularly that of the founder, where a conspiracy of silence

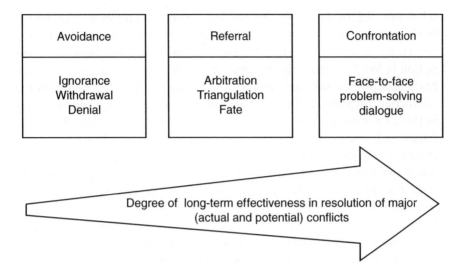

**Figure 4.1** Conflict management strategies

is entered into by all concerned because of ambivalent feelings and an inability to confront the mortality of the outgoing generation.[5] Withdrawal implies there has been at least an initial admission by one or both parties that there is conflict, but a choice is made to disengage in the hope that the contentious issue will disappear. Denial (where one or the other party denies that there is any conflict) may be honest or dishonest, conscious or unconscious. As one sibling in a second-generation family said to one of the authors, 'I have nothing but the greatest respect for my older brother and accept whatever decisions he takes as the CEO.' Unfortunately, it was common knowledge among all the members of the family (and top management of the family firm) that the younger brother detested his sibling, believed the latter was totally incompetent, and harboured strongly negative feelings towards their father because he had not been chosen as CEO.

**Referral**

When the referral strategy is used, there is acknowledged conflict but the parties are unable or unwilling to resolve it themselves. This is a common feature in many families, and the parents or an older sibling often find themselves in the role of official or unofficial arbitrator. It may be about issues as seemingly insignificant as which teenage boy or girl gets to use the family car on Saturday night, who does the dishes tonight or who takes out the rubbish. As the children grow up and enter the family business, the arbitrator may be a trusted non-family employee or even a committee consisting of senior family and non-family members. A second option is for the parties to engage in triangulation, that is, to use a third party as a go-between and spokesman for one or the other person in the conflictual situation. In families, very often it is the mother who is placed in this extremely uncomfortable role. If two siblings are quarrelling or if father and son or daughter are not on speaking terms – for whatever reason, business or family related – the mother is engaged, willingly or not, to pass messages between the parties and try to restore peace. Rarely does this approach resolve the underlying tensions. Finally, one can refer the conflict to fate. Here conflict is acknowledged to exist, but no one is prepared to meet it head on or to use triangulation or arbitration. Again, this strategy is often used in management succession fights. The father (or more rarely the mother) may not be willing to give up the reins of power. The next generation is ready (and, it is to be hoped, competent) to take over but there is no attempt by the patriarch to plan the succession process. What all too often happens is that the successors leave the matter to fate. They simply wait for time to take its inevitable toll. Eventually the 'old man', they say to themselves, will have a stroke, become otherwise incapacitated or die, and hence the conflict will take care of itself – or so they hope. Unfortunately it is often the case that others (such as the family lawyer or accountant) end up in the arbitration role and decide, after returning from the hospital or the cemetery, who will replace the former incumbent.

## Confrontation

It is our belief that the greater the stakes and the more serious the (actual or potential) conflict, the more appropriate is the confrontation strategy. This involves face-to-face dialogue between the parties to identify the basic problem, its causes and alternative solutions. Whenever possible this should be done before the conflict reaches unmanageable proportions. It may not always be possible for them to handle the confrontation process on their own. Luckily there are trained facilitators who can help the parties to find mutually agreeable solutions – although this may not always be possible. One husband and wife team we know, who lead a highly successful media company, established from the start of their marriage one iron-clad rule. Any resentment arising from behaviour that causes a problem for the other partner – whether in the family or the business area – must not be allowed to fester for more than eight hours.

The offended party is required to share his or her concerns with the other – in an open, direct but caring way – before they go to sleep that night. This couple has never needed the intervention of a facilitator or mediator. Confrontation is their preferred conflict-management strategy. Many couples, siblings, parent–child dyads or cousins let the infection develop for as long as eight *years* or more.

Adoption of a good conflict resolution mechanism is of utmost importance in a family-controlled enterprise. Why? The relationships between family members are typically far more complex than among non-family owners or managers. Hermann Hesse, the Nobel Prize winning German writer, captured this phenomenon well when he once said, 'What our mind thinks and says is a fly-excrement compared to the life, relations and kinships that flow beneath the surface.'

Conflict management in families and family businesses is never an easy task, whatever the stage of evolution of the family or its enterprise. Relatively speaking, however, it should be easier in Stage 1 (founder's) or Stage 2 (sibling partnership) than in Stage 3 (cousins' confederation). Typically in the first two stages there are fewer people involved. Furthermore they are members of the same nuclear family who have shared a lifetime together and tend to know each other well. With luck (and hard work) they may have shared ideas on how conflict should be handled. By the time Stage 3 rolls around it is a very different ball game. More people are involved, and they have probably been brought up in different traditions of conflict management. In addition it is probable that relatively fewer members of the family are active in the business. There may well be considerable consensus about various potentially divisive issues among those employed in the family enterprise or who sit on the board, but not among those who are not active in the business. Thus the seeds are sown for destructive conflict based on differing role perceptions (see Chapter 1). This situation gives even further weight to our contention that family institutions are needed even more in Stage 3 companies than in the earlier stages. They may, through open discussion and the establishment of ground rules, obviate conflict or at least provide a venue where healthy confrontation can take place. An example of unhealthy conflict is the following sad story of the Fairfax family.

The earlier descriptors of strong, cohesive and healthy families are examples of values that drive the development of the governance systems of families. They help determine how the family should be directed, controlled and accounted for. As we shall see in subsequent chapters, these family governance systems often have a direct influence on the governance system of the family's enterprise.

**147 Years to Build – One Year to Destroy:
The Demise of the Fairfax Dynasty**

In 1987–88, within one year the business (and the fortune) of the Fairfax family, one of Australia's oldest and wealthiest business dynasties, was destroyed. The reason: a bitter conflict among the members of the family. What happened to that family reminds one of a classical Greek tragedy.

To help the reader to understand the complex affair, we shall first introduce the key players in the drama:

- Sir Warwick Fairfax, fourth generation in the running of the family enterprise and chairman of John Fairfax Limited, the centrepiece of an influential Australian media empire (its flagship: the *Sydney Morning Herald*). Sir Warwick was an autocratic manager, intolerant of criticism, eccentric and a womaniser.
- Sir Vincent Fairfax, a cousin of Sir Warwick, was also in the top management of the family business. Unlike his cousin, he was level-headed and stable and a diligent father and husband.
- Lady Mary Fairfax, third wife of Sir Warwick.
- James Fairfax, son of Sir Warwick from his first marriage.
- Warwick Fairfax junior, son of Sir Warwick and Lady Mary Fairfax.

The family feud that led to the disaster started back in the 1950s, when the fourth generation took up the reins of the family enterprise. Sir Warwick and Sir Vincent Fairfax both had leading positions in the firm and both were on the board of John Fairfax Ltd. The characters of the two cousins could not have been more different. Their extremely different temperaments soon led to a clash, and in 1953 Sir Warwick managed to have his cousin Vincent ousted from the board. Sir Vincent fought the move, but he finally had to give in and leave the board. In 1956, however, he managed to get back in when the company went public. The relationship between the two cousins immediately became as tense as it had been before.

In 1959 a scandal arose when Sir Warwick, then still married to his second wife, became the object of a law suit: one Cedric

Sysmonds claimed that Sir Warwick had induced Sysmonds' wife Mary to leave him. The waves of the scandal swelled high enough for Sir Warwick to be asked to resign as chairman and leave the board altogether. He put up considerable resistance to his removal, as he was convinced that the issue had been whipped up by James (his older son from his first marriage) and his old adversary Sir Vincent in order to oust him. However, in the end he had to step down, but he quickly settled his dispute with Sysmonds and returned to the board in March 1961. In the meantime Mary Sysmonds had become Lady Mary Fairfax, Sir Warwick's third wife. She was never accepted by the family, and Mary never forgave the family for snubbing her.

Things nevertheless went on relatively smoothly until 1976, when Sir Vincent and James came to the conclusion that as Sir Warwick was getting on in age – he was 74 by then – he should give up the chairmanship and leave the board. After much infighting and resistance, Sir Warwick was replaced as chairman by his son James, and Sir Vincent became vice chairman.

Lady Mary and her son Warwick junior would not accept this and, as was revealed in the course of a later court battle, they vowed to avenge 'the family honour' and oust those who had toppled Sir Warwick. Their scheme was complex and very costly: its eventual price tag amounted to A$2.5 billion and resulted in the collapse of the company.

Here are some details of the scheme. In February 1987 Warwick junior borrowed A$30 million to buy back Fairfax shares to help the family's defences against a possible hostile takeover. By the time he had executed this plan, the family's direct control had risen to just over 50 per cent. However, he did not stop there. On 31 August, 1987 he launched a multi-billion-dollar restructuring proposal for John Fairfax Ltd that included a A$1.1 billion takeover bid for the shares of the family and outside shareholders. After much turmoil, in November 1987, the family finally accepted Warwick junior's offer and agreed to sell their shares. A month later the entire board resigned, allowing Warwick junior to take formal control of the company.

It very soon became clear that the price for the takeover had been too high and the company could not service its vast debts. One by one the 'jewels' in the crown of John Fairfax Ltd had to be sold. The A$1.2 billion realised from the asset sales were insufficient to cover the debts. Just before the final curtain fell, what remained of John Fairfax Ltd – still very impressive, although a pale shadow compared of what it had been – was sold to the Canadian publisher Conrad Black for A$1.4 billion, barely enough to cover the remaining debts of A$1.2 billion. That was the end of a once proud family empire.

However strong families do not just 'happen'. Processes and mechanisms, including what we call 'family institutions', must be created to operationalise these evolving value systems. They range from highly informal to highly formal bodies, and of course tend to vary over time and in parallel with the family's life cycle, the ownership stage and the life cycle of the business.

## FAMILY INSTITUTION I: FAMILY MEETING

The simplest and most common family institution is the family meeting, often found in the controlling owner or entrepreneurial stage. This tends to be a very informal get-together and may initially involve only the owner and his or her spouse discussing family and/or business issues. These meetings may be relatively frequent, even daily. 'Pillow talk' has been used as one descriptor. As the children get older they may join in the discussion. In the children's earlier years, meetings tend to focus on purely family issues such as the assignment of chores, weekly allowances, the balance between recreation and study time, the handling of disagreements and so on. The basis of the family's culture and value system is developed at this time. Gradually, family business issues start to appear on the agenda as the parents share information on the rights and responsibilities of ownership and management as well as the joys and disappointments of being a family in business. What is recounted about working in a family business and how it is said will have a major impact on the willingness of the children eventually to join the family firm. These meetings may pave the way for the younger family members to learn directly about the family enterprise by doing part-time work in the evenings and at weekends. Holiday jobs and conditions of employment will probably be agreed in the evening when the family sits around the dining table.

## FAMILY INSTITUTION II: FAMILY ASSEMBLY

As the family matures, and especially once the transition is made to a sibling partnership, each nuclear family unit may continue these informal family meetings with three or even four generations present. But pressure will start to mount to create a forum for discussion between the branches of the owning family. In time these meetings may become more formalised and be relabelled 'family assemblies' or 'family forums'. At the cousins' confederation stage it is almost mandatory to have such assemblies if the family is to avoid the potentially negative forces that come with a larger shareholder group, multiple branches and both active (in the business) and non-active shareholders. Keeping the family interested in itself and its enterprise can be an exceedingly demanding task at this stage. Beyond a certain critical size, possibly 30–40 family members, there will probably be a need to create a family council (see below).

We do not mean to imply that family assemblies are a common feature in business families – or at least not yet. They are seen most often in the United States but are becoming increasingly popular in Europe, Australia, Latin America and other parts of the world. The fundamental purpose of the assembly is to bring the family together so that members can focus on issues of mutual interest to them (*as a family* as well as any matters relating to the *interface between the owning family and its enterprise*). As a general rule, in their simplest form family assemblies are held once or twice a year and allow the family to be updated on issues of interest to the family apart from its ownership role (as well as reports by the CEO and the board on business matters). The ensuing discussion can be quite lively or practically non-existent, depending on the family's culture and degree of closeness to the business.

Families differ on who should take the lead in scheduling and running the family assembly. Often it is the family CEO or the family patriarch who plays this role. In larger families it is the family council that triggers the assembly and chairs the meeting. Our preference is that the lead should be taken by a family member other than the CEO, if for no other reason than the fact that leading the assembly is an excellent management development opportunity (and could avoid conflict of interests). Unrecognised talent may thereby be spotted, which in time could be usefully exploited by the family (and its firm).

A delicate but very important decision is who has the right to be a member of the family assembly. Once again, families vary widely in this regard. There are usually minimum age limits and often restrictions on who has the right to vote. The inclusion of in-laws is often a thorny issue, particularly if they are not allowed to own shares. One Nordic family, which we will use as an example several times throughout the book (we shall call it the 'Bergman' family)[6] has the following to say about its family assembly.

---

### Bergman's Values and Policies: Family Assembly

The Family Assembly is a family meeting which is held annually in connection with the company's Ordinary General Meeting.

At the family assembly the following matters are handled:

- Election of Family Council members.
- Election of Family Review Committee members.[7]
- Approval of various position papers (such as the one on the family's values and policies).
- Other important family matters (if requested).

An extraordinary Family Assembly can be held if requested by more than five members of the family or if the Family Council, the Board of Directors or the company management find it appropriate.

Members of the Family Assembly are:

- All direct descendants of the founding couple, 18 years of age or older.
- All in-laws who have been married to a family member for at least five years.
- Widows/widowers who have been married to a family member for at least five years and who have not remarried.

In-laws vote together with their spouse (one vote/couple) and they represent their spouse in his/her absence. In case of divorce, by definition, ex-spouses are no longer in-laws.

The Family Assembly is chaired by the Chairman of the Family Council, and in his/her absence by the Vice Chairman of the same.

Minutes shall be kept of the Family Assembly meetings and be available to the family.

If it comes to voting at the Family Assembly, the rule is one person (couple), one vote. In order to pass, a proposition has to be supported by more than 50 per cent of those voting. If the voting is equal, the Chairman has the decisive vote. If requested, voting shall be by secret ballot.

---

It is the authors' preference to err on the side of maximising family membership (including in-laws) rather than the opposite. Particularly as ownership becomes more and more separated from management and the family grows bigger with the passing of the generations, it is almost inevitable that proportionately fewer of the owning family will be active in the day-to-day management of the business. Maintaining family cohesion and an enlightened interest in the family and its enterprise in these circumstances is a daunting task. Without an active family assembly it may be nearly impossible to reduce natural centrifugal tendencies, and family owners (particularly the non-active ones) may become very demanding about the liquidity of their shares and/or the amount paid out in dividends. This situation is often the trigger for taking the firm public, which may bring about its demise as a family-controlled enterprise.

## FAMILY INSTITUTION III: THE FAMILY COUNCIL

The family council usually comes into being when the family assembly reaches a certain critical mass and becomes too unwieldy to do all the work necessary to govern the family and play a positive role in the interface between the family and its enterprise. The family council goes by various names, including family supervisory board, inner council and family executive committee. In smaller families its duties can be handled by family meetings or family assemblies. By the time the cousins' confederation stage is reached, it is vital to create a family council.

As with family assemblies, the composition, structure, roles, procedures and so on vary tremendously between family councils. Let us return to the Bergman family to see its approach to the family council.

The authors have some prescriptive views on family councils. There should not be too many members (five to eight). They should be elected on the basis of their ability to do the job (when possible, the criterion should not be that each branch of the family has to be represented). In-laws should be excluded (the unfortunate possibility of divorce has the potential to complicate matters seriously). There should be limited terms of office (so that more family members can gain experience) and no family member of the board of directors or the CEO should be eligible (so as to avoid conflicts of interest).

## Bergman's Values and Policies: Family Council

The Family Council is elected by the Family Assembly.
The role of the Family Council is:

- To be the primary communication link between the family, the Board and the CEO.
- To suggest and discuss names of candidates for Board membership.
- To draft and revise family position papers.
- To deal with other matters of importance to the family.

The Family Council consists of five members representing different interests, areas of competence and age groups within the family.

Members of the Family Council shall be 24 years of age or older and considered qualified for the assignment.

Family members can suggest to the Family Council candidates for Council membership. Proposals, in writing, should be delivered to the Family Council by the end of March. The proposer must have obtained the prior approval of the candidate before submitting his/her name.

The names of the candidates for the Family Council shall be distributed to family members, no later than three weeks before the Family Assembly.

The Family Council shall have a Chairman, a Vice Chairman and a Secretary. The appointment of the Chairman and the Vice Chairman is the responsibility of the Family Assembly.

The work of the Family Council is headed by the Chairman, but matters have to be included on the agenda if requested by family members, Board members, the CEO or the Family Review Committee.

The Family Council should try to reach consensus in all matters handled. If voting is needed, the principle is one person, one vote.

Minutes shall be kept of the Family Council meetings and be available to the family.

The term of office for Family Council members is three years. Each year one or two of the members are in turn to resign. The Chairman and Vice Chairman should not be in turn to resign simultaneously. (A person can be re-elected, no earlier than one year after leaving his/her seat.)

## FAMILY INSTITUTION IV: OTHERS

Active and highly cohesive families may create many other family institutions with a variety of roles and reporting relationships. Most will have a family shareholders committee, which has the final say on all matters that, by law, can only be approved by shareholders. There may be a family nominating committee to propose to the shareholders or the board of directors the names of candidates for the board or the position of CEO. If the family is active in creating educational opportunities for its members (for example learning how to understand financial statements), there may be a family educational committee. If the family places emphasis on socialising and having fun together, there may be a family recreational committee. Some large and rich families have created family offices that provide, directly or indirectly, consulting advice on personal investment planning, estate planning, insurance coverage, career or marriage counselling and a host of other subjects. Others consider that the issue of the terms and conditions of family employment and progress through the company is so important and potentially divisive that an employment committee is formed. This family institution often comprises both family and non-family members and may have advisory or executive powers.

Not uncommon among the list of family institutions is the family's charitable trust or family foundation, which can occupy the energies of many family members and be an important reflection of the family's deeply held values. We return to this subject in the Epilogue.

A rather unusual family institution has been created by Bettys and Taylors (real name), a third-generation British company. It has been labelled 'the constitution committee' and its terms of reference are reproduced in the box overleaf. One of its key tasks is to help manage conflict arising out of how family members are treated in the employment context.

Our list of family institutions is not intended to be exhaustive, just illustrative. In its own way each body can have a lesser or greater impact on the way the family governs itself or on how the family impacts on the governance of the family enterprise.

## FAMILY STATEMENTS

The authors believe that the various family institutions provide opportunities for dialogue, networking, cohesion building, and most importantly,

## The Constitution Committee of Bettys and Taylors

'*1.   The Family Perspective*

A family business has its own particular challenges. One area of difficulty can be the interface between the relaxed, informal, necessarily more emotional side of family life, and the more formal, controlled, unemotional business side of the family. To help avoid conflicts and to act as a buffer, the family is committed to the idea of a Constitution Committee at least two members of which are free of the emotional constraints of family membership and therefore able to act as independent advisors and mediators.

The family should have confidence and trust in the Constitution Committee. The Constitution Committee's decision is final and must be accepted by the family. Although open communication is important, the Constitution Committee reserve the right not to provide an explanation for their decisions. The family undertakes not to place undue pressure on the Constitution Committee to influence the outcome of their deliberations.

*2.   Purpose*

The purpose of the Constitution Committee is to resolve, manage and advise on family, and certain specific shareholder issues . . . where a balanced overview and some degree of independence is helpful or indeed essential. The Constitution Committee has no authority to change the Family Constitution or the Articles of Association but is expected to give effect to the spirit and letter of each of them.

*3.   Composition*

-   The Constitution Committee consists of two non-executive, non-family, non-trustee, non-shareholder Directors *plus* the Chairman of the Board of Directors and the Chairman of the Family Council.
-   The two non-executive Directors serving on the Constitution Committee are appointed annually to the Board and the

Constitution Committee by the Chairman of the Family Council and the Chairman of the Board of Directors, and they may be removed at any time without notice by unanimous agreement of the two Chairmen.

– The appointment of the two non-executive Directors serving on the Constitution Committee should be confirmed by the shareholders at the first Annual General Meeting following their appointment, and every three years thereafter.

– The two non-executive Directors serving on the Constitution Committee should retire no later than their 60th birthday, although this may be extended annually until their 65th birthday, by agreement of the two Chairmen. Annual extensions beyond the age of 65 additionally require the prior written consent of shareholders holding a majority of the issued shares.

– The remuneration of the two non-executive Directors serving on the Constitution Committee is determined by the Chairman of the Board.

– The two non-executive Directors serving on the Constitution Committee are in every other way treated as other ordinary non-executive Directors.

## 4. Resources

– The Constitution Committee may seek such outside advice as it thinks necessary to enable it to reach fair and balanced decisions.

– The Constitution Committee may request the Directors to make available funds in order that they may take outside legal, financial or human resource advice and obtain secretarial services.

– The Constitution Committee may have open access to the Company's auditors, legal advisors and the Company Secretary, and the Family Council.

## 5. Responsibilities

The Constitution Committee is responsible for:
– applying the right of veto in pre-approving family appointments and promotions in the business . . .
– mediation and arbitration of family disciplinary and grievance issues in the business . . .

- monitoring annually the remuneration of family members in the business to ensure fairness . . . and advising the Board of Directors of any concerns.
- administering 'Share Fair Day' [internal stock market] ensuring [the relevant provisions] are honoured, and implementing the relevant provisions of the Articles of Association relating to them.
- approving or vetoing certain share transfers and will provisions relating to bequests of shares . . . and implementing the relevant provisions of the Articles of Association relating to them.
- registering all share transfers and ensuring such transfers satisfy all the [relevant] conditions.
- applying the Compulsory Transfer Procedure . . . and implementing the relevant provisions of the Articles of Association relating to it.
- recommending interim and final dividend payments to the Annual General Meeting (AGM) . . . (in each case of no greater amount than is agreed by the Board of Directors).
- investigation and arbitration of breaches of the Family Constitution.

*6. Decision Making*

The family values consensus as a positive decision making process, but not if it results in inaction or leads to the abandoning of all beliefs, principles, values and policies to something in which no one believes but to which no one objects. In the event of a failure to reach a consensus decision in spite of creative discussion, the Constitution Committee may, in the last resort, fall back on the majority view prevailing.

*7. Meetings & Procedure*

The rules of the Articles of Association governing meetings of the Board of Directors also apply to the Constitution Committee save that the quorum for meetings is two, one of whom is a non-executive Director and one of whom is one of the Chairmen.

The Constitution Committee shall ensure that proper minutes are kept of its meetings, and that copies shall be given to the Company Secretary who shall be authorised to implement the decisions made in those minutes.'

processes for building consensus among the owning family on 'the rules of the game' for the family *per se* (intra-family policies), the acceptable boundaries within which the family enterprise must operate and how the interface between the family and the board of directors/CEO and top management will be managed. In other words the family institutions should make explicit – preferably in written family statements approved by the family assembly or family meeting – what the family stands for, its expectations and its fundamental values. There should be absolute clarity in the differentiation of roles between the family institutions themselves and between them and the board of directors and CEO/top management.

Family statements take a variety of forms and bear a wide range of titles. They may be very general or very specific, focusing on the family, the business or the interface alone, or a hybrid, relatively formal or informal (from a relatively simple letter(s) to the family, the board and/or CEO/top management to a glossy, illustrated, multipage brochure). Here are some titles of such statements:

- Family constitution
- Family strategic plan
- Family vision
- Family mission
- Family code of conduct
- Family protocol
- Family principles
- Family values

- Family policies
- Family culture
- Family creed or credo
- Family objectives
- Family programmes
- Code of understanding
- Family charter

While some students of family business have tried to define clearly the differences between each of these labels, we feel that this effort serves little purpose. One family's credo is another family's code of conduct. One family's values are another family's culture. One family's constitution is another family's charter. For us, it is important that the statements address certain fundamental questions about the governance of the family as well as the governance of the business and the relationship between the two. The answers should reflect the unique qualities of the family and of its business at a given point in time. And the very process of creating these statements may be as important as the final document because of the intensive dialogue that should be undertaken between all the parties to achieve consensus.

Let us reemphasise that it is the *family's* role to prepare the appropriate questions, debate potential answers, gather input from the board, CEO/top management and other important stakeholders, and strive for consensus, which ideally should be published in a single or multiple family statements. The written document(s) should not be considered as engraved in stone but rather revised periodically as circumstances change.

We shall close this chapter by quoting from certain sections of the Bergman family's values and policies as well as (at length) from the Mogi family's constitution. The emphasis will be on how the families view themselves (family *qua* family) rather than on the values that impact directly on the governance of the family enterprise. However, some overlap is inevitable.

Let us first read a synopsis of the Preamble to the Bergman Values and Policies statement. The first page notes that the document was prepared by the family council with the help of two family business consultants. Credit is given to the 'valuable inputs' and comments from the Bergman family (which came largely from the family assembly, the board of directors and the (family) CEO). This is followed by a section on 'purpose'.

---

### Bergman's Values and Policies: Purpose

To serve as a guideline on how we should handle certain for a family company typical issues, in order to avoid unnecessary conflicts and to facilitate the governance and the running of the company in the future.

In this document we want to:

- Recognise important family values
- Recognise important family institutions through which family matters can be handled
- Clarify authority and responsibility between the family and the Board and management of the Company
- Set boundaries within which the Company's strategy should be formulated and implemented
- Clarify policies concerning Governance of the Company, CEO succession, Family Personnel Policy and Transfer of Shares.

This document contains certain principles and recommendations from the Bergman family's point of view, but it is not intended to create any conflict with the bylaws of the Company or the general law, nor to restrict the legal rights of any shareholders of the Company.

---

The 'Purpose' section is followed by an Introduction that briefly traces the history of the company and the family's relationship with it and suggests the need for change, in terms of both the company itself and how the family should relate to it.

---

**Bergman's Values and Policies: Introduction**

Bergman has been in business for almost 150 years, during which period the company has grown from a local company to an important domestic and global actor.

The family has always been strongly engaged in the company, both as owners and in management, influencing the company by the family's values. This, we believe, has had a positive effect on the development of the company.

Today as the family has expanded, we think it is wise to have a mechanism with which we can structure the dialogue between the Family and the company.

Historically the company has been an industrial enterprise. Today, many things have changed within and outside the company. Therefore, we believe it is now appropriate for both the family and the company:

- To look at the possibility of changing the basic form of organisation from an industrial enterprise towards a family-owned investment company with a holding structure
- To look at the strategic boundaries within which the company's future strategy should be formulated and implemented.

---

The following box cites what the Bergman family says about its values.

Experience has shown that one of the most potentially divisive issues in owning families has to do with the 'rules of the game' concerning the right of family members to employment in the enterprise and how they are to be treated in comparison with non-family employees. Some family statements resolve the issue by simply legislating that no member of the family has this right – in whatever capacity. However, how the family resolves the matter will be an important reflection of its value system. The following box reproduces the Bergman position.

---

**Bergman Family Values and Policies: Family Values**

One of the potentially great strengths of family-owned companies is that they are influenced by the family's values in ways that are good for the business, the family and society at large.

It is important that we all, individually and collectively, recognise these values, that we respect them and that we try to safeguard them.

Trust – we should trust and be honest with one another.

Respect and consideration – we should try to understand and respect other people's opinions and integrity.

Communication – we should be open to discussions about various matters and we should try to keep all interest groups well informed.

Continuity – we should respect and build upon the accomplishments of our ancestors.

Commitment – we should look at things with a long-term perspective.

Quality – we should strive to reach perfection in what we do.

Discretion – if a problem should arise, we should try to handle it with the person(s) concerned in a discreet manner and on a confidential basis.

Behaviour – we should keep in mind that it is by what we do, not by whom we are, that we gain respect in society.

For most of us the company is of great importance both socially and financially. Thus, it is in our interest to do our utmost to ensure its successful future development.

We are aware that ownership has its rights, but it also has its responsibilities. We should try to safeguard the interests of other parties concerned, as well as the reputation and attractiveness of the company.

---

For the sake of completeness, here are the other sub-titles in the Bergman Values and Policies statement:

- Family institutions.
- Strategic boundaries for the holding/parent company.
- Financial criteria.
- Governance of the holding/parent company.

- CEO Succession.
- Share transfers.

We shall return to some of these in later chapters.

---

**Bergman's Values and Policies: Family Personnel Policy**

In a company like Bergman there is no room for compromises when it comes to who is employed by the company. We should try to attract and retain the best competence available.

The basic principle is that family members will not be discriminated against or favoured in regard to terms and conditions of employment. Working with another firm before joining the Holding/Parent Company or any of its subsidiaries may be an advantage and is recommended.

Likewise, there is no assumption that the posts of Chairman or CEO of the Holding/Parent Company or any other management position are reserved for family members. The rules of entry, staying and exit (competence being foremost) shall be the same for all – family or non-family.

---

In a quite different vein is the Mogi family constitution. Their enterprise, the Kikkoman Corporation of Japanese soy sauce fame, was founded in the seventeenth century. Their statement has strong philosophical and religious overtones and reflects the family's Buddhist roots. The wording is the result of lengthy discussions between the different family branches and could be labelled a code of interpersonal relations applying to the family and its business. Its 16 articles are reproduced in entirety in the following box:

---

**Mogi Family Constitution[8]**

'Article 1:     All family members desire peace. Never fight, and always respect each other. Ensure progress in business and the perpetuity of family prosperity.

Article 2:     Loving God and Buddha is the source of all virtue. Keeping faith leads to a peaceful mind.

Article 3:     All family members should be polite to each other. If the master is not polite, the others will not follow. Sin is the result of being impolite. Family – young and old, masters and workers – govern themselves by politeness; then peace will be brought of their own accord.

Article 4:     Virtue is the cause, fortune the effect. Never mistake the cause for the effect. Never judge people by whether they are rich or not.

Article 5:     Keep strict discipline. Demand diligence. Preserve order – young and old, master and worker.

Article 6:     Business depends on people. Do not make appointments or dismissals using personal prejudices. Put the right man in the right place. Having men who do what they should brings peace to their minds.

Article 7:     Education of the children is our responsibility to the nation. Train the body and mind with moral, intellectual and physical education.

Article 8:     Approach all living beings with love. Love is fundamental to human beings and the source of a life worth living. Words are the door to fortune and misfortune. A foul mouth hurts oneself and others. A kind tongue keeps everything peaceful. Be careful in every word you speak.

Article 9:     Keep humbleness and diligence, which have been handed down over the years from our forefathers. Make every effort to do as much as you can.

Article 10:     True earning comes from the labour of sweat. speculation is not the best road to follow. Don't do business by taking advantage of another's weakness.

Article 11:     Competition is an important factor in progress, but avoid extreme or unreasonable competition. Strive to prospect together with the public.

Article 12:     Make success or failure clear, judge fairly punishment and reward. Never fail to reward meritorious service, and don't allow a mistake to go unpunished.

Article 13:   Consult with family members when starting a new business. Never try to do anything alone. Always appreciate any profit made by your family.

Article 14:   Don't carelessly fall into debt. Don't recklessly be a guarantor of liability. Don't lend money with the purpose of gaining interest, because you are not a bank.

Article 15:   Save money from your earnings, and give to society as much as you can. But never ask for a reward nor think highly of yourself.

Article 16:   Don't decide important affairs by yourself. Always consult with the people concerned before making a decision. Then employees will have a positive attitude in their work.'

## CONCLUSION

This chapter has focused on various institutions more or less commonly found in families who own enterprises. In particular, emphasis was placed on family meetings, family assemblies and family councils and the roles they can play. They are vital in the governance of the family *qua* family, but they can also be critical in establishing governance boundaries *vis-à-vis* the roles of the board of directors and top management of the family enterprise. These latter governance parameters are often made explicit in family statements – several examples of which will appear in subsequent chapters of this book.

We have stressed the need for (preferably written) family statements that highlight the 'rules of the game' for family, the board of directors and top management. The respective roles of all three should be made explicit. These 'rules' should not be seen as immutable but rather as subject to change as family and family enterprise circumstances evolve.

We ended the chapter with some of the key values held by the Bergman and Mogi families. We believe that strongly held values of this ilk play a vital part in how well the family, the board of directors and top management perform in their respective governance tasks of directing, controlling and accounting for.

NOTES

1. C. E. Aronoff and J. L. Ward, *Family Meetings: How to Build a Stronger Family and a Stronger Business*, Family Business Leadership Series No. 2, Business Owner Resources, Marietta: Georgia, 1992, p. 1.
2. M. F. Whiteside with C. E. Aronoff and J. L. Ward, *How Families Work Together*, Family Leadership Series, No. 4, Business Owner Resources, Marietta: Georgia, 1993,, p. 2.
3. N. Stinnett and J. De Frain, *Secrets of Strong Families*, New York: Berkeley Books, 1985, p. 17. They define 'strong families' as ones with a high level of marital happiness, parent–child relationships that are satisfying to all and mutual needs being met with success.
4. Dr R. Skynner, speech to the Royal Society of the Arts, London, 1993.
5. See I. S. Lansberg, 'The Succession Conspiracy', *Family Business Review*, vol. 1, no. 2, pp. 119–43.
6. The 'Bergman Corporation' was founded in the nineteenth century. The company operates worldwide, has several product lines, sales of more than US$4 billion and 13 000 employees. Its current CEO is a fourth-generation family member. There are some 200 family shareholders and the company is not listed on the stock exchange. It is in the cousins' confederation stage.
7. The family review committee is a rather rare body. It comprises four family members who appoint a chairman from their number. Its role is to review the progress made by the company in implementing the values and policies of the family, which are spelled out in an official document entitled 'Bergman Family Values and Policies'. The committee reports to the board of directors and their main speaking partners are the board, the CEO, the chief financial officer and the company auditors. Members must be at least 24 years of age and considered qualified for the assignment. The tenure of office is four years and re-election is not possible earlier than one year after the seat is relinquished. The family review committee plays a key governance role in terms of verifying compliance with the family's values and policies.
8. Taken from a speech by Mr Yuzaburo Mogi at the Fifth Annual Conference of the Family Business Network, Lausanne, 15–18 September 1994.

# 5 Key Elements of a Governance Structure in a Family Business: The Board of Directors

No man is so foolish but he may sometimes give another good counsel, and no man so wise that he may not easily err if he takes no other counsel than his own. He that is taught only by himself has a fool for a master.

(Ben Jonson, English dramatist and poet, 1572–1637)

In Chapter 3 we indicated that boards typically hold a central position in the corporate governance arena. They indeed represent one of the key elements in a corporate constitution. This is true for family-controlled enterprises as well as for publicly held companies. Because of this pivotal significance, it is necessary to discuss in some depth their specific role, their composition, their working style and the particular problems they may face in family businesses.

The material to be presented here has three major sources. First, it draws on the research that one of the authors conducted (with Ada Demb) in the general area of corporate boards.[1] The second major source is a questionnaire survey conducted between 1992 and 1996 during IMD's educational programme, Leading the Family Business (LFB). Of the 228 participants in LFB, 141 (62 per cent) participated in the survey. This is clearly not a random sample, so the results have to be treated with great care. They nevertheless represent some rare quantitative and qualitative statistical evidence in the corporate governance area with respect to family businesses. It would be a pity not to make use of them. The third source is John L. Ward's ground-breaking work in the area of boards in family businesses.[2]

When discussing the value and role of the board in a family-controlled company, it is important to realise that there may be *legal* as well as *managerial* reasons for the creation of a board.

## THE LEGAL ANGLE

In most countries a family-controlled business is required by law to have a board if it is incorporated. The legal need for a board is even more obvious if the shares of the incorporated business are publicly traded. Depending on the country in which the corporation has its headquarters, it may have a one-tier or a two-tier board. One-tier boards are typically found in anglophone countries and are composed of executive and non-executive members with equal rights and responsibilities. In countries that have adopted the two-tier scheme, there exist *supervisory boards* composed of members who are not involved in the management of the firm (these outsiders can of course be members of the owning family, so long as they are not employed by the firm),[3] and *boards of management*, consisting only of executives of the firm. There is no overlapping membership between the two boards. The two-tier system is used in countries such as Germany, the Netherlands and France, where corporations choose between the two systems.

Even in cases where the law forces a company to appoint a board, the role and clout of that organ can vary substantially; this holds true both for one- and two-tier boards. This means that the role the board will play in a corporation should be carefully discussed and agreed upon by the board and the owning family, in accordance with their specific situation. This flexibility represents a valuable feature of which not too many boards take full advantage.

This leads to the managerial aspect of having a board. If a firm must have a board for legal reasons, it may as well make this obligation worthwhile from a managerial point of view. After all a board costs time and money, so a firm needing one for legal reasons might as well make skilful use of it from a business point of view. Let us take a closer look at the managerial angle.

## THE MANAGERIAL ANGLE

If a family-controlled firm is not incorporated, it is not legally required to have a board. In this case a good number of family-controlled businesses either do not think about creating a board or shy away from setting one up. One of the reasons for this reluctance is the owner's fear of losing some of his or her independence – an aspect that frequently carries a lot of weight for the owner. Indeed an appetite for power and independence is frequently the reason why entrepreneurs strike out on their own in the first place. And yet such owners have to ask themselves whether this attitude may be rather shortsighted. According to a study conducted by Ward in the United States, in more than 80 family-owned companies run by the third or fourth generation, the existence of an active board not controlled by family members turned out to be the most important element in the survival of those firms.[4]

## ADVISORY BOARDS AS A HALF-WAY HOUSE?

In cases where the family is averse to sharing decision-making power with (or even worse, delegating it to) a group of outsiders, the creation of an advisory board may be seen as a possible compromise.

There are several kinds of advisory boards and they are rather popular with large multinationals, where groups of distinguished business, financial or former government leaders come together periodically to advise the top management on policy questions pertaining to the economic, political and social environment of the principal markets where the enterprise is active.[5] In some cases several of these exist per company, each specialising in a particular geographic region.

They do, however, also exist in quite a number of smaller firms and family-controlled companies. In the case of the latter, this is particularly true in two situations: when the family business is not a corporation but, say, a partnership; and when the family business is incorporated and has a legally required board, but that group is composed only of family members and has no arm's-length functions *vis-à-vis* management (a 'paper board'). Making a major mistake that can cause a family business to fail is the constant danger to the isolated CEO who tries to run a business without the help of strong outside aid. In such a case, an advisory board composed of knowledgeable outsiders can possibly offset the management's shortcomings and supplement the 'paper board' in such areas as finance, marketing, personnel and manufacturing technology.[6] There are several objectives in creating an advisory board. The most prominent one is, of course, to counsel top management in specific areas where relevant expertise is not present in the company. Another objective is to provide the isolated CEO with the comfort of a sounding board to test new ideas. A third objective is for the CEO to profit from the excellent business or governmental connections advisory board members may have.

For practical reasons, such a board should not be too large (seven to twelve members) and should meet frequently enough to make its existence meaningful (maybe four times a year). In most cases the advisory boards are chaired by the CEO, though not necessarily. In addition to the CEO, one or two other top management members of the company could belong to this council, which might improve the interface between the advisory board and the firm.

The key advantages of advisory boards are:

- The board members have no legal responsibilities; this reduces the cost of these bodies (no insurance!) and may be an attractive feature for outsiders who do not want to risk their private fortune by joining a board.
- If put together skilfully, they can provide well-rounded, in-depth expertise at a reasonable price.
- Their advice is usually unbiased.
- They require no equity participation and serve only at the discretion of the CEO.
- They may offer new contacts that can lead to additional sales or sources of capital.
- They may represent a source of company continuity, especially in closely held corporations.

There are, however, some major disadvantages as well:[7]

- Some observers feel that setting up an advisory board is not a satisfactory solution. In their opinion it remains unclear whether an advisory board member would be held responsible if management followed his or her advice; after all, the clear-cut, largely undisputed responsibility felt by a fully accountable board has become diluted by the very existence of the advisory board.
- In this situation the CEO is the only person accountable in litigation brought against the company.
- Another major shortcoming of advisory boards is that the shareholders are typically left without representation.

Sir Adrian Cadbury, an eminent figure in the corporate governance field (and who is very familiar with the special situation of family businesses) convincingly summarises people's qualms about advisory boards when he writes, 'Outside advice on a consultancy basis which can be acted on or not as the case may be, does not meet the needs of a family firm in the same way as having external board members with the same responsibility for the future of the firm as the family directors.'[8] Thus there are grave doubts whether advisory boards can serve as a full substitute for a legally constituted board.

Against this backdrop, to us it seems only prudent for a family-controlled company, when it reaches a certain size, to establish a strong board, irrespective of whether or not the company is legally required to do so. Even the most fiercely independent owner–manager would have to admit that his family would sleep better if a strong board existed to take charge if something unforeseen happened to him.

## THE BOARD MEMBER'S ALLEGIANCE

The family may invite an outsider to join the board in the belief that he or she will represent their interests. This of course may be the case in principle, however the matter is somewhat more complex. The basic duty of directors is to act in good faith *in the interest of the company*, and in doing so, to exercise care and skill. It is important to stress that this duty to the company means the shareholders collectively, *both present and future, not the shareholders at a given point in time*. If the family asks aboard a member to approve measures that, in the opinion of the board, would seriously damage or even endanger the company in the long run, a responsible board member would either have to vote against the request or resign (if he or she could not convince the family that their plans were ill-conceived). In the case where the opinions of the board members and the family on what is good for the firm are irreconcilably opposed, the family can of course decide not to reelect that director to the board and replace him or her with somebody else.

The situation would be different if a takeover bid for the company were to be made by a third party. In such a case the board would have to take the position of the controlling family and ask which of the options would be better for the family: selling out or refusing the bid.

## ROLES A BOARD CAN FULFIL IN A FAMILY-CONTROLLED BUSINESS

When discussing the role of the board, a distinction has to be made between *the tasks assigned* to the board and *the degree of involvement* of the board in the handling of these tasks. We will address both questions below. We will first look at what the IMD survey results say about these two questions and then consider the same issues in a more prescriptive way.

In the context of the survey[9], we asked the participants of LFB what they saw as the key tasks (mandate) of boards. Their answers fell into four clusters, which suggests they saw four different board archetypes. These archetypes are located on a continuum (see Figure 5.1). At one extreme of that continuum we find boards with practically no influence whatsoever, and at the other, boards that are actually running the business (with two additional types in between).

The third type of board on the continuum (the board plays a role in strategy, control and hiring top executives) was mentioned 122 times by our respondents, far more than the other roles, each of which was mentioned fewer than twenty times.

It is, however, important to point out that even within this role the degree of involvement of the boards may differ substantially (as will be shown below), ranging from a rather detached 'discuss strategy, support CEO' to a very involved approach: 'set strategy, decide on major investments, challenge business operations'.

Let us now take a closer look at each of the four roles in Figure 5.1.

### Role 1: Board Has Little or No Influence

Advisory boards typically fit this category. Their influence, if they have any, is not based on law, but on factors such as expert knowledge, the track record of the board members or in the power of persuasion. A characteristic example of a survey answer in this category is that most decisions are made prior to board meetings, mainly by the family or family and executives. Other responses include:

**Figure 5.1**   Board archetypes

- The board provides general information.
- Should be loyal to the company.
- Discuss company matters, provide detached discussion partners from outside the family.
- The board has no key tasks.

It is fairly obvious that in this case the board has rather limited value, if any.

### Role 2: Board Protects Family and/or Shareholders

Boards of this type see themselves as having a fiduciary role; they are the guardians of other people's assets. In the survey the following answers were given about the role of this type of board:

- With respect to *shareholders*: defending shareholders, taking care of shareholders interests, developing procedures to handle the increasing number of shareholders, enhancing shareholders' returns, safeguarding shareholders' assets, looking after the owners' interests.
- With respect to *family*: maintaining family bonds and interests, arbitrating quarrels.
- With respect to *mission and culture*: 'developing mission, purpose and values, carrying out the mission, helping to develop a strong culture within the business and the family, formulating a business philosophy.

### Role 3: Board Plays Role in Strategy, Control, Hiring of Top Executives

Within this category the role can be either relatively weak (assisting, guiding and providing advice on strategy, control and hiring) or relatively strong and active (setting the strategy, maximising profits and developing the business forcefully by selecting dynamic executives to lead the company). The tasks mentioned by the respondents were as follows:

- With respect to *management*: hiring and/or firing top executives, supporting the CEO, supervise management, providing the CEO with the comfort of a second opinion from a friendly source.
- With respect to *succession*: planning the succession, providing education for the next generation, ensuring stability and continuity'.
- With respect to *strategy and investment*:

- advising on future trends and opportunities, discussing future plans, guiding management towards strategic goals, defining clear objectives;
- making investment decisions, involvement in mergers and acquisitions, directing the business for future growth, deciding on new products, formulating new ideas, setting the long-term strategy.
- With respect to *control*: evaluating performance, reviewing the business, monitoring executives' performance, evaluating management, monitoring results, monitoring budgets and investments, supervising the execution of business guidelines, asking probing questions with respect to business operations.

In summary, boards playing the third role fulfil rather well the directing and controlling function that is at the heart of the corporate governance process, as we postulated in the previous chapter.

### Role 4: Board has an Executive Role: It is Running the Business

The survey answers characterise this role quite well:

- With respect to *conducting the affairs of the business*: running the business for the benefit of the shareholders, managing the business, taking all major decisions, cash-flow management/production/ marketing, involvement in finance, commercial, sales, research and development.
- With respect to *leadership*: governing all aspects of the business, providing the business with leadership and direction, steering the company, leading and controlling the company.

A case where a family has carved out a very pragmatic role for its board of directors is that of Audemars Piguet, as follows.

## A MORE PRESCRIPTIVE VIEW

Many of the remarks made above were spontaneous and rather personal, so it is advisable to take a somewhat more normative approach to the question of what role a board should or could play in a family-controlled business.

**Audemars Piguet SA: A Pragmatic Use of the Board**

The fame and fortune of Swiss watchmaker Audemars Piguet SA (AP to the cognoscenti) can be partially summed up by statistics: 120 years of tradition, 14 000 watches produced each year, 260 employees (of which 80 are master watchmakers), and more than half of its share capital is held by the descendants of the founders. But above all, AP is among the five most prestigious names in the 'grand luxe' watchmaking world, together with Patek Philippe, Vacheron Constantin, Breguet and Blancpain.

*The Two Dynasties*

Like many other watch companies in the Jura mountains of Switzerland, the company began with a young man, Jules Audemars, making watch movements in his farmhouse. In 1881, six years after he began this work and inspired by entrepreneurial dreams, he and his colleague and best friend Edward Piguet set out to create Audemars Piguet & Cie in their local village. Situated in an isolated border valley, the village became and for more than a century remained the home of some of the best-known names in watchmaking.

Jules, who brought 18 complicated movements with him, became the technical director of the new company, while Edward, who invested SFr.10 000 of his own money, took over the commercial side. Within a few years the two young men had built up an international reputation by keeping a close eye on quality and carrying out all assembly work in-house rather than contracting it out. Initially, much of their work was done on behalf of foreign clients selling the watches under their own name, but soon the company became increasingly well known in the trade as well as among the general public. At the leading edge of contemporary technology, the firm made its name with highly complicated watches incorporating sophisticated features such as perpetual calendars, minute repeaters and the thinnest of movements.

Over subsequent generations, only family members sat in the managerial driver's seat, but in 1956 George Golay was appointed as the first non-family CEO. In 1987, after the unexpected death of Golay, two General Managers (both from outside the family) were appointed: Georges-Henri Meylan and Stephen Urquhart, who hold equal power and possess complementary competencies.

It looks as if the founding dynasties will continue to be involved with the business. One of the Piguet daughters (fourth generation) married Philippe Audemars, an engineer and descendant of the cofounder. They have three children who carry the name Piguet-Audemars. This augurs well for the future.

Jasmin Audemars (fourth generation), president of AP and former editor in chief of the *Journal de Genève*, explained that the strategy for expansion is 'to collaborate with major distributors . . . in order to consolidate our links with key markets or with suppliers to ensure the availability of certain parts'. The expansion programme began in 1991 with the acquisition of 40 per cent of a competing firm, Jaeger-LeCoultre. A representative of that company was invited to join the board of AP, a move that was intended to gain additional expertise.

Of the prestige watchmakers, AP and Patek are now the only ones that are still family controlled. More than half of the shares of AP are held by descendants of the Audemar and Piguet families, and each of these branches has two representatives on the board of directors. Twenty per cent of the shares are held by the LeCoultre family and the two general managers, all of whom have a seat on the board.

The remaining shares changed hands in 1990 when their previous holder, the trading company UTC, became too demanding: it had been the exclusive distributor for the United States and the Middle East, but wanted a larger shareholding and a seat on the board. The owners decided to replace UTC with six general agents. AP ensured the loyalty and motivation of the six new distributors by offering them 25 per cent of the shares.

## The Function of the Board

The eight current board members are considered 'internal' directors. They include the two general managers and representatives of the different shareholder groups. The board meets four times a year, and the agenda is prepared by the president and the management. The directors are very complementary, both in their functions and backgrounds. They are elected for renewable terms of three years, but in practice they are elected for life as the family has no rule about retirement age for board members.

To ensure that the board's decisions would be carried out efficiently, a strategy committee was formed three years ago. It meets once a month and is composed of four board members, including the two general managers and the president. Jasmin Audemars sees the directors as bringing an external perspective, forcing management to think more broadly. 'They are neutral, acting as umpires between the interests of management and the shareholders. The board should operate at the strategic level and not get bogged down in the detail of daily management.' Audemars feels that the new trends concerning boards have forced the board members to become more responsible and vigilant. She also believes that strategies, the vision for the future and product positioning should be established on a consensus basis by the board and be elaborated at that level. This appears to be the right place, as both executive (the two general managers) and non-executive board members meet there. The strategies agreed upon are transmitted throughout the hierarchy and explained to each employee.

## A Spirit of Tradition as a Guide to the Future

'We believe we can survive changes in taste, fashions and habits. Nevertheless, we work hard at forecasting these trends in order to adapt to them while remaining faithful to our long tradition of quality', assures Jasmin Audemars. Since the core product of the company is based on tradition, in order to keep the culture and philosophy alive for the new employees and the forthcoming generation of family members, the descendants of the founders have decided to create a museum. In this unique setting, visitors are now able to retrace the prestigious history of the AP brand name. 'For more than a hundred years, Audemars Piguet has based its reputation on making the most sophisticated mechanical watches. Today, they are simply peerless. They will still be so tomorrow', Jasmin Audemars asserted proudly.

With respect to the possible roles of a board, there are two general rules, originally established in our work with public companies, that make eminent sense for boards in family-controlled businesses. A board is a strain on the resources of a company; it is therefore of great importance that it enhance the success of the family firm. This leads to the first rule: the contribution of a board should be *additive,* that is, it should *improve decisions* and/or *reduce the risks* involved in running the business. Second, *the contribution of the board should be distinctive*, that is, nobody else in the family firm should shoulder the tasks assigned to the board. There is no need for a board to duplicate the work of management (or, for that matter, the family).

With these two guidelines in mind, the family members have to make up their minds about which activities should come under the jurisdiction of the board and to what degree the board should be involved in these activities. Equally, all board members have to ask themselves whether they are comfortable with the role the family has assigned to them. After all, by joining the board the members lend their good name to the company and have a right to judge for themselves whether they believe their influence is commensurate with their exposure.

To stay with the normative: the agreed agenda for the board has to ensure that the board contributes to the key governance tasks discussed in chapter 3 (directing, controlling, accounting for) to a degree commensurate with the role the family wants the board to play. Where should one turn for guidance? Throughout the book, whenever possible we use actual family-controlled companies as reference points. We also cite successful public companies as benchmarks (just as many family companies do), as their boards have to survive the scrutiny of the usually rather rigorous capital markets.

How then do publicly traded companies define the agenda of their boards? During our research, we came across a very successful insurance company that has paid a great deal of attention to the governance question. After considerable internal deliberations they came up with the following key tasks for their board:

- Lead the process to determine the essence, culture and core values of the firm.
- Provide strategic direction and set objectives.
- Establish an effective management team, particularly the managing director, top management and general management.
- Ensure the creation of management processes and policies, police policy application, codetermine the corporate structure.

- Ensure the availability of financial resources.
- Be responsible for effectiveness and continuity of the board.
- Monitor all facets of the operations.
- Protect and promote the firm's image.
- Analyse and interpret environmental influences.
- Report to owners and other interested parties.
- Ensure socially responsible corporate behaviour.
- Secure the existence of an ethical code of conduct.

This list is somewhat all-encompassing – to keep the role of the board manageable in the context of a family-controlled enterprise, the following, more limited list consists of tasks that we consider particularly important in the case of family businesses:

- Securing top management succession.
- Being involved in the strategy process.
- Ensuring the availability of financial resources.
- Monitoring all facets of the operations (control function).
- Reporting to owners and other interested parties.

These five measures cover the general (that is, rather abstract) governance tasks discussed earlier but are translated into manageable, actionable dimensions. We will use them as the organising principle for the remainder of the book. This choice also means that the board we have in mind will be a rather active one.

The Liechtenstein-based Hilti AG, a family-controlled enterprise, has developed an interesting concept of what a board should be as follows.

## THE SIZE AND COMPOSITION OF THE BOARD

The previously mentioned survey of the participants of IMD's Leading the Family Business programme revealed that the size of boards in family-controlled businesses varies markedly. Among those surveyed, the smallest boards had two members, the largest 16. The most common size was six to seven members (see Figure 5.2).

As long-time observers of boards, six to seven members seems to us a reasonable number for normal situations. Unless there is a special reason for a larger board (for example, having to balance the influence of different family branches), six or seven members may well be the upper limit. There are several reasons against larger boards:

- Larger boards are less practical. As the number increases, the more difficult it is to reach a quorum for each meeting; it is more cumbersome to synchronise many calendars than few.
- The effectiveness and efficiency of the board suffer if it becomes bloated – it takes an enormously skilled chairman to keep the discussion on track.
- Much more advantageous group dynamics develop if the board is smaller.
- Last but not least, the dynamics of a small board make it much more difficult for a CEO to manipulate the board.

---

### A 'Working Board' at Hilti

A case where a family-controlled firm has made imaginative use of its board is Hilti AG in Schaan. This very successful family enterprise is involved in construction, the setting up and operation of building sites and the production and marketing of construction materials and tools. Its annual sales volume is more than US$1.7 billion. In Hilti's early years it recognised the need for an active, competent board, what Hilti calls an *Arbeitsverwaltungsrat* (working board). Its non-family members – the number of who, varies from five to seven – have to devote 40 working days per year to their role as Hilti board members, and the chairman of the board is a full-time appointee.

Hilti has established a list of criteria that board members must meet, including entrepreneurial ability, relevant experience and in-depth industry know-how. This list, Hilti believes, facilitates the choice of new board members and succession planning for the board.

The Hilti board members are deeply involved in the development of major company projects, which ensures that the board does not become alienated from the rest of the organisation. The board members have regular discussions with the line managers, an activity that reflects the extent to which the board members are accepted as an integral part of the organisation. As with all its employees, Hilti also arranges management development opportunities for the board members.

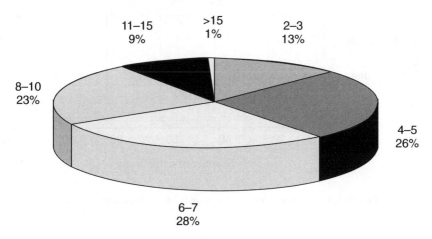

**Figure 5.2**  Number of members on the boards of a sample of family-controlled businesses

## Family Members or Outsiders?

A key question when creating a board for a family-controlled company is *How should that group be composed?* In principle a corporation is free to choose the composition of its board. Likewise, if a family holds the majority of the voting rights it can, according to most legal frameworks, determine the entire composition of the board (this, for instance, is the case in Switzerland).

In general there are three options: the board can be composed of family members only, outsiders only, or a mixture of family members and outsiders. Among the boards of the firms participating in IMD's LFB seminars, a mixture of family and non-family members clearly dominated. Of the 141 boards represented in the sample, 19 per cent were restricted to family members, 2 per cent to non-family members and 79 per cent had mixed boards (see Figure 5.3).

In our view, the decisive criteria for choosing between insiders and outsiders should be the qualifications and the talent of the candidate, not family ties. Although this rule is relatively easy to accept in principle, for many owning families it is very difficult to live by. A recent study of appointment practices for higher positions in Asian family businesses (in Asia family-controlled companies are by far the predominant form of enterprise) justified concerns that family ties rather than ability determine appointments to family firms.[10] Other families have recognised the dangers inherent in such practices and have clearly stipulated in their constitutions that familial relations must not override competence.

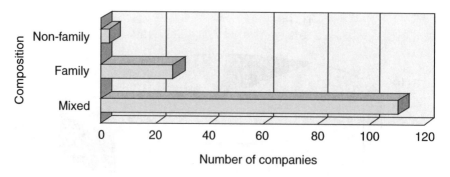

**Figure 5.3**   Composition of the boards of the businesses surveyed

In the boards of the firms in the LFB sample, *non-family board members outnumbered insiders by a slight margin*. When the participants were asked to provide reasons for inviting outsiders, typical responses were:

- They have total independence with no blinders.
- The two non-family members gave our board a certain equilibrium.
- We appreciate receiving control and advice from outside.
- They have standing in the business community and access to major customers.
- They could support the family with their experience in legal, general economic and tax matters.

A systematic compilation of the answers provided the following results:

- They provide expertise, consultancy (mentioned 60 times).
- They are executives in our business (mentioned 20 times).
- They provide objectivity, neutrality, an outside view (mentioned 15 times).
- Because they hold shares in our business or are shareholder representatives (mentioned 13 times).
- To settle family matters, serve as mediators in conflicts, serve as coach, mentor for the younger generation (mentioned 11 times).
- They are employee/union representatives (mentioned 6 times).
- Legal requirements (mentioned 5 times).
- They are close friends (mentioned 3 times).
- They are well-known people (mentioned 3 times).
- The family is too small or the business too big (mentioned 3 times).

The first four points seem to reflect purely business reasons. This observation must, however, be balanced by the adjectives used to describe those people, which show how close they are to the family. It is true that when family members are in the minority on the board they surround themselves with experts, but at the same time they may be good friends. Some of the descriptions were: 'a respected friend', 'a family lawyer', 'an accepted coach', 'somebody who understands family businesses', 'a feeling for our culture and values', 'trust'.

The reasons listed above can be summarised as five general motives for inviting outsiders to join the board. The owners of family businesses hope to reap the following benefits:

- Access to experience and knowledge otherwise not available in the firm.
- Access to the open and honest opinion of people who have no axe to grind.
- The opportunity for demanding and penetrating questions to be levelled at the family and management.
- Trustworthy but confidential advice.
- Valuable business connections.

**Qualifications of Family Board Members**

The point of view is increasingly being shared that successful board-level steerage of a family business in the cousins' confederation stage' requires the best talent that can be found. As a result more and more families – admittedly in many cases not without pain – accept that competence is the minimum attribute that any person, including a family member, must have to be considered as a director. This is also the clear message in the 'Values and Policies' of the Bergman Corporation.

In order better to understand Bergman's guidelines with respect to the board (which are listed in the box below) it is important to stress several points beforehand.

First, it is the clear intent of the family to preserve Bergman as a family company, and to secure and enhance the family fortune.

Second, it is obvious that, in order to stay in business in the long run, the company has to be profitable. Their target, as an average over a business cycle, is a return on equity that is well above the risk-free interest rate.

Third, the family is fully aware of the need to achieve a delicate balance between the accumulation of capital on the one hand and a reasonable distribution of dividends on the other. They express this in the following way: the company has to ensure the build-up of capital, so that it has the financial strength to act when it sees an interesting business opportunity (or to fight off a threat). At the same time it should manage the business in such a way as to ensure that stable dividends are forthcoming (aiming for a dividend pay-out of 20–30 per cent of total profits after taxes).

Fourth, the family feels that they can best build, enhance and control their core business interests and their other assets through a holding/parent company structure. They consider it desirable for the holding/parent company to be 100 per cent family owned, low leveraged and have a balanced portfolio of investments that takes into account the overall risk of the company. The percentage of ownership in different investments and subsidiaries can vary from majority to minority, depending on the type of investment.

Finally, the role of the holding company is:

- To allocate funds between competing investments (existing and new ones).
- To participate actively in the development of the business by monitoring and supporting the subsidiaries (that is, not to be a passive investor).
- To exercise the influence of the family by being represented on the subsidiary board.
- To be involved in the appointment of the subsidiary CEOs.
- To identify and build up management competence.
- To act as trustee of non-strategic assets.

Against this backdrop, the Bergman family has developed a set of guidelines for the board of the holding/parent company, summarised in the box overleaf.

## HOW TO FIND AND SELECT BOARD MEMBERS

Good board members are scarce. Many of the desirable ones are quickly snatched up by public companies, it is not always easy for a family-controlled business to attract good board talent. It is therefore worthwhile to look systematically at the question of finding and selecting board members of the quality required. One way to begin is to list the type of people a family business should *not* invite to join the board:

---

**Bergman's Values and Policies: Board Guidelines**

- The role of the Board is to ensure that the strategy of the Holding/Parent Company is formulated and implemented within the boundaries established by the shareholders [which have been described above].
- The Holding /Parent Company board is composed of family and non-family members. Family shall have the voting majority in the Board. Board membership shall not be life membership.
- Main criteria for being a board member are:
  - Competence
  - Loyalty towards shareholders and other stakeholders
  - A thorough business understanding and a good knowledge of family and company values
  - No conflict of interest with/no dependency (economic or otherwise) on persons or institutions with a conflict of interest with the company)
- Family members can propose new members for the Board to the Family Council. Proposals, in writing, should be delivered to the Family Council by the end of March (each year).
- The term of office for Board members is one year and renewal at the discretion of the Ordinary General Meeting. The retirement age for a Board member is 70 years.

---

- Professional consultants–they usually have conflicting interests.
- Very close personal friends. Some observers feel that while such friends may have the full trust of the family, they may shy away from being rigorous board members. But if they do decide to act rigorously, a highly valued personal relationship may be ruined for the sake of business.
- Retired managers, although one cannot apply this rule automatically. Some retired managers are unquestionably still able to offer valuable advice, while others become 'obsolete' a relatively short time after leaving office.
- Individuals who are on a large number of boards. A board position is no longer a sinecure. Boards, even those in family businesses, are so much in the limelight today that their members have to be able to

devote sufficient time to them. If one assumes (rather arbitrarily) that each board seat in a larger company requires about 20 days per year for sessions and their preparation, it is obvious that executives cannot assume seats on too many boards. Some companies will not invite onto their board any person with more than six other board memberships.

- Competitors–for obvious reasons.

## Who to Invite?

Here again we start with a general rule followed by specific recommendations.

In recent years, particularly in the English-language literature and business world, the question of the independence of board members has been avidly discussed. Purists demand that board members be free of any conflict of interest, that is, they should be truly independent when making decisions, keeping only the well-being of the company in mind. Literally applied, this would exclude the company's banker, suppliers and customers to give but three examples. The question of independence has been taken less seriously in continental Europe; it is known, for instance, that Deutsche Bank, the largest bank in Germany, holds roughly 400 board seats in different companies in Germany and elsewhere, all of whom are their customers as well.

The situation in Switzerland and France is hardly any different from that in Germany. Even in the UK it has been recognised that absolute adherence to the principle of independence may be the equivalent of throwing out the baby with the bath water. First of all, in many established boards there exist age-old, valuable relationships that may violate the letter of the independence postulate, but companies do not want to give them up as the advantages are considered greater than the disadvantages. Second, as we said above, it is difficult to find good board members even with a somewhat relaxed approach to the principle of independence. This problem is compounded if one takes into consideration that restricting the number of board seats one person may hold automatically increases the need for more candidates. Against this background, it is understandable that, as a compromise, it is today widely accepted – even in the English-speaking countries – that it may well suffice for the majority of the non-executive directors to meet the independence criterion.

With this rather general rule for the selection of board members in mind, here are some more concrete suggestions.

The most obvious candidates for boards in family-controlled companies are owner-managers of other family-controlled businesses, preferably ones who have already faced similar challenges to the ones confronting the inviting company.

Other suitable candidates are heads of divisions of larger, publicly traded corporations. They are usually in the younger age range, but nevertheless may be very knowledgeable and more easy to attract as board members than, for instance, the top layer of management in their companies. In addition their own companies may find it desirable for them to gain additional, high-level experience by serving on the board of an interesting family business.

Finally, under normal circumstances a family-controlled business is well advised to look for board members with a good general business sense rather than highly specialised expertise in a given field. Broad, sound business judgement can be usefully applied to a wide range of situations but if the family firm needs highly specialised knowledge for their deliberations at the board level, it can be easily brought in on an *ad hoc* basis.

**How to Spot Good Candidates**

One obvious source of board members are friends and acquaintances of the family controlling the firm. In such cases family members are asked to suggest the names of good prospective candidates. The second most important source are the contact networks of individuals already on the board, as such networks often include suitable candidates. In some countries it is becoming more and more acceptable to use executive search firms to identify prospective board members, and globally active search firms can be particularly helpful if a family is looking for a board member from another national setting.

BOARD TENURE

Because the relationship between the family and board membesr is frequently very personal, it is not surprising that the tenure of board members in family-controlled companies tends to be longer than in large, publicly held corporations. This guarantees both continuity and stability, two qualities that are particularly valuable when the time comes to pass the management baton from one generation to the next. At the same time it is important for the board to be exposed to fresh view points from time to time, so a certain amount of turnover is desirable. Six years might be a reasonable tenure as this would allow new members sufficient time to familiarise themselves with the company and make a fruitful contribution before being replaced.

In this context it is important to highlight a new development aimed at keeping board members on their toes: regular performance evaluation.

## EVALUATING THE PERFORMANCE OF INDIVIDUAL BOARD MEMBERS

The question of evaluating the performance of *individual directors* on a board has been extensively discussed of late in the context of the corporate governance debate. This is not to be confused with evaluation of *the board as a group,* which we will discuss towards the end of this chapter. The response to the idea of judging the performance of individual board members varies. Traditionally minded 'old-timers' on boards find the idea difficult to accept, considering it beneath their dignity to expose themselves to such a procedure. Against this background, it is clear that some owner–managers are wary of ruffling the feathers of good board members by asking them to agree to a formal evaluation of their performance.

Another reason for reluctance to evaluate board members is specific to family-controlled companies. We have observed several cases where chairmen or heads of families have prevented an evaluation because they feared that one or other of their relatives on the board would come out with a poor result. If this should happen, the board member in question is put in a difficult position: on the one hand he or she has almost no choice but to step down; on the other hand his or her pride as co-owner will almost force him or her to rebel against the verdict (and question the whole process). In the light of this, it may be preferable to give up the idea of evaluation in such cases.

However, our research has revealed a newer school of thought whose followers react very differently to the question of evaluation. They argue that since everybody has a 'boss', even board members, and since the shareholders – the natural bosses of the board as they appoint its members – are frequently widely dispersed, meet only rarely and, often cannot judge whether or not a given board member is performing satisfactorily, the next best solution for a performance review is a peer review among the members of the board. This school of thought seems to be gaining sway as the discussion continues.[11] It is important to add that before such reviews are first implemented there is usually scepticism, but it usually disappears once the directors have gone through the process. Some of those reviewed even become enthusiastic advocates of the procedure.

## Limits to Formality

The authors have been involved in developing such evaluation procedures in several large companies, two of them family-controlled businesses. During this work it has become very clear that the procedure requires a healthy amount of sensitivity. As we saw earlier, the job of a board member is anything but sharply defined. This means that by its very nature, such an evaluation has to be largely subjective, with the 'truth' emerging from a multitude of opinions. Of necessity, the degree of formality has to be limited. And this limited formality highlights the important role the chairman has to play in evaluation procedures.

## An Overview over the Process

An overview of the different steps in the process is shown in Figure 5.4.

It is appropriate to go over the five steps in some detail. The starting point is to identify the attributes that are desirable in an 'acceptable director'. The whole board has to be involved in this first task. The following list of required attributes was developed for the board of a large enterprise:

- He/she has a good knowledge of the business, its organisation and culture.
- He/she has a good insight into the industries in which the company is active.
- He/she consistently displays a solid commitment to his/her role as board member (for example prepares well for each board meeting).
- He/she uses his/her knowledge and experience to give the board and management new, strong ideas (distinctive contribution).
- He/she willingly makes his/her contacts in other companies, government agencies or institutions available to the firm.
- His/her participation on the board enhances team performance and development.
- His/her participation on the board is not restricted by conflicts of interest.

- His/her contribution to the discussions enhances the quality of decisions made by the board, and adds dynamism to the value-creation process of the firm 'additive contribution'.
- He/she consistently displays solid judgement.

Guiding us in the development of this list was the principle that such attributes should be observable by the board members in the course of their board work.

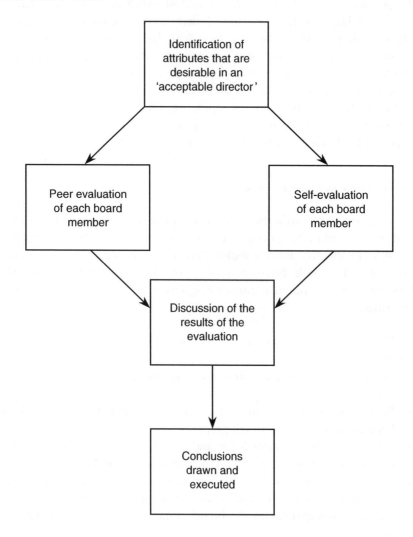

**Figure 5.4** Steps in the peer evaluation process

## Peer and Self-Evaluation

Once agreement on the criteria has been reached, they can be reproduced in a set of simple forms to be filled in by each member of the board. Filling in the form is the first step of a two-part process. First the board members are asked to evaluate each one of their peers. For this task they use a form, the first page of which is shown in Figure 5.5. As can be seen from the form, the directors evaluate their colleagues in two ways: on a scale of one to five and through written comments after each statement. In our experience the latter bring out more subtle points than can be expressed by a numerical rating (furthermore the written comments are usually far more important for the later discussion with the board member than his or her mark on the scale.)

Step two of the process is self-evaluation by each board member: everybody must be given the chance to express how they see their own performance. The self-evaluation may further provide the chairman with interesting, additional information that sheds light on the *de facto* behaviour of a board member. (The same questionnaire is used for the self-evaluation as for the peer evaluation except that 'he/she' is replaced by 'I'.)

It is important to realise that considerable discipline and objectivity is required when completing these questionnaires. Because of the closeness that usually prevails among the members of a board, the temptation to give a lenient evaluation is great. In our experience it is helpful to give board members a reference point by asking, 'How would you rate your colleague if he/she was a member of the board of a first-class, publicly owned company?' This approach usually creates a certain amount of healthy distance between a board member and his or her peers, and this detachment makes it easier to come up with a more objective assessment. In our experience this approach is a good means of revealing not only the strengths but also the weaknesses of a board member.

When such a process is conducted the first time, confidentiality has to be assured; otherwise the board members may not express their honest opinions. In such situations it helps to bring in a trusted third party to compile the questionnaire results in a way that will protect the individual contributors. Just this summary is used in the later stages of the process. Once the board members know how the data are handled and used, any fears are often largely removed. It may well happen that in later evaluation rounds the individual performance of each board member, including that of the chairman, is openly discussed around the board

*Confidential*

**Peer Appraisal**

Name of the appraising board member

...................................................................................................................

Name of the board member appraised

*Please indicate your view as to the following statements by circling the appropriate number on the 1–5 scale (where 1 = Strongly Disagree and 5 = Strongly agree).*

*To allow for the degree of subtlety appropriate for an evaluation process of this kind, space for verbal comments is provided after each statement. You are encouraged to use it to express the nuances of your assessment.*

1.  He/she has a good knowledge of the business, its        1   2   3   4   5
    organisation and culture.
    Comments:

    ...............................................................................................................

    ...............................................................................................................

    ...............................................................................................................

2.  He/she has a good insight into the industries in        1   2   3   4   5
    which our company is active.
    Comments:

    ...............................................................................................................

    ...............................................................................................................

    ...............................................................................................................

3.  He/she consistently displays a solid commitment to      1   2   3   4   5
    the role of board member (e.g. is well-prepared for
    board meetings).
    Comments:

    ...............................................................................................................

    ...............................................................................................................

    ...............................................................................................................

4.  He/she uses her knowledge and experience to             1   2   3   4   5
    motivate the board and management to take
    initiatives (distinctive contribution)
    Comments:

    ...............................................................................................................

    ...............................................................................................................

    ...............................................................................................................

**Figure 5.5**   First page of peer appraisal form

table, but this requires maturity and a good deal of experience with processes of this nature (plus a good dose of self-confidence).

The next step is probably the most important and most delicate: the discussion of the results. As noted above, it is sometimes helpful to ask a trusted outside person to compile the data. The data are used for confidential, one-to-one discussions between the chairman and each board member. If the evaluation turns out to be positive and the criticism is restricted to areas that can be corrected, the chairman and the director in question discuss and make a note of what actions are required so that a record exists for consultation in future evaluation rounds.

If the outcome is strongly negative, and if there is little promise that improvements will result from these discussions, the chairman may suggest that the board member not stand for reelection when his or her tenure is up. This is probably the most elegant and most face-saving solution: asking that person to leave the board immediately would require very important reasons to be given, as such a step would probably stigmatise the board member for the rest of his or her life.

This procedure is painful enough when the director comes from outside the family, but the difficulties are compounded when a family member is asked to leave the board of the family firm, particularly if he or she has been on the board for a long time and has never been challenged before. In our experience it is hardly possible to remove such a person without pain and friction. It is somewhat easier to sever the ties with those who have joined the board relatively recently and who are aware of the possibility of removal. Asking a consistently non-performing board member to leave is, however, necessary if the board is to maintain its credibility. (It is interesting to note that the results of the individual evaluations usually do not come as a surprise. After all, all board members have an opinion on the performance of their peers. Why not look at non-performance systematically and discuss it in a mature way?)

## REMUNERATION OF BOARD MEMBERS

Remuneration of board members is frequently a difficult topic. Here the path to virtue can indeed be narrow. On the one hand the family business cannot get away with offering an insignificant remuneration, as managers of some standing will not feel respected if they are offered the proverbial 'peanuts'. On the other hand the firm should be wary of paying too much, as the board members' independence might be compromised; that is, they could be placed in a quasi-employment relationship. An elegant solution is offered by John Ward, who suggests that the owner–manager divides what he is paid annually by, say, 250 (working days), then pays each board member the resulting amount per day for each day spent on board matters. This provides a logical, defensible basis for figuring out a remuneration that, in principle, puts the board member on a level plane with the owner–manager.

In some countries it has become the custom to offer board members a pension. In our opinion this flies in the face of the independence criterion and is foreign to the concept of board membership as a part-time, 'detached' occupation. In short, we are opposed to it.


## PRACTICAL GUIDELINES THAT HELP BOARDS WORK WELL

For the work of the board to be successful in the long run, the relationship between the board and management has to be governed by 'genuine partnership', which can be translated into a set of down-to-earth guidelines. The more important of these are described below.

### Keep the Board Informed

The management and the owners have to keep the board informed about all important developments in the firm, otherwise sheer self-respect will prompt outside individuals of any calibre to leave the board. Obviously, judgement has to be applied to this guideline, but here again the (probably) correct path is narrow. Some family-controlled firms 'starve' the board of information, while others fall into the trap of overloading the board members with so much paper that important matters no longer catch their attention. Every communication should be concise (that is, it should concentrate on the essentials) and timely. The need for timeliness holds particularly true for bad news. If a well-known or highly reputed personality agrees to join a board, the firm benefits. Therefore when difficulties occur, whether in the firm or in the family, that board member has the right to be informed without delay.

The concept of keeping a board thoroughly informed on a regular basis raises an additional question: should board members – particularly outsiders – have direct access to line managers? Despite the inclination to answer 'yes' in the case of a publicly traded company, such a demand would probably be unrealistic in many family businesses. When a board member of a family-controlled firm wants additional information on, say, intended marketing measures, he or she should turn to the owner–

manager, chairman or CEO, and the latter can then decide whether to answer the question or refer the board member to a marketing specialist in the company (and/or arrange for direct access to that specialist without necessarily being present).

## Hold a Reasonable Number of Board Meetings Each Year

The survey of the participants in IMD's seminars revealed that the number of board meetings they held per year varied widely (see Figure 5.6).

The most common practice (35 per cent of the companies) was to meet three to four times per year; 20 per cent met five to six times a year. The vast majority met every month, quarter or semester. A generalisation about the number of times a board should meet cannot be made without considering additional circumstances, for example the role the family has assigned to the board and the state of health of the company. The broader the role and the rougher the economic times, the greater the need for frequent meetings.

## Determine Who Sets the Agenda

At first sight this appears to be a trivial consideration. However it can seriously affect the board's working atmosphere. It is not disputed that it is the owner's prerogative to set the agenda, but IMD's research on boards indicates that board members place great store on being able to add their 'burning issue' to the agenda.

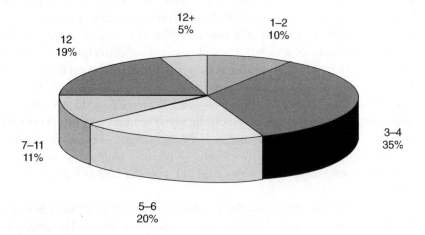

**Figure 5.6** Frequency of survey participants' board meetings (number per annum)

Among the participants of our survey the agenda was set by:

- The chairman (in 28 per cent of the cases).
- The chairman and the CEO (19 per cent of the cases).
- The CEO (16 per cent of the cases).
- In most other cases, setting the agenda was largely a team effort.

### Board Retreats are Important

While routine meetings are typically held on the company's premises, it is highly advisable for the board to have a biannual, weekend retreat away from the business. During such retreats, certain key questions concerning the future of the firm – for example succession and the firm's overall strategic thrust – can be discussed more discreetly and thoroughly. An evening or two away from the office sitting in comfortable surroundings can create an atmosphere that is conducive to relaxed and extended discussions of even difficult questions.

## EVALUATING THE PERFORMANCE OF THE BOARD AS A GROUP

Good boards do not happen by accident. In most cases the members have worked diligently and patiently to improve the performance of their group. Part of this effort should include a board session once a year where members *as a group* ask the question: 'Are we a good board?' We have come across family-controlled companies that have formulated six or seven simple, down-to-earth questions on the overall quality of the board's performance, which the board answers collectively once a year or every other year. More and more schemes to evaluate the performance of the board as a group are appearing in the literature.[12] And yet, the vast majority of the boards in family-controlled businesses do not seem to judge their own performance systematically. The survey of the IMD LFB participants revealed that 64 per cent of the sample (84 boards) had no performance evaluation, 29 per cent (39 boards) claimed to conduct a systematic evaluation and 11 per cent (11 boards) had some kind of an evaluation.

Group self-evaluation (and the resulting corrective measures) is essential if the board wants to benefit from a learning process. The ability to learn is a priceless quality. Arie de Geus, former head of planning of the Royal Dutch Shell Group, expressed it well when he said: 'The ability to learn faster than your competitors may be the only sustainable competitive advantage.'

A good example of how self-appraisal can improve performance is provided by the board of the Campbell Soup Company (a family-influenced business), as the following mini-case demonstrates.


## ALL IN ALL, IT SEEMS WORTHWHILE TO HAVE A BOARD

One of the last questions in our survey was 'Do you in general feel that your board adds value when it comes to managing the business?' Seventy-four per cent of the LFB participants believed that their boards added value when it came to running their business. The results were as follows:

- Boards add value: 101(74%)
- Boards add no value: 21(16%)
- Boards add little or not enough value: 7(10%)

Hence the vast majority of those surveyed felt it worthwhile to have a board in a family-controlled business. A similar study in Italy produced very similar results: of the 62 family businesses surveyed, only eight (or 16 per cent) considered that the boards were not very useful.[13] However in Spain 28 per cent of the participants of a survey felt that boards were not particularly useful, although boards in family businesses were no longer thought of as an 'outlandish' phenomenon: almost three quarters of the family firms surveyed appreciated them.


## CONCLUSION

In this chapter we looked at the board of directors as a key element in the governance structure of a family business. The literature on boards is now very rich, as is our experience of them. All this allowed us to make a comprehensive *tour d'horizon* of the role of boards, their composition, their working style and the cost and time involved in using them.

Boards and the family itself (and its institutions) are two of the three pivots (the third being top management) on which the governance system in a family business turns, and for that reason we have devoted two chapters to them. In order to discharge their governance role effectively, however, they must work together closely in tandem with top management. This requirement will become particularly apparent in Chapters 6–8.

**America's Best Board**

Following the result of a recent survey, *Business Week* elected a family-influenced business, the Campbell Soup Company, as the 1996 winner of America's best board award. According to Business Week (25 November 1996, pp. 62–68), Campbell's governance guidelines 'are among the most stringent and far-reaching in corporate America'. General Electric and IBM ranked second and third respectively.

What makes Campbell's board so special? The rules are written and acted upon, the board reviews and improves the governance standards annually and the evaluation of the board's performance and effectiveness is published, which is probably the best incentive for directors to take their responsibilities seriously.

Campbell first published their corporate governance standards in 1992, and since then the standards have evolved in line with the development of the business. The standards include, among other things, an annual performance evaluation of the CEO, a review of the company's three-year strategic plan and one-year operating plan and a report by the board to the CEO on succession planning and management development. Directors are required to own at least 1000 Campbell shares within a year of election and 3000 shares within three years of election. They all stand for election every year, and no director can stand for reelection after the age of 70. At present, apart from the CEO all directors are independent – 'independent' meaning no present or former employment by the company and no significant financial or personal tie to the company other than share ownership and entitlement to director's fees.

In May 1995, the board's governance committee instigated a new process to evaluate the board's performance and effectiveness. As a first step, all directors completed a board evaluation questionnaire. Each director rated from 1 to 5 (and, in most cases provided written comments) each of the following 15 standards:

- The board knows and understands the company's vision, strategic precepts, strategic plan and operating plan.
- The board reflects its understanding of the company's vision, strategic precepts, strategic plan and operating plan in its discussions and actions on key issues throughout the year.

- Board meetings are conducted in a manner that ensures open communication, meaningful participation and timely resolution of issues.
- Advance board materials contain the right amount of information.
- Board members receive their materials sufficiently in advance of meetings.
- Board members are diligent in preparing for meetings.
- The board reviews and adopts an annual operating budget and regularly monitors performance against it throughout the year.
- The board regularly monitors the company's income statement, balance sheet and cash flow.
- The board reviews and adopts an annual capital budget and receives regular written or oral reports of performance against it throughout the year.
- In tracking company performance, the board regularly considers the performance of peer companies.
- The board regularly reviews the performance of the CEO.
- The board and/or the compensation/organisation committee regularly reviews the performance and ethics of the senior officers.
- The correlation between executive pay and company performance is regularly considered by the board and/or the compensation committee.
- The board reviews succession plans for the CEO and senior management.
- The trigger level for board or committee involvement in major business policies and decisions is appropriate.

This process led to the identification of areas the board felt were its greatest strengths: (1) attention to company performance versus competition, (2) timeliness and adequacy of written board materials, (3) connection of pay to performance and (4) the board's involvement in setting and tracking performance in relationship to budgets.

Conversely the board identified the following areas where improvement was needed.

- Increasing the amount of board time devoted to long-range strategic planning.

- Broadening and diversifying the skills of directors.
- Encouraging the active participation of all directors in meetings.
- Upgrading the quality of the committees' reports to the board regarding their deliberations.

Specific steps were taken in early 1996 to improve these areas. At the end of fiscal year 1996 the directors were asked to assess the progress made, and it was concluded that there had been significant improvement in all four areas.

It is worth noting that, in a parallel development, Campbell's market value has tripled since 1990.

NOTES

1.  A. Demb and F. F. Neubauer, *The Corporate Board: Confronting the Paradoxes*, New York: Oxford University Press, 1992.
2.  J. L. Ward, *Creating Effective Boards for Private Enterprise*, San Francisco: Jossey-Bass, 1991.
3.  In some countries, firms are required to have labour representatives on the board. Although they are insiders, they are typically not involved in the management of the firm.
4.  Ward, *Creating Effective Boards*, op. cit., p. 30.
5.  W. C. Turner, 'International Advisory Councils', *Directors & Boards*, Winter 1996, pp. 43–8.
6.  'Advisory Board', *Small Business Report*, May 1982, pp. 11–14.
7.  J. K. Loudon, 'The Liability of Advisory Boards', *Directors & Boards*, Spring 1986, pp. 19–20.
8.  A. Cadbury, *The role of directors in family firms, The Director's Manual*, Hemel Hempstead: Director Books in association with the Institute of Directors, 1993, ch. D3, p. 12.
9.  For the statistical work that drew the pertinent points out of the survey, the authors are indebted to Denise Kenyon-Rouvinez, Research Associate at IMD.
10. P. N. Pant and V. G. Rajadhyaksha, 'Partnership with Asian Family Business – What Every Multinational Corporation Should Know', *Long Range Planning*, vol. 29, no. 6, p. 813.
11. Report of the NACD Blue Ribbon Group on Director Professionalism, Washington, 1996, p. 41.
12. A. Demb and F. F. Neubauer, *The Corporate Board*, op. cit., pp. 183–185 or Report of the NACD Blue Ribbon Commission on Director Professionalism, op. cit., pp. 15–31.
13. G. Corbetta and S. Tomaselli, 'Boards of Directors in Italian Family Businesses', *Family Business Review*, vol. 9, no. 4 (1996), p. 414.

# Part IV
# The Directing Task of Corporate Governance: Key Measures

## INTRODUCTION

In Part IV we take a closer look at the first three of the governance measures identified in Part III as ways and means of discharging the directing task in corporate governance. We devote one chapter to each and show how the board typically spearheads the handling of the task, close cooperation with the family and top management.

Chapter 6 looks at CEO succession, first from within the family and then from outside.

In Chapter 7 we look into the ways and means the board can use to get the family (and top management) involved in establishing a vision and strategy for the firm.

In Chapter 8 we look into aspects of financial strategy, that is, ways of securing the financial resources the firm (and the family) needs in order to function well. Questions such as whether or not to go public play a major role here.

Earlier efforts to improve corporate governance (for example the Cadbury Report) have been criticised for placing too much emphasis on *conformance* (to certain behavioural standards, for instance), rather than stressing the *economic performance* of the firm. This is one of the reasons why we devote more attention in this book to the directing side of governance rather than, for instance, the controlling side.

# 6 Securing CEO Succession as a Key Governance Measure in a Family Business

No matter how much wisdom may go into planning, whether it be an insurance program, an armed invasion of a continent, or a campaign to reduce the inroads of disease, the measure of its success always will be the spirit and mettle of the individuals engaged in its execution. No matter how much treasure may support a project, or how elaborate its organisation, or how detailed and farsighted its operational scheme, the human element is always the central one.

(Dwight D. Eisenhower, former US President, 1890–1969)

Any broad review[1] of the literature on family enterprises will come to two conclusions:

- CEO succession is by far the most commonly addressed issue.
- A (if not *the*) critical determinant of whether or not a firm remains in the hands of the founding family is the latter's ability to manage the succession process.

A further confirmation of the importance of succession has come from our experience with the participants (all from family enterprises) in IMD's LFB programme. At the start of each seminar we ask, 'Why did you choose to come to this particular programme?' In the ten years of LFB's existence, the most repeated response has been, 'To find solutions to the problems of making the transition between the generations in terms of management succession', or words to that effect. And when they say 'succession' they are talking about replacing the CEO, the leader of their family enterprise.

The first part of this chapter is devoted to the issues associated with appointing a new CEO from within the family. In the second part we will look at the appointment of a non-family member to the position of CEO.

Both processes have one thing in common: they are usually fraught with difficulties.


## APPOINTING A FAMILY MEMBER AS THE NEW CEO

Academics, researchers, consultants and family members alike put management succession at the top of their list of priorities. In the authors' opinion, they are right to do so. The appointment of the next CEO is not so much a personnel decision (although it is that too) but a strategic one and possibly the most important one that has to be made in any generation, whatever the stage in the life cycle of the firm. If indeed Raph Waldo Emerson, the American philosopher, was correct in concluding that 'an organisation is the lengthened shadow of a man' or, we would add, a woman, then surely that person is the CEO. CEOs are usually the key determinants of the success or failure of the family firm. The CEO is also a pivotal figure in the three governance tasks we have identified: Directing, controlling and accounting for. Together with the board, he or she is most often identified in the public's mind with the directing function.

### Succession as a Planned Process and Event

Management succession is both a process and an event. The latter, of course, is the formal transfer of power from the outgoing generation (the successee) to the incoming CEO (the successor).[2] The former refers to a series of identifiable steps over time whose purpose is to ensure that the eventual successor will be ready to undertake the difficult task of CEO when the time comes.[3] It is our belief that a formal management succession plan enhances the probability that the shift between the generations will be accomplished in the best interests of the family and the business. As Lansberg has stated, 'One of the most significant factors determining the continuity of the family firm from one generation to the next is whether the succession process is planned.'[4] Barach *et al.* echo this conclusion: 'CEOs of family firms and their successors can benefit from a thoughtful career planning for the next generation because goals of both the firm and the individuals are involved. Care given to the career paths of the next generation is an essential part of the implementation strategy of family firms.'[5]

Unfortunately, research and anecdotal evidence indicate that such planning is the exception rather than the rule, in spite of the above noted preoccupation with management succession. We hypothesise that this state of affairs explains to a considerable degree why family enterprises have such poor longevity records,[6] as we outlined in Chapter 1. Even when there is planning, it is often in terms of the event and not the process. It seems that relatively few family business leaders think about their own succession until they are well into their sixties or experience a life-threatening crisis. Yet we believe that planning for management succession should start, at the latest, on the day that a new CEO takes over. The goal is to put in place a system that will ensure the leadership talent necessary to replace the CEO is available at that inevitable future date when he or she can no longer remain in charge. We strongly support the conclusion of Foster of the Center for Creative Leadership, who says:

> The ability to develop leadership in the successor generation is crucial to the survival and growth of family-owned and family-managed businesses. In order to successfully make the transition from one generation to the next, family businesses must design a process of grooming and developing the successor generation of the family into skilled leaders who can shepherd the business through the inevitable crises, changes, and growth of the competitive future.[7]

In his trail-blazing study, Malone attempted to understand what factors tended to influence the degree of what he called 'continuity planning' in family business.[8] This concept reflects our formulation of planned management succession. He offered six propositions that he felt, *a priori*, would be positively correlated with extent, level or degree of continuity planning. He anticipated a positive correlation between the degree of continuity planning and the following:

- The size of the business.
- The amount of strategic planning.
- The level of perceived family harmony.
- The percentage of outsiders on the board.[9]
- The age of owner–managers.
- The degree of internality[10] of the owner–manager's locus of control.

Even though the sample was small (58 CEOs) and restricted to one industry (timber) in one country (the United States), his results are both intriguing and disquieting. His statistical analysis produced the following findings.

There was no significant positive correlation with the *size of the business*. Even relatively large enterprises were not engaging in continuity planning. This could be very bad news for the numerous employees, heirs and communities that depend on these companies.

The more *strategic planning* there was, the higher the probability that business continuity was being planned. An explanation of this could well be that family firms active in strategic planning have come to the realisation that succession planning must be a fundamental component of strategic planning.

There was a positive correlation between family harmony and continuity planning. One explanation could be that if the family is in harmony, it is much easier to discuss succession and set up appropriate systems for preparing the next generation to take over. A family in serious conflict may find this task next to impossible.

While the correlation between the *percentage of outsiders on the board* and continuity planning turned out to be positive, one must exercise caution when interpreting the results. They could mean that outsiders are more able to influence (because of their supposed independence) the CEO to establish a management succession process. Alternatively the very fact that the CEO wants outsiders on his or her board implies that the owner–manager is open to discussion with others, either inside or outside the firm, on management succession issues. The data do not allow us to conclude anything about the role of non-family board members in the continuity planning process.

Unfortunately the proposition that the *age of the owner–manager* is positively correlated with continuity planning was not statistically confirmed. It seems that the prospect of declining health or death does not necessarily prompt continuity planning. For too many aging CEOs it is not a question of 'when I die', but 'if I die'.

According to Malone, earlier research implies that those with an *internal locus of control* tend to be more proactive and intent on having a direct influence on the future. His research confirmed a positive correlation between the amount of continuity planning and the degree of internal focus of control.


## A SUCCESSION SUCCESS STORY

The media, 'tell it all' books and the academic literature are full of stories describing in lurid detail the failure of family enterprises to manage the succession process successfully. We would like to break with this tradition by describing a family company where the transition was made painlessly and had a positive outcome (see box below). The names used are fictitious but the family company is real. The focus is on passing the baton between the second and third generations.

---

### Machine Tools S.A. (MTSA)

MTSA was founded in 1935 by Georges Marchand when he was 30 years old. He borrowed money from friends and family and used this, plus his own savings to build a small machine tool plant in the French-speaking part of Switzerland. He was a very typical founder in the sense that the business was an extension of his personality, and he devoted almost every waking hour to managing even the smallest detail.

His wife Marie had given birth to their first child, Albert, in 1933, two years before Georges quit his previous job as a welder on various construction projects in the area. One year after the founding of MTSA their second child, Denise, was born.

Between 1935 and 1975 Georges built up the business to the point where it had more than 500 employees and was one of the largest and most profitable firms in its market niche in Switzerland. Daughter Denise never showed any interest in joining the firm. However Albert showed considerable enthusiasm about working for the family company even before he completed his secondary education. Georges was very proud of his son's educational achievements as he himself was, as he often declared, a 'self-made man' with little formal education. So in 1953, at the age of 20, Albert became his father's assistant, heir apparent and right-hand man. At his father's side he learned the business in the classical master–apprentice fashion. Albert was often frustrated by his father's autocratic behaviour and wished that Georges would give him more responsibility, more quickly. Still, his respect for his father's entrepreneurial ability and his love of the business kept him patiently waiting for his chance to become CEO when Georges finally decided to step down.

In 1975, at the age of 70 and in failing health, Georges decided abruptly that the time had come. Within the space of one day there was a new CEO and at last Albert, at the age of 42, took charge.

Georges had also decided to give control of the voting stock to his son and a minority position to Denise. Rather unusually for a family company, Georges cut off all ties with the company he had created and let Albert get on with the job.

Albert married Sonia in 1956 and they had three children: Suzanne (born in 1957), Pierre (1959) and Xavier (1962). The family was warm and loving and there was easy communication between the two generations and among the siblings. A special time of each day during the children's childhood was the evening meal, when the family shared the day's events. The children talked about their successes and failures, their hopes and concerns, Sonia about her life as a full-time homemaker and Albert about the company and the challenges of being the owner–manager of a growing organisation. Both triumphs and disappointments were discussed in a calm tone. Albert always tried to bring out what each member of the family had learned from the day's activities.

Of course there were inevitable disagreements and periodic clashes among the siblings. The family rule in such cases was that they should try to work out the problem themselves. If unsuccessful, then the matter would be 'kicked upstairs' to Sonia and/or Albert for mediation and, if necessary, arbitration.

All three children turned out to be excellent students. In their early teens Pierre and Xavier started to show an interest in MTSA (Suzanne never became excited about the business), and Albert offered them the opportunity to do minor jobs in their free time. Some school holidays were spent on the shop floor learning the basic skills needed to produce high-quality machine tools. Both boys were well accepted by the employees and were perceived as genuinely interested in acquiring knowledge from their older and more skilled coworkers.

Suzanne finished her secondary school education, married young and became a locally famous artisan, producing first-rate cut-out paper works of art. Pierre received a degree in economics from the University of Geneva in 1983, while Xavier, with his father's full approval, decided to pursue his studies in the United States – in 1985 he received a BSc in information technology.

Upon graduation at the age of 24, Pierre joined MTSA in an entry-level position in the finance department. Over the course of the next 11 years he worked in all the major departments and was appointed vice president of finance and accounting in 1994. As

Pierre moved up the chain of command, his father made it clear to his son's superiors that they should treat him like any other employee and that Pierre should be given objective feedback on his performance. Where weaknesses were discerned, they were to coach Pierre and suggest appropriate training and development opportunities. Albert was to be kept informed of his son's progress. On no occasion did the CEO overrule a decision made by one of his son's superiors concerning Pierre's career development.

Xavier's career path was somewhat different. When he graduated in 1985 he decided to join a renowned American consulting firm, which gave him the chance (and eventually an excellent reputation) to use information technology to improve the manufacturing operations of various client companies. This he did for three years and enjoyed every minute of it, but finally decided he was homesick for Switzerland and wanted to return. A phone call to his father confirmed that Albert would be delighted to have him join MTSA, as would Pierre. So in 1988 Xavier joined the family firm. After discussions with members of the board of directors of the company (by now MTSA was triple the size it had been when Albert took over) and the vice president of personnel, Albert decided to charge Xavier with the task of creating a brand new staff department to apply information technology to both manufacturing and administrative operations. From the start Xavier reported to Albert. The younger son was warmly accepted into the fold by all employees, his parents and his siblings.

In February 1995, at the age of 62 Albert suffered a massive heart attack that almost killed him. The doctors' advised him to step down from the CEO position as staying on would endanger his recovery. After a short discussion with his wife Sonia, his decision was made – for the sake of the family and the business he had to pass on the baton as soon as possible. The three external members of the board (Albert being the only other member) were consulted and all four agreed that the vice president of manufacturing, who had been with Albert since he took over from his father, would be appointed acting CEO.

Meanwhile the family and business crisis provoked by Albert's heart attack presented a real dilemma for Pierre and Xavier – the only other family members active in the business. Pierre had been with MTSA longer than his brother Xavier and was the older of the two. On the other hand Xavier had had excellent outside experience and had made a significant contribution to cost reduction during his seven years with the company. Both brothers felt entitled to the job of CEO. In line with the tradition established in their pre-teen years, they agreed to try to resolve their problem – this time by going off to the Swiss Alps for a skiing weekend. There were heated discussions over fondue dinners, but by Sunday night their respective positions had not changed. They decided to submit the issue to Albert.

By then Albert was well enough to resume the role of mediator/arbitrator. The three met in Albert's bedroom to try to resolve the conflict. Albert listened carefully to his two sons' self-serving arguments, delivered in calm, measured tones. He said he would do some thinking and let them know what he had decided. His next step was to call a consultative meeting of the three external directors, the vice president of manufacturing and the vice president of personnel – all trusted colleagues who knew the family well.

After several days Albert asked his two sons, the two vice presidents and the three board members to meet him at home – this time in the living room as he was feeling stronger. He announced that he would appoint a succession committee, which he would chair, of all those present, minus the two siblings. Their task was to supply him with answers to the following:

- What should be the profile of the next CEO – in terms of experience, abilities, interests and so on – if they were to maximise the chances of MTSA moving into the twenty-first century as a successful family-controlled if not family-managed company?
- Which five people, in their opinion, fulfilled the above criteria – whether family or non-family, internal or external to the firm?
- Could they agree on one person as being 'the best'?
- What should his role be in the immediate future *vis-à-vis* the family and its enterprise?

Pierre, Xavier and all others present supported Albert's plan. The succession committee reported back to Albert two weeks later with their responses to the four-part mandate:

- They had prepared a job description of the future CEO given the strategic direction of the family firm, and derived from that the qualities the candidate needed to fill this role.

- The names of Pierre and Xavier had been placed on the shortlist, plus three highly qualified executives not currently working for MTSA.
- There was consensus that on balance Pierre was the most qualified.
- Albert should officially step down as CEO as soon as he, as majority shareholder, decided who would replace him. The other members of the board would approve whomever he chose from the list of five candidates. If Albert's health permitted, and if he so desired he should remain as non-executive chairman of the board.

Albert warmly thanked the succession committee for their recommendations and said he would do some further thinking.

Albert's next step was to call the first meeting of what subsequently became known as the family council: Sonia, Suzanne, Pierre and Xavier. He passed on in detail the report of the succession committee. Xavier expressed his disappointment at not being chosen as the front-running candidate, but stated clearly and with no vindictiveness that if Albert chose Pierre as his successor, he would accept that decision and stay with the family firm. Sonia and Suzanne said that their only concern was that whoever was chosen would be the best man for the job and that the family would stay united. Pierre had little to say except that he would accept whatever his father decided.

During the next week Albert held informal, off the record conversations with his banker, lawyer, major supplier and two of his most important customers. He showed them the shortlist of five drawn up by the succession committee, and while there was no outright favourite the majority favoured Pierre as Albert's successor.

On 5 May 1995 the board of directors of MTSA prepared a press release announcing that Pierre Marchand had been appointed CEO of MTSA and that his father would retain the post of chairman of the board. This information was provided to the employees before being sent to the media. What was not announced was that Pierre would hold 51 per cent of the voting shares and his brother 49 per cent. For Suzanne, other financial arrangements had been made, which were felt by all the family members to be equitable.

**Commentary**

To many readers, especially those families who own a business and have lived through the all too common trauma of management succession between the generations, the MTSA story may read like a fairy tale. But as an old song proclaims, 'Fairy tales can come true, it can happen to you.' That it happened this way with the Marchands was not due solely to chance. There was hard work, conflict and above all a serious attempt by Albert to establish a planning 'process' and an 'event' management protocol that maximised the probability that not only would the interests of the business be safeguarded, but that the family would stay together.

Let us analyse some of the key elements that brought about this positive conclusion:

- Socialisation of the third generation into the rights and responsibilities of managing and owning an enterprise started very early – around the dinner table as the children were growing up.
- The family's culture stressed caring and mutual respect.
- Certain conflict management procedures were accepted and honoured from the start.
- The children were allowed to pursue their own natural interests and talents, and success was celebrated in whatever field they chose.
- There was no precondition that acceptance as a fully fledged family member meant being active in the business.
- None of the third generation was forced to join the family firm; for both Pierre and Xavier, it was a fully voluntary decision, and a warm welcome awaited them when they chose to join.
- Both in-company (Pierre) and external experience (Xavier) were valued, and even before they joined the firm on a full-time basis, both brothers had a grasp of the essentials of the business.
- Pierre in particular was treated in a non-preferential way as he made his way up the ladder. He was given equivalent challenges and opportunities as his coworkers. Vitally, and all too rarely in family companies, he received constructive feedback on his performance. There was career planning for him as there was for all management – not just family members.[11]
- After Albert's heart attack decisions had to be made quickly, but they were not rushed and were not made without due consideration.

- Albert did not dictate the final decision on his succession, he sought multiple inputs.
- The succession committee played a pivotal role in answering the four questions posed by Albert. Their immediate mandate was not only to consider the two logical family candidates, but others had to be put on the shortlist. Albert was genuinely interested in finding the *most qualified* successor.
- Other significant stakeholders such as the banker, lawyer, major suppliers and important customers were consulted.
- Likewise the family, including the two brothers, were involved in the final decision.
- Planning was done with regard to Albert's future role.

In our opinion Albert achieved his three primary objectives:

- To ensure that the most competent person received the baton.
- To build consensus around the final choice amongst all family members, the board, key non-family top-management and other external stakeholders.
- To find a useful and viable role for himself after the transition.

While of necessity the MTSA case has been truncated, it still stands out as an all too rare example of an admirable attempt by an enlightened owner–manager to manage the succession process in the best interests of the family and the business. As a postscript, Xavier was promoted to vice president of manufacturing upon the retirement of his predecessor, Pierre is still CEO, both brothers are now on the board and Albert remains as chairman. One additional board member is now serving, which makes the board composition three family and four non-family 'externals'.

## THE PAIN OF PARTING

Why is it that the MTSA story is so uncommon? Why is it that most family CEOs, especially founders, find it so difficult to step down?

One way to start to answer these questions is to examine what could be called 'departure styles', each with different implications for the succes-see, the successor, the business and the family.[12] They are neither mutually exclusive nor exhaustive.

- The 'hedonist' departs voluntarily to pursue cultural or sporting activities/hobbies that he or she has never had the time to do before and cuts off all contact with the family firm. This person is the archetypical 'totally retired'.
- The 'ambassador' gives up the CEO post but may stay on or go on the board of directors and acts as the firm's external networker builder. He may represent the family, for example, in industrial associations or not-for-profit community organisations.
- The 'mentor' cuts his official ties with the family enterprise but is available, when asked, to coach and counsel his successor.
- The 'reborn entrepreneur' retires early, may retain contact with the firm but starts his or her own non-competing enterprise. This is often done just for the fun of it, to relive the thrills of starting something afresh.
- The 'general' (named after the American General Douglas Mac-Arthur, who vowed he would return to the Philippines after his initial defeat in the Second World War) agrees to step down or is forced to leave but spends all his time plotting to return as the *de facto* if not *de jure* CEO.
- The 'monarch' refuses to depart, even at a very advanced age, and usually dies on the job. Too rarely is there anyone ready or willing or capable of replacing the 'old man' when nature takes its inevitable course.

Unfortunately the history of family enterprises is littered with monarchs and generals who have played a decisive part in the demise of family firms. It is easy to be cynical and accusatory about the 'generals' and 'monarchs'. Often, however, the blame should be shared. As Lansberg has clearly demonstrated,[13] key stakeholders, especially other family members, may conspire to keep the issue of management succession off the agenda. Placing the issue on the priority list means having to confront the incumbent with the reality of his or her own mortality, no pleasant task. It also means that the family itself will have to come to grips with the eventual loss of a respected, often revered, even loved, paternal (or maternal) figure. Ambivalence abounds. Many families just cannot deal with it. The result is little or no pressure on the incumbent to launch the necessary succession process.

In other cases a management succession process may exist, but no internal candidate, family or otherwise, is deemed competent to replace the incumbent when the time comes. This can trigger the decision to sell the family firm. Alternatively a candidate may be chosen and appointed, only to find him- or herself in a firefight with other family members, non-family managers and/or other stakeholders who refuse to accept the incumbent's choice. Chaos is almost inevitable in such instances and can lead to the breakdown of the family and/or the firm.

In a deeply psychological sense, the successee may be grappling with issues of which he or she may not even be conscious. Levinson (1971) has said it best:

> For the entrepreneur, the business is essentially an extension of himself, a medium for his personal gratification and achievement above all. And if he is concerned about what happens to his business after he passes on, that concern usually takes the form of thinking of the kind of monument he will leave behind.[14]

And too often he concludes that his enterprise cannot live without him, and the longer he stays, the more difficult it is for him to step down.

There is abundant evidence that family CEOs tend to hold their positions much longer than their counterparts in public companies. It is now common for the tenure of the latter to be five to ten years at most. In family companies the founders often stay around for 25 years or more. A recent death notice in the *International Herald Tribune* eulogised a founder who had led his family's firm *for 45 years*. So if Levinson is right, this would explain why there is an overabundance of 'generals' and 'monarchs' in the histories of many family enterprises.

Even when a succession planning system has been put in place, the timing of the succession may be too late, as the following anecdote illustrates. This paraphrased conversation took place between a father (CEO) and his eldest son in the former's Paris office:

*Father*: My son, I have wonderful news for you. I have decided to retire in four months. You, as I have said so often over the years, are my chosen successor as CEO. Furthermore, you will own 75 per cent of the voting shares and will be totally in charge!

*Son*: With respect, dear father, the proposition is ridiculous. You are now 92 and I am 67. My only goal is to retire with my wife to our country estate in Provence.

The sad ending of this story is that the 75-year-old family enterprise was sold to a large multinational, and father and son never spoke to each other again.

The final explanation of why the final passing of the baton between the generations can be difficult comes from the work of Davis and Tagiuri.[15] Their research led to a life stage matrix that describes the quality of the relationship between father and sons working together in the family business as each aged. They concluded the following:

- When the father's age is 41–50 and the son's age is 17–22, the relationship is relatively problematic.
- When the father's age is 51–60 and the son's age is 23–33, the relationship is relatively harmonious.
- When the father's age is 61–70 and the son's age is 34–40, the relationship is once again relatively problematic. This is just the period when the generational transition could be expected to start.

Davis and Tagiuri conclude that the explanation of the second problematical stage lies in the typical characteristics and inner feelings that the father and son are likely to have in their respective age brackets. The father is faced with a lot of internal turmoil and anxiety. He is becoming very aware of what the loss of his controlling position in the company will mean in terms of diminished power, respect and earning capacity. He may have a deepseated fear of retirement. What will he do with his time? What kind of life style can he afford? Is there life after retirement at all? His behaviour during this period may reflect his need to show that he still has authority and his skills are as sharply honed as ever. Meanwhile his son is at a very different life stage. His needs are security, independence and recognition. There may be a conflictual relationship with his wife, his siblings, or even old friends and mentors. Nor does he typically have much trust in authority figures of any kind.

Is it any surprise, then, that in so many families the changeover period is so stressful and often unsuccessful? Davis and Tagiuri's research provides a salutary warning to all families in business that there may be rough waters ahead. Awareness of this can greatly facilitate accommodation on the part of both generations as the succession event approaches.

Over the centuries the Beretta family, one of Italy's oldest family business dynasties, has developed an approach that is very different from the one chosen by MTSA. The following mini-case describes their pragmatic but unusual way of handling the succession issue in difficult circumstances.

**Beretta: Securing Succession Through Adoption**

What more could a marketing man dream of if he wanted to promote a brand and its legend than for the product to be used by James Bond, the legendary Agent 007?

For more than 500 years, the Beretta family has supplied kings, presidents and sportsmen with one product: handguns. In the process Beretta has become one of the oldest industrial dynasties, building a name for itself that today is synonymous with precision, efficiency and tradition.

*The Background*

The dynasty began with Bartolomeo Beretta, born at the end of the fifteenth century, who was the ironmaster in a village in what was then the Republic of Venice. Bartolemeo's weapon-making art has been handed down through the generations of his descendants, and today the thirteenth generation runs the company.

Originally Beretta was only active in its region of origin. In 1815, thanks to Napoleon's numerous wars and battles, the company had the opportunity to expand internationally. Guiseppe Beretta began to sell his products across borders, thus not only establishing the brand internationally, but also turning the growing company into one of the pillars of industry in northern Italy. His son Pietro took advantage of the conflicts of his time and built Beretta into the largest manufacturer of handguns in Europe. Beretta's fame was solidified by the development of a semi-automatic pistol in 1915 and its adoption by the Italian army. Lately the company has won the favour of NATO as well as that of the US army, which gave Beretta an impressive contract for its 9mm pistol, a more recent innovation.

*'Prudenza e Audacia'*

The secret of Beretta's success may well be encapsulated in the three words that are engraved above the entrance to the Beretta Palace: 'Prudenza e audacia' – prudence and audacity, a combination that has characterised the behaviour of the family throughout the generations. Each generation embraced technical innovations in weapon making as they came along and combined this readiness with a sense of pride, efficiency and quality. During the five centuries of the company's existence, at least ten major changes in the manufacturing technology of their products have been absorbed and applied in their workshops. In the 1980s, for instance, Beretta installed an up-to-date computerised system for designing and manufacturing pistols. This has not, however, caused them to forget their roots. Today, in parallel with their modern products, they still produce a range of guns, all made by hand (and snatched up by collectors), that are symbols of and witnesses to Beretta's history.

The fact that the family palace has always been located next to the factory has made the linkage between the family and the business natural. Successive generations of children were introduced to the family's business activities, and quite a number of them entered the company as soon as they finished school. This traditional proximity has engendered an uncomplicated relationship between the members of the family and the business.

As the result of a tacit agreement, throughout the centuries family members were offered jobs in areas such as marketing, public affairs and manufacturing. The only selection rule was the approval of the 'Padrone Beretta', the head of the family. This centuries-old tradition is still by and large in place, and as a result, more than ten family members are presently active in the firm. It is interesting to note, however, that leadership in the area that has been the forte of the Beretta family throughout the centuries, namely the technology side, has also been open to gifted outsiders who were able to bring in the new technology of the period in question.

## Succession à la Beretta

The Beretta family found a sober, pragmatic solution to the issue that vexes many family businesses, namely the succession question. Whenever possible the oldest son took over the leadership of the firm from the father. However an heir apparent either did not exist or was not considered capable of running the business, the 'Padrone Beretta' would choose a gifted young man from another branch of the family and officially adopt him. For that reason, throughout the centuries all the leaders of the company have borne the name Beretta. At the same time, ownership of the business has always been concentrated in the hands of the head of the business, and as a result the splitting up of shares and the division of responsibilities has been avoided (and a certain pruning of the family tree achieved).

Only after the Second World War did the family briefly depart from the age-old governance practices. In 1957 Pietro Beretta – the last old-style Padrone, who effectively owned 100 per cent of the shares – after 54 years of reign and with no son of his own, decided to divide the stock among his two brothers and his sister. The two brothers ran the firm as partners, both holding the title of managing director. None of them had children, so in line with the age-old tradition one of them adopted Hugo, the son of his sister, who in 1992 became president of the firm (again amalgamating the ownership in one pair of hands, if one forgets about the 36 per cent of shares that in the meantime have ended up in the possession of the Italian government as the result of a new law requiring the government to have a stake in key suppliers of the armed forces of the country).

### Room for Outsiders

Beretta has always been a niche player with a limited need for capital. As a result it has been relatively easy for the family to maintain its dominant role. For generations the firm had only one manufacturing site: its factory in the Trompia Valley in northern Italy. Relatively recently it added a second one, in Maryland, as its contract with the US armed forces stipulates that the M6 pistol must be manufactured in the United States. The combined employment in both factories amounts to 1300 people, who together generate a sales volume in the neighbourhood of 100 billion lira. While the present Padrone – in line with the family tradition – sees his role primarily as that of supervisor, marketing person and ambassador of the firm, the everyday running of the factories is left to talented non-family managers, who are supported by a board that mainly consists of outsiders, trusted friends of the family.

The present Padrone, Hugo, who is in his fifties, has two sons. The oldest is 34 years old, has a business degree from an American university and will probably inherit the throne, if his father finds him worthy. The younger son is 32 years old and has had a technically oriented education. Both are presently working for the company, in charge of special projects and involved in important decisions – just like their forebears over the centuries.

## ADVICE TO SUCCESSEE

No two top management successions in family firms are identical. Therefore it is unwise to give advice to the successee without mastering the details of the case in question. Nonetheless experience has shown that there are a few basic 'rules', which if followed can greatly facilitate the successful transition between the generations. The following are some of the most important.

### Start Early

Management succession should be seen as both a process and an event. The earlier the successee starts planning the transition, the better. The process should be considered as starting at the very latest when he or she – family or non-family – becomes CEO. When transitions take place *within* the family, the process may have started much earlier, the youngest generation being socialised into the rights and responsibilities of owning and managing the family firm well before they become teenagers, as in the MTSA case. Unfortunately, all too often no systematic effort is devoted to this vital task by the successee and no one around them has the courage to urge them forward, Lansberg's so-called 'succession conspiracy'. Upon their death, premature or otherwise, there may be no logical, competent successors waiting in the wings.

### Create Career Development Systems

The successees should convince themselves that the key criterion for determining their replacement must be competence and not blood. If the most competent turns out to be a member of the owning family, so much the better. But competence does not come about by osmosis. Systems must be established so that all employees, and particularly those who have the potential to replace the CEO, have the opportunity to gain expertise over time. This requires the setting of realistic objectives and standards, providing challenging assignments and diverse experiences, offering education and training as appropriate and ensuring feedback on performance. The last of these is by no means automatic in the case of, say, the son or daughter of the CEO. Non-family superiors may be loath to provide objective feedback to persons who may end up being the big boss and owner! However, in the final analysis, it is the responsibility of the present CEO to ensure that such systems are in place and functioning well.

## Seek Advice

Eventually the successee, it is to be hoped, will want to start to narrow the list of potential successors. Particularly in family companies, this task is too important to be left to the CEO alone. One source of valuable input can be the truly independent external members of the board of directors. Alternatively, trusted, senior, non-family managers can be asked for their assessments. In some instances it may be wise to turn to older, share-holding family members for their advice or to the family council. Many family enterprises have left the compiling of the short list and the final choice of successor to parties other than the successee. However when ownership control is in the hands of the outgoing CEO this strategy may be difficult or even foolhardy.

## Build Consensus

The successee will serve his or her company and heir apparent well by trying to obtain a consensus about the choice of successor. This will ease the eventual transition enormously. All the key stakeholders should be considered in this process, including the board of directors, senior non-family management, important customers and suppliers, the bank manager and influential family members, to name a few. Not least important is the chosen successor him- or herself. Just as no one, especially a family member, should be forced to join the family firm, no one should be forced to assume the mantle of the outgoing CEO. It should be a totally voluntary act entered into with enthusiasm and confidence and not just because 'that's what the old man wants'.

The unsuccessful candidates deserve to be told the reasons why another person was chosen. Ideally they will accept that the better man or woman won and will loyally support the successor when the transition is effected. This may not always be possible, and there is the risk that some of them will leave the firm.

## Clarify the Phasing-Out Process

All those who have a stake in the enterprise (not the least of whom is the successor) will be looking to the outgoing CEO for clear signals as to his or her intentions. Now that the successor is known and, with luck, there is consensus on the choice, they will want to know what is going to happen when. Will the transition be abrupt or will the successor be given additional executive duties incrementally? Has a specific date been chosen for the passing of the baton? What will the outgoing CEO be doing upon his or her retirement? Will he or she be available to the successor for advice and guidance? Will he or she sit on the board of directors? All those in the system, especially the successor, need to know the successee's intentions.

**Plan for Retirement**

The successee cannot be clear about the phasing-out process until he or she has decided what to do after giving up the day-to-day control of the family enterprise and until he has completed his estate planning. This is vitally important and should not be taken lightly. Clearly the CEO needs to have financial security for him- or herself and his or her partner. Without it, it would be stupid to give up the salary and fringe benefits that go with the post of CEO. Outside advisors can be very useful in designing the total package necessary for the outgoing CEO to live in the desired manner.

**Stick to Plans**

Once the phasing-out process is announced and the retirement plan is finalised, the best advice to the successee is to stick to the plan. Barring unforeseen and very unusual circumstances, there should be no need to renege on the arrangements, particularly if the other 'rules' noted above have been followed. 'Generals', in these circumstances, are seen more as burdens than facilitators.

## ADVICE TO THE SUCCESSOR

While it is the authors' conviction that in family enterprises the responsibility for stage-managing the succession process and event lies with the successee, this does not preclude advice being offered to the successor. In what follows, the assumption is that the heir apparent is a family member. However much of what we say applies, *mutatis mutandis*, to a potential successor who is not a family member.

## Maximise Educational Opportunities

Whether or not a family member intends to become the next CEO, or even join the family firm, acquiring a solid education is a 'must' in today's competitive world. If the intention is to go into the business, relevant technical training and management education (possibly to the MBA level) will be a definite advantage.

## Acquire Outside Experience

In many family firms, the potential family successors join the company immediately upon graduation. It is our belief that it is advantageous for the family, the business and the successor to delay his or her entry for some years. There are three basic reasons for this recommendation. First, it is often difficult for family members to discern what their true market value is if their whole careers are spent inside the family firm. For their own sake, if for no other reason, it is vital that they receive valid feedback on their worth from objective sources. Second, if they prove successful in someone else's firm and then decide to work for the family enterprise, their entry will be enormously facilitated. Their families, fellow employees and other stakeholders will know that they have proved their competence and that their entry into the company is not based solely on possession of the family name. Third, if a family member fails, is shown to be incompetent or not cut out for a career in business, it is preferable for this to take place outside the family firm as this will significantly reduce the embarrassment of the family itself and all others connected with the family's firm.

## Examine Motivation for Entry

As our colleague at IMD, Joachim Schwass, has often suggested, it is eminently desirable for a family member to examine his or her motivations before deciding to join the family firm. Is it because it is the only job offer around? Is it because the family has always assumed that person will come on board and the potential successor wants to be seen as the obedient family member? Is it because the person fears that by not joining the family firm, he or she will be at a competitive disadvantage *vis-à-vis* the siblings when inheritance time comes around? Or is it because he or she feels that the education, experience and interests so far acquired would be useful for the family enterprise and he or she can contribute significantly to the further development of the firm? From the authors' viewpoint, the last of these should be the preferred reason for wanting to join the business.

### Anticipate Special Hurdles

If the potential successor is working full-time in the family firm, he or she will soon learn that being a member of the owning family and employee presents hurdles that few if any of the coworkers have to face. While each situation is unique, research by Foster indicates that special challenges are faced by family heirs apparent.[16] They may be held to higher performance standards on a given job – not only by fellow employees and their direct superiors but also by other family members inside and outside the firm. The person should expect to be in the spotlight constantly and his or her behaviour will be watched and judged more closley and more critically than that of others. It may be more difficult to establish warm, close relations with colleagues simply because the person is 'family'. There may even be outright avoidance or hostility and explicit or implicit accusations of nepotism. Potential family successors often also have to balance doing the job with representing the family on projects, task forces and committees inside or outside the firm. Finally, there will be a need to balance work with the demands of one's nuclear family and extended family, whether or not these are active in the business. Anticipating these hurdles will allow the potential successor to develop coping strategies. Not all will be able to cope, and in this case leaving the family enterprise may be the best strategy for all concerned.

### Influence Career Development

We stated earlier that the key responsibility for succession planning lies with the successee, but this does not mean that potential successors should be inactive. Potential successors, just like other employees, have the right to demand clear goals, objectives and expectations. They need to know on what basis their performance is to be evaluated. They have the right to request training and education in areas where they feel weak and to seek counselling and coaching help as needed. In many cases the correct strategy for potential successors is to try to persuade their superiors to provide multifunctional experience. The career development goal should not only be deepening but also broadening in order as to increase the chance of making it to the shortlist when the time for succession arrives.

## Call for Honest Feedback

Any well-designed career development system, one of whose purposes is to provide a pool of competent potential successors to the CEO, must have a built-in feedback mechanism. In the case of family businesses this is so important that we list it as a separate item of advice to the successor: get honest feedback on your performance. In family enterprises it can be extremely difficult for family members to receive objective performance evaluation from non-family superiors, as already stated. After all, this subordinate may one day be the boss. In the MTSA case we saw how Albert instructed his managers to make honest comments to Pierre as he worked his way up the organisation. In that particular instance it seemed to work, but this may not always be possible, even if the potential successor has asked for it. One solution in such instances is to ask for a mentor, often a trusted senior non-family manager, who can track the potential successor's progress and provide unbiased feedback and counsel over the years. Many family firms have found mentoring a most powerful developmental tool.

## Become Acquainted with Successee

Let us assume that a family member has made it to the shortlist of potential successors. If the career path followed so far has not permitted close, personal contact with the CEO – family or non-family – this is the time to engage in dialogue, to learn directly from the outgoing CEO his or her view of the past, present and future of the family and its enterprise. What strategic visions does the successee have? What are his or her plans upon retirement? What role, if any, does he or she hope to play after the fateful day? What we are suggesting is a *dialogue*. This is also the moment for the potential successor to share his or her own personal strategic visions for the family enterprise. Ideally there is a competitive process at work, and the views held by all on the shortlist are a vitally important component of the information on which the final decision will be based.

## Build Alliances

If the potential successor's hat is still in the ring and he or she sincerely believes that being appointed the next CEO is right for the family and its business, bridges have to be built (if this has not already been done) with other key stakeholders or those who will influence the final decision, especially members of the family. They should be given the opportunity to gauge the relative competencies of the candidates so that their advice, if requested, will be based on information and impressions received directly from the candidates.

**Make a Deal with the Successee**

Once the choice is made, it is up to the successor to come to an agreement with the predecessor on the actual process to be followed in the handing over of power. When will the successee step down? When and how will the announcement be made? What happens in the interim in terms of the distribution of roles and responsibilities between the incoming and the outgoing CEO? What will the outgoing CEO be doing after the event? What can the successor do to facilitate the outgoing CEO's transition to a very changed daily existence? Achieving consensus on these questions will enormously facilitate the changeover. Depending on the family concerned it may be advisable to put the deal down in writing, to be referred to in the event of future problems.

## POSITIVE CORRELATES OF THE EASE OF TRANSITION

Handler cites some of her earlier research on the next generation's succession experience. Here is what she found after in-depth interviews with 32 successors:

- 'The more a next-generation family member has achieved fulfilment of three needs (career interests, psychosocial needs, and life stage needs) in the context of the family firm, the more likely it is that the individual will have a positive succession experience.'
- 'The more a next-generation family member has the potential or the ability to exercise personal influence in the family business, the more likely it is that the individual will have a positive succession experience.'
- 'The more a next-generation family member achieves mutual respect and understanding with the predecessor in succession, the more likely it is that the individual will have a positive succession experience.'

- 'The more the siblings can accommodate rather than conflict with one another regarding the family business, the more likely it is that the individual will have a positive succession experience.'
- 'The greater the commitment to family business perpetuation as a family value, the more likely it is that the individual will have a positive succession experience (except when the commitment is to business means rather than business ends).'
- 'The greater the existence of separation strains due to family involvement in the business, the less likely it is that the individual will have a positive succession experience.'[17]

Some recent research[18] provides further helpful hints on easing the transition between generations. With regard to the successor, the longer he or she has been employed by the firm and the better prepared he or she is to take on the top post, the easier the transition. The more of the following there are in the family relationship, the easier the transition:

- Trust
- Openness
- Cooperation
- Respect
- Lack of defensiveness
- Lack of conflict
- Lack of resentfulness.

Also positively correlated with the ease of transition were the following:

- The existence of a formal succession plan.
- The existence of a plan to train successors.
- Having a board of directors/advisors that is dominated by insiders.

Lastly, and very importantly, the easier the transition, the higher the return on equity, net profits and sales growth rate. Clearly, successful management of the succession process pays off on the bottom line as well.

## APPOINTING A NON-FAMILY CEO

If a family that owns an enterprise comes to the conclusion that there is nobody in the family with the interest and/or ability to run the firm, and assuming they do not wish to sell the firm, they have no choice but to look outside the family for a replacement CEO. This step is typically dramatic and, as a rule, very complex.

Why dramatic? The drama has a material and a psychological aspect. From the material point of view, such a step means entrusting a non-family member with the care and development of what is probably the family's most important asset. This can easily be perceived as a major material risk. This risk is intensified (as we will see) if the new non-family CEO comes from outside the company. From the psychological point of view, there could be a fear that the identity and character of the firm, as shaped by the family over a long period of time, may be lost if an outsider takes the rudder of the family ship and steers his or her own course. This switch could be compared to the changeover from a hereditary monarch to an elected president as head of state.

If a non-family CEO is to head the family enterprise at least two essential ingredients are required: a capable CEO who is willing to tie his professional lot to that of the family, which usually has a much stronger sense of ownership than a widely dispersed group of distant shareholders (this implies, in some respects, that the environment may be more restrictive for the family company CEO than his counterpart in a public company); and a well-balanced family that will allow the new head to spread his or her wings. While a highly entrepreneurial CEO is desirable, entrusting him or her with the power that goes with that position means that appropriate precautions have to be taken to protect the interests of the family. In short, a governance issue *par excellence.*

Appointing a non-family CEO may be simple or complex. There are cases where the succession takes place in an orderly and routine fashion. As retirement approaches, the incumbent family CEO and the board take steps to identify a qualified person to take over the job in a non-crisis context. Much more complex is when such a move is triggered by an unexpected event, for example the position of CEO has suddenly become vacant because of terminal illness or death. The process of succession differs vastly in the two instances.

To add a further layer of complexity: the new CEO may be somebody who has been working for the family enterprise for quite some time (which means the family knows him or her relatively well) or may come from outside the business. Our research shows that companies in general (that is, not only family-controlled enterprises) tend to appoint CEOs from within; only about 30 per cent of new CEOs come from outside. The reason for this preference was explained to us by an experienced chairman: if you go outside to find a new CEO, your batting average goes down to about 50 per cent.

These different starting positions – routine versus sudden, from within the company versus from outside – can of course occur in many variations. We will restrict ourselves to looking at the three most important ones. In searching for solutions we will use public corporations as a model, for two reasons. Large family-controlled companies frequently consider public enterprises as their natural benchmarks; and public companies can also be confronted with the three situations to be investigated. Once a situation is understood generically (by looking at a public company's typical reaction to it), it is easy to identify the special aspects that have to be added to the discussion *vis-à-vis* a family firm.

### Situation 1: the succession takes place in a routine fashion and the CEO post is filled from within the firm

In such a case the process typically goes through two stages.

*The initiation stage.* The first stage is to initiate the process. Who 'kicks it off'? Our research shows that in the situation we are discussing here, the CEO normally initiates the process. Ideally, as was mentioned earlier, a number of years before the CEO is due to retire a formal process should be set in motion, and it should not take too long to identify a likely candidate (or better still, *candidates*).

The situation where an incumbent CEO refuses to leave his or her position is not uncommon in family-controlled firms. As the earlier discussion of departure styles showed, 'generals' and 'monarchs' are not rare in family company circumstances. In these situations an active board can be of enormous help to the family by insisting that a succession process be launched.

*The identification and grooming stage.* Regardless of which approach to identifying a candidate (or candidates) is eventually chosen, at the beginning of the process it makes a great deal of sense for the board and the CEO to give some thought to the world in which the new CEO will have to lead the company. This may remove some blinkers and prevent the incumbent CEO from trying to come up with a clone of him- or herself.

While constructing a scenario of the world to come may narrow the choice of CEO somewhat, it is not sufficient in itself. More sophisticated methods are needed. In this identification phase, two modes of selecting a candidate seem to prevail: the 'relay process' and the 'horse race'. Let us look first at the 'relay process'.

As observed by Richard Vancil in his seminal research in the area,[19] the most common pattern in CEO succession is to select an heir apparent several years before the incumbent CEO is expected to step down. Somewhat analogous to a relay race, the two executives work as a team until the CEO passes the baton (the CEO position) to his teammate. During the grooming phase leading up to this point, the candidate should be evaluated annually and assigned new tasks, both to broaden his or her experience and to test his or her abilities in different roles. It is obvious that in this mode, the incumbent CEO drives the process. He or she would, however, be well advised to keep the board of directors informed about and involved in the process from the beginning. The CEO should regularly apprise at least key board members (if not the full board) of his or her evaluations and the progress of the potential successor. The contender should furthermore be invited to make presentations to the board so that the non-executives can gain a first-hand impression as well. The final decision should be relatively easy towards the end of the process.

If the CEO, the board and the family identify several non-family CEO candidates in the present management team of the company and feel uneasy about making an early choice, they might want to use the second approach: the 'horse race'. This is less common than the relay process, but it has been discussed increasingly in the business press. Two examples in the United States have received widespread publicity: the three-way horse race at General Electric, in which Jack Welch beat two other contenders; and Citicorp, where Walter Wriston presided over a race for the top spot that John Reed won against Thomas Theobald. (We have come across similar 'horse races' in Europe, particularly in the UK.) The essence of the approach is that the candidates are informed that they are in the running for the top managerial job and are then closely observed by the CEO and the board. In order to allow the non-executives to get to know them thoroughly the candidates are invited to the regular board meetings, where they have a seat and voice but no vote. This situation can last up to one year (as was the case at General Electric). Towards the end of the 'race', the board and the CEO select the preferred candidate and discuss their choice with the family.

Vancil calls the approach an exciting event yielding a winner – and several losers. This hints at some of the dangers involved. A 'horse race' tends to inflict wounds on individuals and may well split the organisation. In addition the 'loser' has almost no choice but to leave the company, which means that the firm is probably going to lose top talent (as happened in the case of Citicorp). One may argue that this danger is always present if one obvious contender is picked over another, be they overt candidates or not. However in a 'horse race' salt is rubbed into the wound because one candidate is considered superior to the other by the board and the family. This makes it very difficult for the loser to stay on. These shortcomings notwithstanding, and although Jack Welch, winner of one of these 'horse races', has publicly expressed doubts about it, the method has its followers.

Under both approaches, if everything develops as the incumbent CEO and the board hope and expect (that is, at least one of the candidates meets their expectations) the formal appointment at the end of the process should be a relatively simple affair. It is worth mentioning that under the 'relay' approach, the influence of the outgoing CEO is obviously relatively strong, probably stronger than in the 'horse race', where the board is more deeply involved. For the family (which is typically heavily represented on the board), this means that the 'horse race' gives them more direct influence over the choice. However even under the 'relay' approach it would be very surprising if the family were not intimately involved in the choice – it may just happen more behind the scenes.

### Situation 2: the succession takes place in a routine fashion but a non-family member from outside the firm is brought in as CEO

If for any reason the board and the family fail to come up with a suitable non-family candidate inside the firm or prefer to open up the choice to insiders and outsiders alike, the situation changes substantially. The urge to search for an outsider may be particularly pronounced in a desperate turnaround situation, where the existing management has long tried in vain to refloat an ailing company. In such a situation the board may have reached the conclusion that there is no one in the company with the ability to relaunch the company. This, for instance, was the case at IBM, where outsider Lou Gerstner was chosen to replace John Akers. In such cases the board – *de facto* or formally – frequently forms a small committee (which may include the incumbent CEO) to spearhead the process. They may get the full board to establish a list of qualities they are looking for in the new CEO. This list is important, but should not be overvalued. Its advantage is that it allows the board members to synchronise their thoughts; it also gives some focus to the search. It may be, however, that some of the key criteria go out the window the moment a candidate comes along who, according to some of the remaining criteria, is overwhelmingly attractive. Hence the list of criteria should not be allowed to become a straightjacket.

When looking for a possible CEO candidate from other firms, it is becoming more and more common for companies to employ executive search consultants. Their net can usually be cast wider than that of a board or a CEO (this is particularly true when it comes to international candidates). Some companies employ two headhunters rather than one, for interesting reasons. An executive search firm may, for ethical reasons, not be able to approach a very suitable candidate as they have recently placed him or her in another position. However if a second firm with no prior contact with that person is in a more suitable position to convince him or her to leave that position. This situation occurred with IBM's appointment of Lou Gerstner. The board of IBM had hired two head-hunters, but it turned out that a relatively short time before, one of them had placed Gerstner in the top position at Reynolds Nabisco and thus could not go back to him; the second search company was, however, free to approach him and he eventually became the CEO and chairman of 'Big Blue'.

Before making the final decision, the board committee and selected board members have to talk to a number of candidates. These are, of course, delicate discussions that have to be kept secret, as many candidates do not want to be publicly associated with the search, particularly if they do not get the job in the end.

Making the final choice means judging people, but at the CEO level this cannot be done with the help of formal analytical tools. The problem is too complex and egos of the candidates may be too big to allow themselves to be subjected to a formal assessment. The choice has to be largely intuitive. Fortunately board members are typically mature, ex-perienced business men and women; during their long careers they have had to judge many people, so they usually have a good deal of experience-based intuition at their command. If there is one job that a seasoned board member can do well, it is probably this one.

Here again the role of the family should not be underestimated. If there are no key family representatives on the board to participate *ex-officio* in the selection), those in the running will have to be introduced to representatives of the family. In these cases, particular care has to be given to the secrecy of the process. The wish for such a meeting is by no means one-sided; any candidate worth his or her salt will insist on such a meeting in order better to understand the intentions of the family with respect to the business.

After the choice has been made, the CEO elect should join the organisation as soon as possible. A meaningful transition period from the old to the new CEO should be planned, but it should not last too long, as the outgoing CEO may rather quickly become a lame duck.

**Situation 3: a new CEO is appointed after his or her predecessor was asked to leave or died suddenly and there is no family member to step into the position**

In this third case, the replacement can come from inside or outside the company. Boards usually give themselves a reasonable amount of time to find a successor. In the case of IBM and Lou Gerstner, the board allowed themselves three months. During this period any of the approaches mentioned above – with the obvious exception of the 'horse race' – can be employed.

With the CEO gone, it is clear that in situation three the board typically plays a key role in finding a new CEO. In such a constellation, their responsibility to the company and the family grows significantly. This is also a situation where the family, as responsible owners, are called upon to be actively involved. After all the aim is to find the best talent available to run the family enterprise.

Once the choice has been made, it has to be made public without delay, particularly if the company's shares are publicly traded. Otherwise the company will violate the stock market regulations in many countries. Obviously the choice of a new CEO is also of great importance to outside shareholders.

In the case of situation three, the new CEO does not enjoy the luxury of a smooth and gradual changeover between him/her and his/her predecessor; he or she is immediately thrown in at the deep end.

At the beginning of this chapter we said that the choice of a new CEO is a strategic rather than a purely personnel decision. As we see a role for the board and the family in helping to set the strategic direction of the enterprise while at the same time recognising that it is not easy for these two parties to be intimately involved in formulating the details of a technical strategy, influencing a strategy by choosing the CEO is a powerful tool for the board and family to steer the course of the firm. Choosing a CEO comes down to judging people. And as judging talent is one of the traditional strengths of the seasoned business people who typically make up competent boards, it should not be surprising that the act of selecting a CEO has been called 'the finest hour of the board'.

Let us finish with another quotation from the Bergman family statement. It clearly differentiates the roles of the various governance institutions in this extremely important decision – a recommendation we have made several times before.

---

**Bergman's Values and Policies: CEO Succession**

The CEO of the Holding/Parent Company shall be appointed by the Board of Directors after consultation with the Family Council. It is the Chairman of the Board who leads the nomination process of the CEO, but other Board members can also initiate the process if the Chairman does not move or act.

The Board is responsible for drawing up the contract with the chosen CEO, defining the terms and conditions under which he/she is hired.

The CEO must be a competent person.

It is desirable that either the Chairman of the Board or the CEO be a family member.

---

## CONCLUSION

One of the main figures in the governance system of any family enterprise is the CEO. We argue that the appointment of the CEO is a key *strategic* decision that must be made at least once every generation. The authors further believe that – to the advantage of both the family and its business – a well-thought-out management succession process (career planning being a significant part thereof) will maximise the chances of finding a competent successor and ensure a smooth leadership transition between the generations.

It is the successee who is mainly responsible for ensuring a viable management succession process and guaranteeing that the actual handing over of power is well conducted. We have made several recommendations in this respect. We have likewise offered advice to the other key actor or actress in this process – the successor.

Planning succession is neither commonplace nor easy, particularly in family enterprises. We have spotlighted some of the main reasons why. It is our hope that this chapter will help family companies to retain the reins of executive power. The authors tend to agree with a statement made by Donnelly in one of the earliest articles published by the *Harvard Business Review* on the family enterprise:

There is an overriding advantage that a succession of competent family managers can provide to a business enterprise – continuity and a deeply felt sense of corporate purpose. These two elements seem to be increasingly important in a society where change and break-up of traditional institutions are normal.[20]

Our bias is clearly on keeping the family *in* the business whenever possible and when desired by the family, though not unconditionally. We strongly adhere to the principal that the final decision on the appointment of a successor should be based on *competence* and not blood. All things being relatively equal, the nod should go to the family member. Otherwise, to keep the company viable a non-family CEO is the more appropriate choice.

Selecting a non-family manager as the next CEO is usually complex and difficult, particularly the first time it happens. The problems of selection are further compounded if the candidate comes from outside the firm. In such a situation, a solid, well-functioning board can be of invaluable help to the family. It would, however, be wrong to assume that the family can abdicate their responsibility to help fill the top job in the firm. They must work very closely with the board in order to be as sure as humanly possible that the right person, the *most competent,* is picked.

## NOTES

1. For a comprehensive summary of the research carried out from 1953 to 1993 on succession in family business, see W. C. Wendy, 'Succession in Family Business: A Review of the Research', *Family Business Review*, vol. VII, no. 2 (Summer 1994).

2. As we shall see later in this chapter, the passing of the baton can be gradual or very abrupt (for example on the death of the founder or incumbent CEO). It can be argued that the formal transfer of power (*de jure*) may be much less important than the moment when the successor has truly (*de facto*) taken over the reins. The time lag between the two in many family companies can be very long – sometimes years.

3. Longenecker and Schoen have provided a seven-step model that they entitle 'Framework of Analysis Stages of Father–Son Succession'. The steps are labelled as follows: pre-business, introductory, introductory-functional, functional, advanced-functional, early succession and late succession. See J. G. Longenecker and J. E. Schoen, 'Management Succession in the Family Business', in C. E. Aronoff, J. H. Astrachan and J. L. Ward, *Family Business Sourcebook II*, Marietta: Georgia, Business Owner Resources, 1996, pp. 87–92. We shall draw from their model later in this chapter.

4. I. S. Lansberg, 'The Succession Conspiracy', *Family Business Review*, vol. 1, no. 2, (1988), p. 120. We highly recommend this classic article, especially to

founders and owner–managers who are having trouble coming to grips with their own succession.

5. Quoted in D. A. Kirby and T. J. Lee, 'Research Note: Succession Management in Family Firms in the North East of England', *Family Business Review*, vol. ix, no. 1 (Spring 1996), pp. 72–80.

6. This conclusion is shared by Malone: 'firms that consciously plan for continuity are more likely to survive'. S. C. Malone, 'Selected Correlates of Business Continuity Planning in the Family Business', *Family Business Review*, vol. 2, no. 4 (1989), p. 341.

7. A. Turner Foster, 'Developing Leadership in the Successor Generation', *Family Business Review*, vol. 8, no. 3 (Fall 1995), p. 201.

8. Malone, 'Selected Correlates', op, cit., pp. 341–53.

9. Malone does not define 'outsiders'. We assume he means non-family, non-executive directors.

10. A person whose locus of control is internal believes he or she has considerable control over his or her destiny. If the locus of control is felt to be external, the person feels that he or she has relatively little control over his or her own destiny.

11. Compared with the Murdoch family, the Marchands moved rather slowly in giving the heir apparent increasing responsibility within the family firm! Lachlan Murdoch, Rupert Murdoch's oldest son, received his degree from Princeton University in 1994. During the same year he became general manager of News Corporation's Queensland Newspapers, and in July 1995 became publisher of *The Australian* newspaper. By December 1995 he was on the board of News Limited, News Corporation's Australian division. In April 1997 it was announced by his father that Lachlan had been appointed as managing director of News Ltd at the age of 25. Of his two siblings, only Elizabeth, 28, is said still to be in the running to replace Rupert Murdoch, 66, at the top of the media empire. At the time of writing, the father had not indicated any intention to retire.

12. The following discussion on departure styles has been influenced by and some of the labels taken from J. Sonnenfeld, *The Hero's Farewell*, New York: Oxford University Press, 1988.

13. Lansberg, 'The Succession Conspiracy', op. cit.

14. H. Levinson, 'Conflicts that Plague the Family Business', *Harvard Business Review*, March–April 1971, p. 91.

15. J. Davis and R. Tagiuri, *Life Stages and Father–Son Work Relations*, Owner Managed Business Institute Santa Barbara, 1989.

16. Foster, 'Developing Leadership', op. cit., pp. 206–7.

17. W. C. Handler, 'Succession in Family Business: Review of the Research', *Family Business Review*, vol. vii, no. 2, pp. 141–2.

18. M. H. Morris, R. W. Williams and D. Nel, 'Factors influencing family business succession', *International Journal of Entrepreneurial Behaviour and Research*, vol. 2, no. 3, pp. 68–81.

19. R. F. Vancil, *Passing the Baton*, Boston, Mass.: Harvard University Press, 1987.

20. R. G. Donnelly, 'The Family Business', *Harvard Business Review*, July–August 1964, pp. 101–2.

# 7 Vision and Strategy as Key Governance Measures in Family Business

Columbus found a world, and had no chart save one that Faith deciphered in the skies
(George Santayana, Spanish-born American philosopher, 1863–1952)

Have you ever heard of Joshua Slocum? Probably not. Slocum was the first person to attempt to sail alone around the world.[1] On 24 April 1895, at the age of 51, he set sail from Boston in a boat that was about 12 meters long. Just over three years later, on 27 June 1898, he anchored again off Newport, the first solo sailor to circumnavigate the globe. The money he needed had been earned as he went.

What makes Slocum such an interesting person is that he was capable of achieving his dreams with only the very limited means at his disposal: an old sailboat that he himself had repaired and made seaworthy. His navigation equipment was minimal: a sextant and an alarm clock that, in the course of the voyage, lost its minute hand. If one considers how important the exact measurement of time is for determining nautical position, then it is even more amazing that after a 43-day (or 4000-mile) voyage in the Pacific – during which time he never met another boat or touched inhabited land – he succeeded in arriving exactly where he had planned to arrive – at the Nuku Hiva Atoll in the Marquesas islands.

Slocum did not delay his voyage until he had accumulated enough money: he did not search for sponsors, he did not lament the lack of help from the government or his adverse circumstances. He simply carried out his plan with what he had.

He had one plus though, which today is as decisive as it was in his time for any entrepreneurial activity: he had the vision, the strategy and he

167

was in total command of the means at his disposal. He not only knew what he wanted, he also had the intellectual capacity, the experience, the will to make his ideas come true.[2]

This little story, as we shall see, is an appropriate introduction to this chapter.

When we discussed the concept of corporate governance in Chapter 3, we stressed that there are two major governance tasks: the task of directing the enterprise and the task of controlling it (the latter, as we said then, also includes accounting for the enterprise). In this chapter we continue to deal with the directing function of the board. This governance task was described very well by Sir Adrian Cadbury, former CEO and chairman of Cadbury-Schweppes.[3] In his book *The Company Chairman*, Sir Adrian writes:

> It is the board's responsibility to determine the aims of the company and to decide on the strategy, the plans, and policies for carrying out those aims. This is the job of *direction,* which alone the board can do and on which it needs to focus its attention. There is a natural temptation for boards to stray from the more abstract issues of directing to the more hands-on issues of management . . . Management issues are more immediate and easier to get to grips with than questions of strategy. But the board has appointed managers to turn its decision into action and it must allow them to do so.[4]

In a family-controlled business, it is quite obvious that the family as owners can be particularly interested in helping to establish the strategy of their firm. Here we take strategy to mean 'choosing from among different options with respect to the long-term direction of the enterprise'. The desire to have a say in such important decisions is even more understandable if the business happens to be the main family asset.

As already mentioned in Chapter 5, which dealt with the board proper, despite the strength and legitimacy of their desire, there are usually practical limits to the family's involvement in shaping the firm's strategy, unless the firm is relatively small and the business easy to understand. As the firm grows in size and complexity (and the distance between the family and the business quite naturally increases), the involvement of family members in setting strategy is not dissimilar to that of a detached, non-executive board member in a large publicly traded company: meaningful involvement in strategy setting becomes difficult. The reasons for this are obvious:

- Typically there is a shortage of expertise in both groups – family members and non-executive board members – when it comes to making a substantive contribution to the technical aspects of a detailed strategy that differentiates the firm from its competitors in the market place.
- In many companies strategic planning is an ongoing process; non-executives and some members of larger families are typically not around often and long enough to participate in that process.
- Both groups, non-executives as well as remote family shareholders, normally do not have the appropriate resources (for example staff) to equip themselves properly for a thorough discussion with management on questions of strategy. This puts them at a distinct disadvantage *vis-à-vis* the full-time, resource-rich management.

This latter situation prompted Sir Owen Green, former chairman of BTR in the UK, to make a caustic remark about the role of outside directors in strategy that can also be applied to remote family members (one only has to replace 'non-executive director' by 'remote family shareholder'):

> The idea of non-executive directors making significant contributions to strategy is not very realistic. As an analogy one recalls the eminent contribution to the strategy of war made by von Clausewitz, de Gaulle and Guderian, all men steeped in the technology of the subject. In contrast, the contributions to strategy by Churchill and his cabinets and Hitler and his political posse have not been well received.[5]

While Sir Owen's remarks may go too far for many tastes, they contain a kernel of truth. This does not mean, however, that the family members in general or their selected representatives (on the board or in the family council), for example, should be totally excluded from influencing the future course of their firm. As was mentioned earlier, there exist certain approaches to establishing the future direction of an enterprise where somewhat distant contributors can be meaningfully involved in the creation of a vision for the enterprise. Such a vision can afterwards be turned into a more detailed strategy by top management.

## THE CONCEPT OF A VISION

### The Generic Concept

A breathtaking example of a vision in the broad sense is the memorable speech made by Martin Luther King Jr on 28 August 1963 in Washington, a speech that many believe will enter history as one of the greatest speeches of the twentieth century. Its leitmotif – 'I have a dream' – still gives many people goosebumps when they hear a recording of it today. This was a great moment in the long struggle for civil rights and it triggered far-reaching legislative measures by the US Congress.

Here are a few words about the background. Born in 1929, Martin Luther King Jr was a black Baptist minister, as were both his father and his grandfather before him. He was an articulate, intelligent person with an academic background (he was awarded a PhD in 1955). He soon made civil rights his life-long concern. In his work he was strongly influenced by Gandhi's idea of non-violent direct action to bring about social change (for example sit-ins, marches and so on).

In 1955 he was pastor of a church in Montgomery, Alabama, deep in the American South. On 1 December of that year, Mrs Rosa Parks refused to surrender her bus seat in Montgomery to a white and was promptly arrested for violating the city's segregation laws. As president of the Montgomery Improvement Association, King organised a boycott of the town's buses. This effort led to the desegregation of Montgomery buses one year later, and caused Martin Luther King to rise to national prominence. Buoyed by this success, King founded the Southern Christian Leadership Conference (SCLC), which became a mass movement preaching active non-violence to free the American minorities. He became a public figure, either revered or hated by both blacks and whites. King was under constant FBI surveillance, and was unsupported by President Eisenhower but championed by John F. Kennedy (this helped Kennedy to win his first election).

In 1963 King led the historic march on Washington that culminated in the famous speech at the Lincoln Memorial before an inter-racial audience estimated at 200 000 people. The speech is reproduced in part in the box on p. 172. In his passionate plea, King painted a powerful vision of an America worth living in and fighting for, a desired future state. Even in print his words glow, but they were overpowering when delivered by him. The vision inspired the people assembled in the Mall to overcome their sagging morale and strive for the achievement of one goal: the securing of their civil rights. By juxtaposing his vision – the result everybody at the Mall wanted – with the reality they faced back home, the memorable speech created a strong constructive tension to bring about racial equality. A vision like the one presented by Martin Luther King can provide a lasting source of energy for an organisation.

The Southern Christian Leadership Conference played a major role in the passage of the Civil Rights Act of 1964, which forced the desegregation of housing and outlawed discrimination in publicly owned facilities and employment. The same year Martin Luther King received the Nobel Peace Prize. Four years later, in March 1969, he was assassinated in Memphis, Tennessee, by a white Southerner.

It is obvious that the approach used by King was not without serious dangers. Some people might say it came close to demagogy, and it was obviously only justifiable because it was legitimised by a just cause. In business, leaders with similar charisma can frequently be found among the founding fathers of many firms. As in politics, such an approach is not without risks. Flamboyant entrepreneurs can indeed take a company 'over the cliff', as the case of Metallgesellschaft showed in Germany only a few years ago, when an extremely persuasive CEO led the twelfth largest German company to the brink of bankruptcy by irresponsibly overextending its business in oil derivatives. Despite this danger, we should nevertheless realise that our capitalist system is built on these entrepreneurs. As Charles M. Schwab – an entrepreneur *par excellence* and founder of the United States Steel Corporation – once said, 'A man to carry on a successful business must have imagination. He must see things in a vision, a dream of the whole thing'. It is one of the most prominent roles of a board to make sure that such charismatic leaders, despite their exciting ideas, keep their feet on the ground.

**Vision in a Business Setting**

Visioning processes are one of the most recent tools designed to establish the long-term direction of a business. 'When a manager or a whole organisation holds a reasonably clear image of a desirable future, that's vision', asserts Hal Leavitt, one of the pioneers in this field. He calls visionary managers 'pathfinders': 'The futures that interest pathfinders are imagined, not predicted.'[6] Unfortunately the word vision is a loaded one. For people not familiar with it, the word (and the tool with which it is associated) conveys the idea of something 'airy-fairy'. Nothing could be further from the truth. In a business setting a vision is a relatively concrete answer to the question: 'What do we want to have created in this company in, say, five or ten years time?' In the light of this question,

**'I Have a Dream': Speech by Martin Luther King Jr, 28 August 1963**

. . . I am not unmindful that some of you have come here out of great trials and tribulations. Some of you have come fresh from narrow cells. Some of you have come from areas where your quest for freedom left you battered by the storms of persecution and staggered by the winds of police brutality. You have been the veterans of creative suffering. Continue to work with the faith that unearned suffering is redemptive.

Go back to Mississippi, go back to Alabama, go back to Georgia, go back to Louisiana, go back to the slums and ghettos of our northern cities, knowing that somehow this situation can and will be changed. Let us not wallow in the valley of despair.

I say to you today, my friends, that in spite of the difficulties and frustrations of the moment, I still have a dream. It is a dream deeply rooted in the American dream.

I have a dream that one day this nation will rise up and live out the true meaning of its creed: 'We hold these truths to be self-evident: that all men are created equal.'

I have a dream that one day on the red hills of Georgia the sons of former slaves and the sons of former slaveowners will be able to sit down together at a table of brotherhood.

I have a dream that one day even the state of Mississippi, a desert state, sweltering with the heat of injustice and oppression, will be transformed into an oasis of freedom and justice.

I have a dream that my four children will one day live in a nation where they will not be judged by the colour of their skin but by the content of their character.

I have a dream today.

I have a dream that one day the state of Alabama, whose governor's lips are presently dripping with the words of interposition and nullification, will be transformed into a situation where little black boys and black girls will be able to join hands with little white boys and white girls and walk together as sisters and brothers.

I have a dream today.

I have a dream that one day every valley shall be exalted, every hill and mountain shall be made low, the rough places will be made plain, and the crooked places will be made straight, and the glory of the Lord shall be revealed, and all flesh shall see it together.

This is our hope. This is the faith with which I return to the South. With this faith we will be able to hew out of the mountain of despair a stone of hope. With this faith we will be able to transform the jangling discords of our nation into a beautiful symphony of brotherhood. With this faith we will be able to work together, to pray together, to struggle together, to go to jail together, to stand up for freedom together, knowing that we will be free one day.

This will be the day when all of God's children will be able to sing with a new meaning, 'My country, 'tis of thee, sweet land of liberty, of thee I sing. Land where my fathers died, land of the pilgrim's pride, from every mountainside, let freedom ring.'

And if America is to be a great nation this must become true. So let freedom ring from the prodigious hilltops of New Hampshire. Let freedom ring from the mighty mountains of New York. Let freedom ring from the heightening Alleghenies of Pennsylvania!

Let freedom ring from the snow-capped Rockies of Colorado!

Let freedom ring from the curvaceous peaks of California!

But not only that; let freedom ring from Stone Mountain of Georgia!

Let freedom ring from Lookout Mountain of Tennessee!

Let freedom ring from every hill and every molehill of Mississippi. From every mountainside, let freedom ring.

When we let freedom ring, when we let it ring from every village and every hamlet, from every state and every city, we will be able to speed up that day when all of God's children, black men and white men, Jews and Gentiles, Protestants and Catholics, will be able to join hands and sing in the words of the old Negro spiritual, 'Free at last! free at last! thank God Almighty, we are free at last!'

a definition of the term corporate vision could be: 'A corporate vision is a mental image of a desirable state of the firm in five or ten years time.'

Such an image can be explicitly formulated and written down. It has the advantage that it can be communicated and shared by others in the firm (and not only known to the creator of the vision). The concept is, however, equally valid if the vision exists only in the mind of the entrepreneur as a mental image of the future state. Implicit visions are more common than explicit ones. The following is a classical example.

At the age of 27 William Paley took over CBS. At the time (1927) the company had no radio stations of its own, did not figure large in the industry (which was dominated by NBC) and was in fact making losses. Within a span of ten years Paley built up a network of 114 stations, and the company made US$28 million in profits in 1936. Four decades later – with Paley still heading CBS – the company was a key player in the broadcasting industry. The role his implicit vision played in this success is well described by David Halberstam:

> What Paley had from the start was a sense of vision, a sense of what might be. It was as if he could sit in New York in his tiny office with his almost bankrupt company and see not just his own desk, or the row of potential advertisers outside along Madison Avenue, but millions of American people out in the hinterland, so many of them out there, almost alone, . . . with almost no form of entertainment other than the radio. It was his sense, his confidence that he could reach them, that he had something for them that made him different. He could envision an audience when there was in fact no audience. He not only had the vision, he knew how to harness it.[7]

We will come across a few more implicit visions later on in this chapter. As the implicit visions are obviously more difficult for an outsider to grasp (as long as they are not implemented), our main (but not exclusive ) emphasis will be on explicit visions.

The above statements should make clear that the concept of a corporate vision, as we are using it here, has nothing in common with two other tools typically used in companies in this context:

- It should not be confused with the one-line slogans that are frequently offered as vision statements; these are, at best, parts of a full vision statement.
- Nor is it the same as conventional strategic five-year plans.

As we will see in more detail later, a well-prepared vision statement is a carefully worded, inspiring document, usually consisting of several pages that describe an exciting future state of the firm.

Let us explain in more detail why in our view a vision statement should not be confused with traditional five-year plans.

- First, a strategic plan is typically a forecast. A vision, in contrast, is an expression of 'a future imagined' (Leavitt) by business leaders. As Walt Disney once said, 'If you can dream it, you can do it', a statement that has a very familiar ring for many founding fathers of family enterprises.
- Second, typical strategic planning is incremental in nature: $x$ per cent plus per year. It has certain extrapolating qualities and rarely questions the business fundamentally. In contrast a visioning process is discontinuous. It represents a step function: one jumps, say, ten years ahead (by asking where one wants to be at that point in time) and describes in vivid terms a desired future state of the organisation. Thereafter one looks back and raises the question, 'What would we have to do today to achieve that future state in due time?'
- Third, under these circumstances it is understandable that strategic planning very rarely gives rise to a vision; rather visions are established in a process that is separate from that of strategic planning. Strategic planning often becomes the means of realising that vision, as Figure 7.1 illustrates.

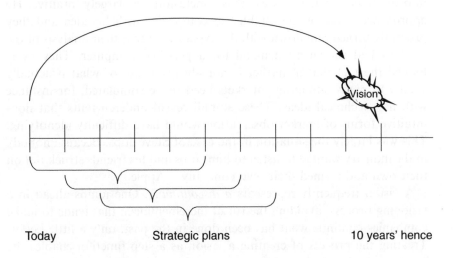

**Figure 7.1** Strategic planning as a means of realising a vision

Visioning forms part of *the entrepreneurial side of management*. The hallmark of the entrepreneur is that he or she sees opportunities where nobody else sees them. He or she reads the environment differently than 'the pack' and responds to it in a unique way, with a unique service or product. And as entrepreneurs typically venture into new, uncharted territory, they frequently have to act on little data and a large amount of intuition; this makes it difficult for them to back up their ideas with reliable statistics. Joseph Schumpeter, the Austro-American economist who has made the entrepreneur the central figure in his thinking and writing, explained the economic development of nations by the presence of great entrepreneurs. In his seminal book *The Theory of Economic Development* he writes,

> Here the success of everything depends upon intuition, the capacities of seeing things in a way which afterwards proves to be true, even though it cannot be established at the moment, and of grasping the essential fact, discarding the unessential, even though one can give no account of the principles by which this is done.[8]

A telling example of such a situation is that of Steve Jobs and the personal computer. As a young creative member of the computer industry and deeply involved in that market, Jobs came to the conclusion that substantial business could be generated by putting computing power into the hands of the masses. This conclusion was largely intuitive. He approached some of the established companies with his idea and they promptly turned him down with the explanation that their analysis of the markets had shown no demand for a personal computer. They overlooked the fact that a market is not always aware of what it actually wants. In many situations, markets need to be stimulated, for instance with new technical ideas. These stimuli reveal undercurrents that nonintuitive forms of market observation would have difficulty identifying. This was largely the situation in the case of Steve Jobs. Because nobody in the industry wanted to listen to him, Jobs and his friends struck out on their own and formed their own company – Apple.

A vision frequently represents *a discontinuity*. One jumps ahead in a visioning process, avoiding the rut of incrementalism that tends to make companies continue what has been done in the past, only a little better. Treating the process of creating a vision as a step function enables the company to break out of the routine of traditional strategic planning. This breaking with the past is another key characteristic of the approach of visionary managers and can lead to a redefinition of their industries. Here are two examples:

- The creation of the Swatch watch involved breaking away from the conventional approaches to watchmaking. Just about everything – design, production methods, pricing, distribution systems – had to be reconceptualised to allow the company (SMH in Neuchâtel, Switzerland) to open up new market segments at the bottom of the pyramid of customers.
- IKEA, a family business by most counts, is another example of an entrepreneur redefining an industry, namely furniture retailing. Ingvar Kamprad's ideas could not have been realised within the confines of the traditional furniture business and the old paradigms had to be abandoned.

## THE PRACTICE OF VISIONING

The idea of creating a vision for their firm is attractive to many family business leaders. They are, however, frequently rather helpless when it comes to the practical aspect of the process: What does a concrete business vision look like? What are its main components? How does one go about establishing a vision for a family business? These questions will be answered in the remainder of this chapter.

### The Building Blocks of a Vision

Collins and Porras have done ground-breaking work in this area. Figure 7.2 summarises the two building blocks of a vision. We shall look at each in turn.

#### The Core Ideology

One of the key elements of a vision is the core ideology of the firm, shown on the left-hand side of the yin/yang symbol. According to Collins and Porras, 'Core ideology defines the enduring character of an organisation, a consistent identity that transcends product or market life cycles, technological breakthroughs, management fads and individual leaders.'[9] They insist that the most lasting and significant contribution of those who build visionary companies is the core ideology. It provides the glue that holds the company together.

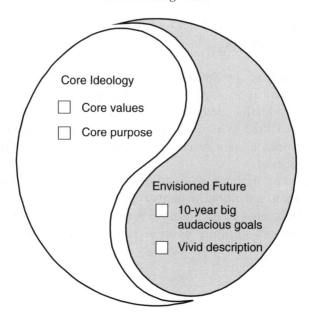

**Source**:   Collins and Porras (1996).[10]

**Figure 7.2**   The building blocks of a vision

The core ideology is composed of core values and the core purpose. The core values are the organisation's essential and enduring tenets – a small set of general guiding principles, not to be confused with specific operating practices. They must not be compromised for financial gain or short-term expediency. The core purpose is the firm's fundamental reason for existence beyond just making money, a perpetual guiding star on questions such as why are we in business?

An example of a core ideology is the well-known creed of Johnson & Johnson. The current revision is reprinted below. It was originally written by R. W. Johnson Jr in 1943.

Typically, strong core ideologies are key characteristics of family businesses. In some cases they are expressed in writing, in others they are just lived (which does not mean that they are less powerful). Linking the visioning process so closely to the core ideology, the core values and family ethics gives it a special quality and lifts it far above traditional planning techniques. It is interesting to note that the actual content of a company's core ideology is of lesser importance than the authenticity of the ideology and the extent to which the company adheres to that ideology.[11]

**Johnson & Johnson's Credo**

We believe that our first responsibility is to the doctors, nurses,
and patients, to mothers and fathers and all others who use our
products and services.
In meeting their needs everything we do must be of high quality.
We must constantly strive to reduce our costs
in order to maintain reasonable prices.
Customers' orders must be serviced promptly and accurately.
Our suppliers and distributors must have an opportunity to make
a fair profit.

We are responsible to our employees,
the men and women who work with us throughout the world.
Everyone must be considered as an individual.
We must respect their dignity and recognize their merit.
They must have a sense of security in their jobs.
Compensation must be fair and adequate,
and working conditions clean, orderly and safe.
We must be mindful of ways to help our employees fulfil
their family responsibilities.
Employees must feel free to make suggestions and complaints.
There must be equal opportunity for employment, development
and advancement for those qualified.
We must provide competent management,
and their actions must be just and ethical.

We are responsible to the communities in which we live and work
and to the world community as well.
We must be good citizens – support good works and charities
and bear our fair share of the taxes.
We must encourage civic improvements and better health
and education.
We must maintain in good order
thr property we are privileged to use,
protecting the environment and natural resources.

Our final responsibilty is to our stockholders.
Business must make a sound profit.
We must experiment with new ideas.

Research must be carried on, innovative programs developed
and mistakes paid for.
New equipment must be purchased, new facilities provided
and new products launched.
Reserves must be created to provide for adverse times.
When we operate according to these principles, the stockholders
should realize a fair return.

*Used by permission of Johnson & Johnson.*

*The Envisioned Future*

Let us now turn to the right-hand side of the yin/yang symbol in Figure
7.2. The two concepts listed there – '10-year big audacious goals' and a
'vivid description of the future "strategic architecture" of the company' –
are closely related to each other. The concept of strategic architecture was
created by Gary Hamel and P. K. Prahalad; we shall draw on their work
but use the concept in a slightly different form.[12] Strategic architecture is
basically a high-level blueprint of the desired future state of the firm. The
term architecture is well chosen. On the one hand an architect must be
capable of dreaming of something not yet created; on the other hand, he
must be able to produce a blueprint for turning the dream into reality.
According to Hamel and Prahalad, an architect is both a dreamer and a
draftsman; an architect marries art with structural engineering.

   To build a strategic architecture, the participants in the visioning
process must first determine the following:

- The *benefits*, or *'functionalities'* that will be offered to the customer.
- The new *core competencies* that will be needed to create those benefits.
- How the customer *interface* will have to change to allow customers to
  access those benefits – all of them with a time horizon of five to ten
  years.

Thinking in 'functionalities' allows the company to escape the narrow
view of 'What is our product or service?' Hamel and Prahalad give several
examples of moving from thinking in products and services to thinking in
functionalities.[13] The following is one of them.

Question: What is the functionality of a blackboard or a flipchart? Answer: to share information among a small group. But if each individual wishes to have a copy, the blackboard cannot be put through a copying machine or stuffed in a brief case. What is the obvious answer? The obvious answer, if one conceives the product in functionality rather than pencil and paper terms, is an electronic whiteboard with a built-in scanner and copying system. (It wasn't the blackboard manufacturers who came up with this idea, but the Japanese electronics firm Oki Electric Industry Co. Ltd.)

A *core competence* is a bundle of skills and technologies that enables the company to provide a particular benefit (a 'functionality') to customers. At Sony for instance the benefit is 'pocketability', and the core competence is miniaturisation. There are obviously many more examples of this nature.

It goes without saying that a strategic architecture has to be reasonably concrete and spelled out in some detail; one-line 'motherhood' slogans do not qualify as vision statements. On the other hand a strategic architecture is not a detailed plan either. Its nature in this respect can best be explained with the help of a cartographic analogy. A strategic architecture is a general map of interstate highways, not a detailed map of city streets. It is specific enough to provide a general sense of direction, but does not detail every street along the way[14]. The details will be provided by the strategic plans that management will draw up in due time to fill the gap between the present and the desired future state of the firm.

One point is of great importance in this context. Once the content of the future strategic architecture has been agreed upon, it is necessary to write it up in a way that excites those people who have to turn it into reality. The great problem in industry today is to motivate middle management, be they in family-controlled businesses or publicly owned firms. These employees are typically well-educated and intelligent. They need to feel that the company they work for is the right cause to which to devote their lives. In short they want to be committed emotionally as well as rationally. A well-written vision statement can help to achieve that goal. Antoine de Saint-Exupéry (1900–44) expressed this beautifully when he wrote:

If you want to build a ship
Do not bring men together
To fell timber, prepare tools,
Assign tasks and think about easing work . . .
Rather teach your men the longing for the wide, endless sea.

One other important point: a vision statement is most credible if the final version is not written by a staff member but by the CEO or chairman him- or herself. After all, in the words of St Augustin of Hippo, 'In you must burn . . . [that which] you want to ignite in others'.

Let us now turn to the '10-year audacious goals' on the right-hand side of the yin/yang diagram in Figure 7.2. There is research evidence that visionary companies use audacious goals to stimulate exceptional progress.[15] The concept has been around for a while. In a speech he gave in 1988 in St Gallen, Switzerland, Sir John Harvey-Jones, then chairman of ICI, said:

> I believe we need a clearer understanding of the role of corporate vision or, as I prefer to denote it, a corporate dream . . . I believe that every business should have its dream since it is essential that a board of a large corporation should have a shared dream and the CEO a personal dream as well. *Dreams do not have to be demonstrably achievable although it helps if there is some broad indication of scale. They must not be precise but they have to be ambitious far beyond the capabilities of day to day operations. They have to attract the hearts and the minds of the people who have to accomplish them* [emphasis added].

A company that claims to have extensively and systematically benefited from big audacious goals is General Electric. They call these goals 'stretch', as this quote from their annual report 1995 shows:

> Stretch is a concept that would have produced smirks, if not laughter in the GE of three or four years ago, because it essentially means using dreams to set business targets – with no real idea of how to get there. If you do know how to get there – it's not a stretch target. We certainly didn't have a clue how we were going to get to ten inventory turns when we set that target. But we are getting there, and as soon as we become sure we can do it – it's time for another stretch.
>
> The CEO of Yokogawa, our Japanese partner in the Medical Systems business, calls this concept 'bullet-train thinking', that is, if you want a ten-miles-per-hour increase in train speed, you tinker with horsepower – but if you want to double its speed, you have to break out of both conventional thinking and conventional performance expectations.
>
> Stretch allows organisations to set the bar higher than they ever dreamed possible.

A big audacious goal that forms part of a vision statement engages people; it reaches out and grabs them. It is tangible, energising and highly focused.

> People get it right away; it takes little or no explanation. For example, NASA's 1960s moon mission didn't need a committee of wordsmiths to spend endless hours turning the goal into a verbose, impossible-to-remember . . . statement. The goal itself was so easy to grasp – so compelling in its own right – that it could be said in 100 different ways and yet be easily understood by everyone . . .'[16]

There are four types of big audacious goals.[17]

- Target goals: these can be quantitative (for example GE demands from its businesses that they become number one or number two in their markets world wide); they can also be qualitative, such as Apple's goal to 'put computing power into the hands of the masses'.
- Common enemy goals such as 'Beat Caterpillar' (Komatsu)
- Role-model goals such as 'Become the Rolls Royce of our industry.'
- Internal-transformation goals, such as that of GE: 'We set out to shape a global enterprise that preserved the classic big-company advantages – while eliminating the big company drawbacks. What we wanted to build was . . . an enterprise with the reach and resources of a big company – the body of a big company – but the thirst to learn, the compulsion to share and the bias for action – the soul – of a small company'.[18]

*Why Use the Yin/Yang Symbol in a Vision Statement?*

We used the Chinese yin/yang symbol in Exhibit 7.2 because it serves a particular purpose here. It has its origins in dualistic Chinese philosophy and indicates that seemingly contradictory elements can and – in real life – must be achieved simultaneously. It is quite obvious that, for instance, certain core ideologies and, say, audacious goals can stand in opposition to each other. They can actually be contradictory. They thus represent a paradox. The philosopher Howard Slaatte describes a paradox as 'an idea involving two opposing thoughts which, however contradictory, are equally necessary to convey a more imposing, illuminating, life-related or provocative insight into truth than either factor in its own right. What the mind seemingly cannot think, it must think; what reason is reluctant to express, it must express.'[19]

Paradoxes abound in business, and they are at the heart of the visioning process. Once sensitised, we discover them in all aspects of business life and observe that managers deal with them every day. They are actually a facet of all human experience, beautifully summarised by F. Scott Fitzgerald: 'The test of a first-rate intellect is the ability to hold two opposed ideas in mind at the same time and still retain the ability to function.'[20]

## HOW A VISION CAN BE CREATED

The creation of a vision is always the result of a process. But attempts to structure such a process run the risk of robbing this highly creative, entrepreneurial activity of its vitality. We must live with that risk.

That the creation of a vision has to be based on a process does not mean that there are handy formulas to turn this into a simple task. We can, however, say that there seem to be three approaches to visioning:[21]

- The introspective approach.
- The interactive approach.
- A combination of the introspective and interactive approaches.

In the *introspective approach* the vision is created by one person. A good example here would be Edwin Land, creator of the Polaroid camera and founder of the Polaroid Corporation. Land has described the way he came to envision the camera that revolutionised photography:

> One day when we were vacationing in Santa Fe in 1943 my daughter, Jennifer, who was then three, asked me why she could not see the picture I had just taken of her. As I walked around that charming town, I undertook the task of solving the puzzle she had set for me. Within an hour the camera, the film and the physical chemistry became so clear that with a great sense of excitement I hurried to the place where a friend was staying to describe to him in detail a dry camera which would give a picture immediately after exposure. In my mind it was so real that I spent several hours on this description.[22]

When reading this story one could easily assume that the idea of the Polaroid camera sprang fully blown from nowhere. Breakthroughs of this nature are, of course, somewhat more complex. As K. Ohmae, the influential Japanese thinker in the area of strategy, once pointed out, the kinds of event described by Land, like great works of art, do indeed originate in insights that are beyond the reach of conscious analysis, but they also call for a high degree of technical mastery. Land had spent years in the laboratory perfecting the polarisation process, schooling his scientific and inventive abilities, practising and repeating, learning his craft. His inspiration thus sprang from a fertile background.[23]

The *interactive approach* lies at the other end of the spectrum. Members of a group – managers, board members and/or family members – hammer out a shared vision for their organisation during intense discussions. The strength of this approach is captured well by a Brazilian saying: 'If one person dreams, it is only a dream; if many dream jointly, it is the beginning of something new.' (It may well be that articulation of that vision, the pulling together of the results of the discussion, is left to one person.) A practical example of this approach will be described later in this chapter.

As with the introspective approach, in the *combination of introspective and interactive approaches* one individual is important. But unlike the Land case, where a leap of the imagination resulted in a complete design, in this way of proceeding the vision results from a number of small insights, discrete moments of inspiration discussed with other persons in the organisation and continuously refined. An example of this approach is Jan Carlzon's work, which revolutionised the airline SAS.

## A PROVEN PROCESS

We would like to describe here a visioning process we developed at IMD and applied successfully in a number of companies. (In terms of the discussion above, our vision-creating approach was interactive.) Figure 7.3 provides a thumbnail sketch of the elements of the process.

### The Participants

In the case of a family-controlled company, the composition of the groups participating in the process can vary. One could use the board consisting of family members only or at least with a good representation of the family. This group should be augmented by key members of management. It may also be helpful to call in a process specialist who has experience of running processes of this nature. It is also possible to include the family council in the process; they could be very helpful in convincing the family of the new vision. Their credibility will be particularly high if they have been actively involved in developing the vision.

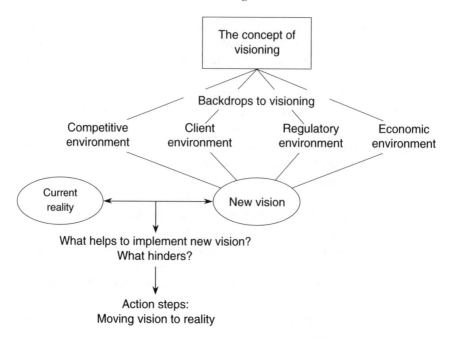

**Figure 7.3**    IMD's interactive approach to visioning

## The Steps of the Process Proper

As shown in the top line of Figure 7.3, the process starts with a session to familiarise the participants with the concept of a vision (pretty much along the lines discussed in this chapter) and the steps to be followed. Then comes the process itself. In line with the classical thinking on visions, our approach depends on two things: the ability of the participants to read the world surrounding the company differently 'from the pack' (that is, differently from other companies); and the ability of the participants to create a mental image of a desired future state of the organisation. A brief look at both of these is appropriate.

### New Ways of Looking at the World

A key characteristic of an entrepreneurial personality is that he or she spots the opportunities offered by the environment before anybody else sees them. To allow the participants to take a fresh look at their world, they are exposed to brief statements on breaks in different environments pertinent to the company (in Figure 7.3 this is called 'backdrop to visioning'). The environmental domains in the figure are taken from a practical example. For every company embarking on such a process, the domains have to be selected very carefully in response to the specific situation in which that company finds itself. These brief presentations are made by specialists in the fields. They are asked to be concise and succinct, stressing the changes (that is, discontinuities) they expect to happen in the different environmental domains. After each presentation, the participants have to ask themselves what these changes mean to the company and discuss their views. These discussions typically result in a lively *tour d'horizon* of the major changes that are expected to take place in the world surrounding the family business and in a better, shared understanding of what they mean to the firm.

### A Desired Future State

With these discussions in mind, each participant is then asked to write a lively article in response to the question, 'What would you like your favourite business journal or financial newspaper to write about your company five (or ten) years from now?' To help the participants create that vision of the company, they are provided with a detailed mandate that directs their attention to certain concrete and salient points that should be addressed in a meaningful, practical vision statement. These instructions ensure that the key elements of a vision – as those shown in the yin/yang symbol in Figure 7.1 – are addressed by the participants. In our experience the participants appreciate the opportunity to lean back and 'reinvent' their company in a risk-free way.

After extensive discussions these individual visions are shared among the participants. Finally, one vision statement is hammered out. The chairman typically plays a major role in writing up the shared statement. The outcome is usually a three- to four-page statement describing in rather vivid but concrete terms the desired future state of the company. This step is typically seen as very stimulating and thought-provoking by the participants.

Once the vision statement has been completed and polished, it is necessary to present it to and discuss it with the family assembly as their support is of utmost importance for the subsequent implementation phase. It is equally important to relay the outcome to those layers of management who have not directly participated in the process. After all, it is they who have to realise the vision. The lion's share of this burden falls on the chairman and/or the CEO. As one CEO aptly put it, 'From that point on I turn into a preacher man.'

**Comparison with Current Reality**

In the next phase of the process the vision statement is largely in the domain of management. In order to implement the vision, it has be compared with the current reality. In this context, management is asked to work 'from the vision'. That is, they are invited to put themselves mentally into the desired future state of the organisation (as it is described in the vision statement), and then ask what needs to happen today for that vision to be realised. This becomes the task of the traditional strategic planning staff, with the vision as their 'guiding star'.

The visioning process typically leads to strong emotional involvement on the part of the participants. It is also quite strenuous, although the effort is well spent. As two knowledgeable observers once said, 'If there is a spark of genius in the leadership function at all, it must lie in this transcending ability . . . to assemble – out of all the variety of images, signals, forecasts and alternatives – a clearly articulated vision of the future that is at once simple, easily understood, clearly desirable and energising'.[24]

## CONCLUSION

In this chapter we have looked at ways of getting the family, board and top management meaningfully involved in setting the long-term direction of the firm. We recognise that it is quite difficult for a remote, non-active family member to make a contribution. A possible way of overcoming this is to involve the family in a visioning process. While this process is driven by the board and top management, it allows the family to become meaningful participants in the process of directing the firm towards a promising future. Faithful to our intent to serve the family business practitioner first and foremost, we have also outlined a practical visioning process that we have applied in a number of companies.

## NOTES

1. H. U. Bodenmann, *Turbulente Zeiten*, Zürich: Weltwoche–ABC–Verlag, 1994, pp. 100–1.
2. Ibid., p. 101.
3. Sir Adrian Cadbury, as noted earlier, gained world-wide recognition for the work of the Committee on the Financial Aspects of Corporate Governance

– the Cadbury Committee. Under Sir Adrian's chairmanship the committee formulated far-reaching recommendations on corporate governance. In order to prevent lawmakers from stepping in and legislating corporate governance more tightly in the UK, British industry largely implemented the suggested measures. While Cadbury-Schweppes is no longer family-controlled, it is still heavily influenced by the spirit and values of the Cadbury family. The present chairman is Dominic Cadbury, the younger brother of Sir Adrian.

4. A. Cadbury, *The Company Chairman*, new edition, Hemel Hempstead: Director Books, 1995, p. 15.
5. *Corporate Governance: An International Review*, October 1995, p. 242.
6. H. J. Leavitt, *Corporate Pathfinders*, Homewood, Ill.: Dow Jones-Irving, 1986, p. 62.
7. D. Halberstam, *The Powers That Be*, New York: Dell, 1979, p. 40.
8. For more information on the concept of intuition and its role in management see J. Parikh, in cooperation with F. Neubauer and A. Lank, *Intuition: The New Frontier of Management*, Oxford: Basil Blackwell, 1994.
9. J. C. Collins and J. I. Porras, 'Building your Company's Vision', *Harvard Business Review*, September–October 1996, p. 66.
10. Figure 7.2 is a somewhat modified version of a figure that appeared in ibid., p. 67.
11. Ibid., p. 87.
12. G. Hamel and P. K. Prahalad, *Competing for the Future*, Boston, Mass.: Harvard Business School Press, 1994, pp. 107–26.
13. Ibid., pp. 108–9.
14. Ibid., pp. 108–9.
15. Collins and Porras, 'Building your Company's Vision', op. cit., pp. 73–4.
16. Ibid., p. 73.
17. Ibid., p. 72.
18. GE Annual Report 1995, p. 2.
19. H. A. Slaatte, *The Pertinence of the Paradox*, New York: Humanities Press, 1968, p. 4.
20. Cited in A. Demb and F. F. Neubauer, *The Corporate Board: Confronting the Paradoxes*, New York: Oxford University Press, 1992, p. 5.
21. F. Westley and H. Mintzberg, 'Visionary leadership and strategic management', *Strategic Management Journal*, vol. 10, (1989), p. 22.
22. E. Land, 'The most basic form of creativity', *Time*, 26 June, 1972, p. 84.
23. F. Westley and H. Mintzberg, 'Visionary Leadership', op. cit., p. 19.
24. W. Bennis and B. Nanus, *Leaders*, New York: Harper & Row, 1985.

# 8 Securing Financial Resources as a Key Governance Measure

Can anybody remember when the times were not hard, and money not scarce?

(Ralph Waldo Emerson, American philosopher, 1803–82)

In a recent IMD Survey of 200 family businesses with between 20 and 2000 employees and representing 20 nationalities, the respondents were asked whether they had ever considered going public with the shares of their family businesses. No less than 40 per cent answered in the affirmative. To the follow-up question 'Do you think you may issue shares to the public within the next ten years?' almost a quarter of the sample (23 per cent) answered in the affirmative and a remarkable 43 per cent responded 'Maybe'. This means that roughly two thirds of the companies had considered or were seriously considering floating their companies on the stock exchange.[1] Whether to offer shares to the public is obviously a key issue for the owners of family businesses, and therefore warrants detailed examination.

The reasons for going public cover a broad spectrum. At one end of that spectrum is the case where it is considered ideal to build up a business forcefully and introduce it to the stock exchange at the most suitable point in time to reap a handsome price that will enable the owners to live comfortably thereafter (and to even consider embarking on new ventures). This attitude is rather common in the anglophone countries, particularly the United States. At the other end of the spectrum are cases where the family may not be particularly keen to give up control of the business, but the firm has been growing so rapidly that its further development can no longer be financed internally. The enormous need for capital in cases where the business has had the good fortune to grow rapidly is frequently underestimated by entrepreneurs, particularly if they come from a purely technical background and have had limited managerial experience. They sometimes do not realise that rapidly growing businesses – as attractive as they obviously are for many reasons – absorb liquid resources in the way that sponges absorb water, in large quantities relative to their size.

The need for liquidity in family businesses is either caused by the capital requirements of the business proper or it has its origins in the liquidity needs of the family shareholders. Let us first take a look at the question of how to satisfy the liquidity needs of the business.

## LIQUIDITY NEEDS OF THE BUSINESS AND HOW TO SATISFY THEM

As this is not a book on how to finance a family business we will restrict ourselves to some financially oriented remarks, in principle related to aspects of corporate governance. As we saw earlier, securing financial resources is a classical corporate governance task. This holds particularly true for family businesses, where the issue is frequently intertwined with aspects of ownership. Several of the institutions of a corporate constitution are called upon when the crucial question of how to finance the business is tackled: the board, top management and, of course, the family.

The capital needs of a family business can be satisfied in a number of ways:

- Through internally generated cash flows.
- Through additional capital injections by current shareholders.
- By broadening the circle of shareholders (without floating shares on the stock exchange), for instance, by inviting employees, directors or investment institutions to buy shares.
- Through loans from insiders and/or third parties.
- By selling parts of the business that do not belong to the core activities of the firm. A good example in this context is FAG Kugelfischer Georg Schäfer AG, a German company active in roller bearing products and technologies, which is controlled by the Schäfer family (the family owns 51 per cent of the shares). As part of its turnaround strategy the company sold 13 subsidiaries, including hydraulic brakes, textile machinery accessories, metrology and industrial gauging and control systems. By 1992 the move had brought no less than DM 740 million into the coffers of Kugelfischer.[2] In this type of decision, the

desire to maintain control and the cost of capital are two of the criteria typically used to make a choice.

One other important way of securing additional capital is, of course, to go public. In principle there are two ways for a privately owned firm to go public. The first approach is to issue a proportion of the existing shares, which does not increase the firm's liquidity but provides the present shareholders with more cash. The second method is to issue additional shares, thereby increasing the capital of the company by the amount paid for the new stock. Both options usually bring 'outsiders' into the firm, with all the consequences that such a move involves.

The decision to float shares on the stock exchange is usually a watershed for the family and the firm, involving, among other things, a major change in the confidentiality enjoyed by a privately owned company. A good case in point here is the venerable German pharmaceutical and chemical company E. Merck in Darmstadt (Germany), which was founded in 1827 and has been controlled ever since by the founding family. In 1995 the company decided to change their legal structure and to place 25 per cent of the newly created share capital on the Frankfurt, Zürich and London Stock Exchanges (in addition, some of these shares were privately placed in the United States.) The more than DM 2 billion raised in the transaction bolstered Merck's financial reserves, which had shrunk as the result of a brisk expansion of the firm's activities. The decision to go to the stock exchange had been made unanimously by the family assembly. Although it was a big event in the history of Merck, this step, in the opinion of Hans Joachim Langmann, a family member and CEO of Merck, will not change the nature of Merck as a family business.[3] As this case shows, the source of such important governance decisions is the family, but the driving force in preparing such a step and eventually carrying it out will, of course, be the board and management.

Going public is a highly complex matter comprising many dimensions: the price at which the shares are to be introduced, the point in time for the introduction, the preparation of the market and so on. Any family business contemplating such a move will need the expert advice of specialists in the field. In addition tax considerations frequently play a major role in these decisions; here again the need for expert advice is obvious, all the more so since the tax regimes differ markedly from country to country. In a book like this, where general corporate governance issues are the subject, we have to restrict ourselves to some general remarks on the pros and cons of such a step.[4]

## THE BENEFITS OF GOING PUBLIC

There are six obvious advantages of offering the shares of a family-controlled business on the stock exchange, as follows.[5]

### Improved Marketability of Shares

After a family company has gone public, the family shareholders find themselves in a more favourable position. Rather than holding stock with limited marketability, their shares can now (in principle) be sold at a fairly predictable price on the open market. In addition it is much easier to use them as collateral for loans.

At first sight it could be thought that this argument belongs more properly to the next section of this chapter, where we discuss how the liquidity needs of shareholders (rather than the company) can be satisfied. This is to a certain degree true. However, improving the marketability of the shares also increases the flexibility of the company to look after its own capital needs.

### Improvement of the Financial Position of the Firm

As shown by the Merck example above, selling shares to the general public improves the financial position of the firm. A stronger balance sheet and greater financial health typically increase the ability of the firm to take out loans (not to mention improving its leverage when negotiating the terms of such loans). In addition, the fact that the stock has arm's-length value makes it easier for the firm to use its stock for a share swap when an acquisition is made.

### Solution for Inheritance Tax Issues

The often serious liquidity problems experienced by families faced with inheritance taxes are usually shifted to the company, as the family rarely has sufficient personal funds to cover the tax entirely. This means that the firm has to make financial provisions for such an event if the sudden drain on the resources of the firm caused by the demise of a family member with a major shareholding is not to endanger the company. Having the firm's stock on the exchange allows it to sell shares at a favourable point in time to generate the funds needed to pay the inheritance taxes. The same applies to individual family members when responsibility for the payment of inheritance taxes has not been shifted to the company.

## Potential Increase in the Value of the Shares

One possible benefit of going public is that the value of the stock may rise above the stock price estimated by an investment banker on behalf of the family. The reason may be twofold. First, the estimate will probably be on the conservative side – for understandable reasons. If this is the case, the market quotation may produce a more realistic (that is, higher) price. Second, investors may be willing to pay a higher price because of the greater credibility sometimes attributed to public companies, the improved marketability of the shares and the transparency of the accounts, which in some cases, are a valuable by-product of going public.

## Improved Ability to Offer Incentives to Employees

Family businesses compete with public companies for talented employees, and in some business cultures they therefore have to offer stock incentives that are similar to those offered by publicly traded firms, for instance stock options and stock purchase programmes. These incentives are of course more attractive if the shares of the company are on the stock exchange. Furthermore the many complications that arise with the other shareholders in a closely held company are avoided, which means that share schemes as incentives are easier to implement.

## Increased Prestige

Going public gives a family business greater visibility. Its name and products frequently become better known as the press will report on it at least once a year when the annual accounts are presented. Furthermore there is a popular misconception that the family business is an inefficient or ineffective form of organisation. Some observers see a company's willingness to have at least some of its shares in the public's hands as an indication of an enlightened owner who is more inclined to accept non-family senior executives and directors. This and the other commitments that go with the status of a public company – greater transparency with respect to facts and figures, accounts audited by a public accountant and so on – in the eyes of some investors suggest increased managerial professionalism.

## THE DISADVANTAGES OF GOING PUBLIC

As the saying goes, where there is a lot of light, there are also many shadows. What then are the key disadvantages of going public? The following are a few important ones.

### Loss of Privacy

Of all the changes that occur when a company goes public, perhaps none is more disturbing to the family than the loss of secrecy. For instance any privileges given to family members will have to be made public. In our experience family businesses are usually quite thrifty and careful with perks to family members, but going public may require them to disclose any perks that are given – a fearful thought for many families. This is illustrated by the case of W. R. Grace.

Although W. R. Grace is not a family business in the strict sense of the term, until 1995 it had been dominated for generations by the Grace family, who treated it as their personal fiefdom despite the fact that their share ownership had dwindled to an insignificant percentage. At one point a non-family CEO insisted that the fiduciary duties of the board *vis-à-vis* the other shareholders demanded the publication of the perks and advantages the Grace family received from the company – with devastating consequences for the CEO: Peter Grace convinced the board to remove him. In the end Peter Grace was likewise forced to relinquish his chairmanship at the insistence of institutional investors in the company.[6]

In addition, quite legitimate family financial transactions that can be handled discretely before going public may have to be revealed to the public after the introduction of the firm's shares on the stock exchange. This is an uncomfortable situation for many old time family share-holders.

### The Fear of Takeover

When a company goes public, and assuming enough shares have been issued, it is possible for an outside investor (who might even be a competitor) to wrest control from the family owners, with all the obvious consequences. One way of protecting against such a move is for the family to hold onto the voting majority, either by restricting the sale to less than 50 per cent or by creating share categories with restricted voting rights that are sold to third parties. This is a common practice, although the restricted voting rights diminish the value of the shares in the eyes of investors.

### Changes to the Board

A public company is required to have a board of directors, the members of which are charged with quite far-reaching fiduciary and other responsibilities, as we saw in Chapter 5. These responsibilities may force the board to become much more active than the family-dominated board of the pre-stock-exchange period. That is, they will be forced to scrutinise the actions of management much more thoroughly. There is another side to that coin though. It is also the case that the new members of the board, reflecting the new shareholder structure, may bring with them a good deal of additional know-how and experience that management and the family can use skilfully. Although the family can legally shape the composition of the board as long as it has the majority, it is quite obvious that the board can no longer be used as a sinecure for any old uncle in the family. This comes as a nasty surprise to some families, as in the past they may have used board membership as a convenient means of pacifying different branches of the family that otherwise would have felt disadvantaged for one reason or another.

### Increased Formality, Higher Expectations

Broadening the circle of shareholders beyond the family will frequently make the interface between the company and the shareholders more formal. This and reduced familiarity among the key actors may well slow down the decision-making process of the company. Furthermore, once the shares are on the market, investors will compare their performance to that of any other investments they may have. In some cultures this may lead to a short-term orientation among the new shareholders, an attitude that is far removed from acceptance of the 'patient money' the family used to provide.

The dictate of quarterly statements typically increases pressure on management to perform well, which of course is beneficial provided it is not at the expense of the long-term development of the firm.

### Additional Costs

The initial cost of going public is substantial. It can be as high as 10 per cent of the offering price. The underwriter's commission, legal fees, printing costs, registration and auditing cost have to be taken into account. The necessary paperwork will include substantial disclosure of financial information, as well as other company figures and performance data. Key executives will discover that a surprising amount of time has to be devoted to informing shareholders, present as well as prospective, and the general public. In some cases it will be necessary to upgrade the existing management systems (for example, accounting) so that the firm can react promptly to the increased demand for certain kinds of data.

Going public is not a route to hidden treasures, as the following mini-case shows.

Let us now turn to the liquidity needs of the shareholders and what can be done about them.

## THE LIQUIDITY NEEDS OF SHAREHOLDERS AND HOW TO SATISFY THEM

There are two reasons why shareholders may need liquidity:[7]

- An *immediate* (large) liquidity need is caused by a shareholder's unexpected personal need for cash or the wish of a shareholder to part from the family business altogether (sell out).
- A *structural* liquidity need arises when family shareholders feel that more liquidity and financial flexibility should be given to the owners.

First a word about *immediate liquidity needs* and *the wish to sell out*. There is little the company can do to prevent unexpected personal financial needs; they are under (or beyond) the control of the individual shareholder affected by them. This means the company just has to deal with then when they occur. The desire to sell out, on the other hand, can be for reasons over which the company or family may have at least some influence and can take remedial measures. For instance the shareholder may be disenchanted with the way the company is conducting its business, or may feel that his or her involvement is having no impact on the way the company is run. If these negative feelings are spotted early enough, the family might be able to deal with them and keep the shareholder in the flock, thus removing the need for liquid funds to pay off the shareholder.[8]

*Structural liquidity needs* by a family shareholder may be rooted in the fact that the shares of family businesses frequently have no or limited marketability, even if the family members are not prevented by a

### Levi Strauss: A Company that Went Public but Returned to Being a Family Business

Levi Strauss & Co was founded in 1853 by Levi Strauss. After decades of growth and successful family ownership, in 1971 the family shareholders decided to float the world's most famous manufacturer of jeans on the stock exchange.

The company changed its name to Levi Strauss Associates and new shares with a par value of US$0.10 were issued, although the family retained a controlling interest. Soon after the company started to diversify. Additional factories were opened and the range was extended to include skiwear. The outcome was a disaster.

By 1984 the caring family culture had gone, numbers now mattered more than people. Profits fell dramatically from US$200million to US$40million. The price of the shares dropped from $50 to $23 and rumours of takeover spread. The Strauss and Haas families, descendants of Levi Strauss, who still owned some 40 per cent of the company, reacted energetically by replacing the non-family CEO with Robert Haas, then aged 40. One of his first decisions was to return the company to private hands in a $1.7 billion leveraged buy-out (LBO) in July 1985. The price offered for the transaction was $50 per share, almost twice the market value.

The family regained majority ownership and Robert Haas started to rationalise production. In a year he closed 23 production plants and made 7000 workers redundant. His efforts paid off – by 1989 profits had climbed above the $250million level for the first time in the history of the company, and by 1992 all loans had been repaid. In 1995 net sales reached $6707million and net earnings $735million (a return on sales of 11 per cent).

In April 1996 Levi Strauss completed its second leveraged buyout at a cost of $4.3 billion. The transaction took place at $265 per share. As a result of this second buyout the company is now solely owned by descendants of the founder and senior management. Although Robert Haas said that the primary objectives of the transaction were to ensure 'long-term, stable and consistent ownership and maintain corporate social responsibility', there might have been another reason at the back of his mind: private companies are not required to disclose sensitive information – which could be misused by competitors – and they also save considerable management time and money by not having to publish quarterly and annual reports.

The company was public for only 25 years of its 144-year history; it is now back in the hands of a family that is more keen than ever to keep it private and to safeguard its freedom to choose the strategy and culture it feels most appropriate for the future of the company.

shareholders' agreement from selling their shares freely. Another reason for structural liquidity needs might be that a shareholder – particularly if his or her investments are undiversified – considers it undesirable to have all his or her eggs in one basket and thus seeks to spread the investment risks. The crux of all of this is that it is frequently not easy to satisfy the immediate and structural liquidity needs of shareholders as their main assets – shares in the family business – are not easily disposed of, and doing so will affect other family members.

How can this issue be handled? In principle there are two solutions:

- To float all or a proportion of the company's shares on the stock exchange. The pros and the cons of this option were discussed above.
- To create an internal company market for the shares.

## CREATION OF AN INTERNAL MARKET

The great advantage of a well-functioning external market is that the price of a product (or a share, for that matter) is determined by the interaction of a number of independent parties. The classical description of this process came from Adam Smith, who as early as 1776 in his *Wealth of Nations* stated that value 'is adjusted . . . not by any accurate measure, but by the higgling and bargaining of the market, . . . [a] sort of rough equality which, though it is not exact, is sufficient for carrying on the business of common life.' As this freely functioning market is not available to many family-controlled firms, they try to create an internal market that comes as close as possible to the ideal described by Adam Smith.

The mechanisms companies have developed in this respect vary widely. The solutions we came across in our dealings with family enterprises seem to share certain features; we will look at them by using three particular examples as illustrations. They are based on real companies, but we have disguised them.

The first case is a large, globally active, very successful health care company. The shares are on the stock exchange, but the family holds the voting majority. We shall call this firm the Delta Corporation.

The second case is a multibillion dollar company that produces and markets worldwide four different categories of high-tech products, including sophisticated heavy machinery. The company has a large number of shareholders, and members of the fifth generation of the founder's family are gradually taking over the reigns of the firm (that is, they have joined the board but are not significantly represented in management). The shares of the company are all in the hands of family members, not on the stock exchange. There are three classes of shares, two of them non-voting. The firm is Bergman AB, the disguised company to which we have referred in earlier chapters.

The third case is a large, successful, multinational chemical company. The shares are on the stock exchange, but the voting majority is still in the hands of the family, now in its fourth generation. Let us call this firm Conches Cie.

We now turn to the key elements of an internal market. The first is very widespread in family businesses.

### A Shareholders' Agreement or Pool

One typical ingredient of an internal market is an agreement among the family members to give the family first refusal should one of them ever consider selling his or her shares.

Such an agreement does not necessarily have to cover all the shares, for instance it does not usually encompass non-voting shares (this is the case in Bergman AB). Such an agreement is particularly important when some of the shares are already in the hands of third parties and the stocks held by the family give them a relatively narrow voting majority (which is the case with Delta Corporation). Under these circumstances, were a shareholder to leave the flock and sell his or her shares to a non-family party, the impact would be dramatic in many respects. For example the premium that typically goes with majority voting power would disappear, which would of course devalue the shareholding of all the family members. Furthermore the family would lose its grip on the company: for instance they could no longer unilaterally determine the composition of the board, and thus would no longer be able to govern the overall direction of the firm and choose the CEO (among other things).

It is not always easy to convince all family shareholders to join the pool. This was the case in Conches Cie, where some dissident members of the family refused to sign the agreement. Even if this does not immediately threaten the majority of the family, it is an awkward situation. In such cases the natural cohesion among the family members can serve to prevent these shareholders from straying too far from the common interest.

*Selling a Shareholding*

As discussed above in connection with liquidity needs, it is not uncommon that once in a while a family shareholder wants to sell some or all of his or her shares.

The larger the family becomes, the smaller the individual shareholdings usually are (unless a 'pruning of the family tree' has taken place). A frequently observed parallel development is that allegiance to the family enterprise weakens, and as a result some of the shareholders may wish to sell their holdings. This has happened in Bergman AB, and likewise in Delta Corp., but not recently. In Conches Cie it does happen, but rarely. As these internal sales are almost always a complicated matter, many companies (among them Delta Corp.) expressly discourage their members from trying to sell.

*Ways to Determine a Sales Price*

Another common ingredient of an internal market is the need to determine the price of stock to be sold within the family. There are of course ways of tackling this challenge. In the case of Bergman AB, the public accountant of the firm, a long-time associate of the company who enjoys the trust of the family, is asked to come up with a reasonable price. (He uses multiples of earnings paid as share prices for comparable companies on the stock exchange to come up with a price estimate.) Although the final price is ultimately hammered out between seller and buyer, the public accountant's estimates are usually heeded.

*Mechanisms for Finding Buyers*

How does one identify potential buyers in an internal market? Here again the methods differ markedly. In the case of Conches Cie, where several branches of the family now exist, the seller must first offer his or her shares to the other members of his or her family branch. If nobody in the branch is interested, the shares are offered to all other shareholders in the family. Should none of them be willing to buy, the shares are acquired by a pool whose financial resources were obtained from an earlier public share issue. The price in this case is not an issue, as arm's-length stock prices are available. In order to discourage such deals, the seller has to accept a 10 per cent (or other) discount if the pool buys.

In Bergman AB the first and most natural way is for two family members – seller and buyer – to seek each other out in an informal way and strike a deal between themselves. In some cases the legal department of the firm functions as a facilitator: the party wishing to sell contacts the company lawyer and indicates his or her intent. The lawyer is usually aware of who in the family might be interested in buying. He brings the two parties together and thus serves as a kind of broker. This method is the most important one at Bergman AB.

The second method in Bergman AB is via a company that is controlled by the family and holds about 15 per cent of the capital of the main family business. A proportion of the dividends this company receives is used to buy shares from those family members who wish to sell. Sometimes the accumulated dividends are not enough to pay for the shares and the seller may have to wait some time for the necessary funds to accumulate. This method, which was instituted as early as the 1940s and was considered a success, has lately drawn some criticism from the family, particularly as it has been used to bail out family members who cannot keep their personal finances in order. The critics feel that this is an inappropriate way to tie up a fairly large chunk of the family fortune.

The third method employed by Bergman AB is to ask friendly foundations or other family businesses to absorb some of the family shares, even if only for a short period. A similar service is offered to those organisations should they face the situation where part of the family wants to sell some or all of their shares and nobody in the family proper wishes to buy them.

There are cases where the degree of freedom for a family shareholder to sell is very limited indeed. In Delta Corp., where a small family forms the voting majority of the company, the stock exchange value of the shares – like that of many health care companies – has increased strongly in the last two decades. If one of the pool members decides to sell his or her shares, a complex procedure exists to handle the matter. These intricate and complicated provisions however, are not much use as the market value of the existing blocks of shares is so high that none of the other shareholders would be able to acquire them without getting into serious debt.

As the above examples show, satisfying the liquidity needs of family business stockholders by selling shares is a highly complex matter. The issue therefore occupies the minds of a considerable number of owners of family businesses. This complexity is the price they must pay for the freedom to conduct financial dealings with no outside interference.

An example of the skilful handling many of the issues raised in this chapter is the approach taken by the well-known Hermès SA.

## Hermès SA: Publicly Traded, Privately Owned

Hermès SA is a French manufacturer of elegant, upmarket luggage, clothing, and accessories. Established in the nineteenth century as a manufacturer of leather goods, the company later diversified into silk goods (about 36 per cent), ready-to-wear clothing (12 per cent) and perfume (7.5 per cent). Although more than 50 per cent of annual sales were still generated in Europe in the 1990s, the Asia–Pacific region contributed nearly one third of annual revenues and the United States accounted for 11 per cent of the yearly turnover. Hermès enjoyed average annual sales increases of 24 per cent from 1986 to mid 1996.

Since the late 1980s the business has been led by Jean-Louis Dumas, a fifth-generation descendant of the founder. He has been credited with building Hermès' world-wide retailing empire by directing an intensive strategic programme and imposing a strong family influence.

### Constructing a Strong Financial Structure (Going Public)

Under pressure from some factions of the extended family, Hermès made its first stock offering in June 1993, but more than 80 per cent of the equity remained in the hands of 56 family members, six of whom retained 5–10 per cent stakes. The equity sale generated more excitement than the semi-annual Hermès sales: the 425000 shares, which were floated at $55 each, were oversubscribed by a factor of 34 and went to approximately 4000 outside shareholders. The equity sale helped reduce family tensions by allowing some members to liquidate their holdings without squabbling over share valuations. The family members now had shares with a fluctuating official value, and if they wanted to sell shares in order to buy houses or cars, they could do so without affecting the market. The owning family views itself as having improved its stability while retaining its strong family influence on the firm. They see themselves as a public company with a 'Fort Knox-type' of family culture.

### Developing Financial Autonomy

Hermès has been able to stick to its principle of self-financing, although it has often taken risks. To avoid financial dependence on the banks but still supply the capital required for new projects, approximately 15 per cent of the profits has traditionally been reinvested in the company.

### Retaining the Family Influence

According to the owners, the family firm is based on a democratic monarchy and involves the following.

- Strong leadership by the CEO, who is part of the extended family. (41 family members in the sixth generation).
- A structure to maintain the family influence: a strategy committee composed of 17 family representatives.
- A board of directors composed mainly of family members. Ten of the twelve directors are descendants of the founder.
- Written company regulations and a family constitution with rules for selling and buying shares, limited family voting rights and so on. These were established after the company went public.
- Non-family buyers and divorced family members may own shares but have no voting rights, so as to avoid dilution of the voting rights.
- A majority of 75 per cent is needed to change the company statutes as well as the top person – this rule is designed to keep the family intact.

The owning family wants Hermès to remain a family firm. They believe that it is desirable, but not imperative, that the CEO be a family member. What is imperative to them is that this person is chosen by the family representatives. They also strongly believe that all really important decisions should be made at the ordinary and extraordinary meetings and that the family should have majority control over these meetings (in their opinion, if the family does not have that control, even if the CEO is appointed by the family the company will lose some of its family character).

At an early age the youngest generation is directly immersed in the tradition of the company. The youngsters regularly participate in organised tours of subsidiaries and company suppliers in order to get a stronger feeling for the products and their creation.

*Stimulating Family Pride*

According to Jean-Louis Dumas, 'the secret of our company lies in a job well done. Everyone should be proud of doing their best. This type of pride is not arrogance, but tempered by humility and shared enthusiasm . . . We are more proud thinking that the fruit of our labours will be harvested by our grandchildren. The main idea is that yesterday's ship is ancestral and it is our duty to conserve it even though we did not build it. The only valid criterion of our satisfaction is whether, if thanks to some miracle our grandfather returned to life, he would pat us on the back and tell us that we have done a good job.'[9]

CONCLUSION

This chapter has dealt with two aspects of the realm of finance: the liquidity needs of the firm and the liquidity needs of the family – both of which must be addressed by the governance system.

Several ways of handling both have been considered, highlighting both the positives and the negatives. With very few exceptions, these approaches touch on the very nature and character of the family business and therefore must be handled with great sensitivity. Once again, advice from a solid board can guide the family across this difficult territory.

NOTES

1. M. Wagen, 'What about going public?', *Family Business Network Newsletter,* no. 11, March 1995, p. 8.
2. 'Kugelfischer's ruthless survival route', *Financial Times,* 19 July, 1994, p. 18.
3. 'Der Börsengang wird den Charakter von Merck nicht verändern', *Frankfurter Allgemeine Zeitung,* 29 April, 1995, p. 18.
4. We are grateful to Monica Wagen, research associate at IMD, Lausanne, who has done extensive work in this area in connection with her doctoral dissertation and has allowed us to draw on it in this section.
5. M. Wagen, 'Perspectives on going public', *Family Business,* Spring 1996, pp. 31–4.
6. W. R. Grace & Co., IMD case series written by Scott Bissessar under the supervision of Fred Neubauer, Lausanne, 1996.
7. M. Bruel, *A Model of Liquidity in Family Business,* doctoral dissertation, University of Groningen, the Netherlands, 1994, p. 43.
8. For an example of how one family attempted to increase the potential impact of non-active shareholders, see the material on the Bergman family business workshop in the Epilogue.
9. From a speech by Jean-Louis Dumas, CEO and President of Hermès International, at the Annual Conference of the Family Business Network, Madrid, September 1995.

# Part V
# Handling the Controlling Task of Corporate Governance

## INTRODUCTION

In Chapter 9 we discuss what is needed for the different elements of the governance structure – the family, the board and top management – to control the firm effectively and efficiently. In this context, we will also look briefly at ways of accounting for the activities of the firm (reporting *vis-à-vis* third parties with a legitimate interest in such information).

# 9 Control as a Key Governance Measure

I claim not to have controlled events, but confess plainly that events have controlled me

(Abraham Lincoln, US president, 1809–65)

On Friday, February 24, 1995 at 7:15 in the morning, Peter Baring, the Chairman of the oldest Merchant Bank in the United Kingdom, received a call from Singapore that he had been dreading: a 'big hole' in the accounts was confirmed. Just how big was not yet known, but it was clearly greater than the bank's capital. A 'rogue' trader had run up massive losses[1] on unauthorised derivatives dealings in the Far East, which threatened to bring down the bank. Following time-honoured tradition, Baring sought an interview with the Governor of the Bank of England. Because the Governor, Eddy George, was away on a skiing holiday, Baring was seen by Rupert Pennant-Rea, the Deputy Governor. Senior representatives of 15 or so UK Clearing and Merchant banks were called to the Bank of England. There was frenzied activity throughout the weekend. On receiving the news, George immediately returned from Geneva, and the assembled bankers and their professional advisors were asked to put together a rescue package, although the extent of Baring's obligations was not known. Neither the Bank of England nor the Treasury would provide a 'cap', or limit, to the potential liability, and the Chancellor of the Exchequer, Kenneth Clark, would not sanction the application of public funds. The bankers were not prepared to take an unquantified risk with their shareholders' funds . . . . No deal could be agreed upon and all departed despondent. On the following Monday morning, administrators were appointed and a pillar of the UK banking establishment was allowed to fail.[2]

Barings Bank was established in 1762 by Protestant immigrants from Holland. The family business was originally based on the textile trade and later expanded into banking. The bank made its early fortune from trade, particularly with the Americas; it benefited from various wars and was involved in funding the Napoleonic wars. Its influence was such that the

209

Duc de Richelieu, French soldier and statesman, once said: 'There are six great powers in Europe: England, France, Prussia, Austria, Russia and the Baring Brothers.'

Despite some ups and downs in its more than 200 years of history, the bank had remained an aristocratic, 'blue blood' bank. It numbered the present queen among its clients, and there were five title holders in the extended family. It was known to be oldfashioned, recruiting from 'Eton and the army'. Its income was derived from corporate finance fees, corporate debt funding and asset management. It had a significant blue chip client base.

In the 1980s Barings was still a family-owned bank, the ordinary shares being held by descendants of the founders and their charitable foundations. Operating control lay with the directors (and an internal auditing department, established in the mid 1980s). Much changed in 1984 with the approach of the 'Big Bang', when Barings – like many others – acquired a stockbroking business, their first involvement in equity securities. Henderson Crosthwaite (Far East), which had strong Asian connections and was run by Christopher Heath, became Barings Securities Limited (BSL). It had been a partnership and therefore had no outside shareholders to worry about. Its ethos was different though, and there was a big cultural gap. Barings' strong classical banking ethic conflicted with Heath's 'salesman' approach. There were other clashes as well: corporate finance versus trading, team players versus individualists, trust and strong personal relationships versus quick results and a 'hire and fire' approach.

Heath ran BSL as a one-man band with hardly any management structure in place. As early as 1992 the system of management and internal controls was known to be weak. BSL was driven by the front office, and communications between front and back office were poor. The rapid expansion in the late 1980s following the acquisition of personnel, offices and markets was not accompanied by the development of commensurate controls. No internal audit function was in place until the end of 1992.

BSL made big profits in the late 1980s as a result of the Tokyo Stock Exchange boom. By mid-1992, due to a significant market downturn, BSL was losing money. The Board demanded a new strategy. Following restructuring, Heath stepped down and then left altogether in early 1993, together with other senior staff and the whole derivatives team. They were replaced by people from corporate finance with no background in derivatives dealings. Attempts were made to impose more controls. A matrix management structure was put into place, and BSL was combined with Baring Brothers (BB&Co), the merchant banking arm, to form

Baring Investment Bank (BIB). Cultural differences over control were never fully resolved. In fact the management structure changed three times after 1992. A number of serious personal conflicts amongst the senior management affected their operating performance. Basically there was neither clarity of responsibility nor stability.

Following the Kidder, Peabody disaster in New York, the board commissioned an internal risk review on the question of whether a similar disaster could happen in Barings. The review was inconclusive and the matter was taken no further.

That was the backdrop to the activities of Nick Leeson, one of the key figures in the drama. Leeson joined Barings in 1989 to work for BSL's futures and options settlement department, having previously done something similar at Morgan Stanley. His background differed markedly from that of typical BB&Co associates. He was a plasterer's son who had been educated at a comprehensive rather than a public school and had received poor A-level results. Still, Leeson became a competent and well-regarded member of the settlements team, and when problems arose in the Far East because of rapid expansion, he and others were sent to Hong Kong and then Jakarta to sort out the matter. On their return to London, it was generally acknowledged that they had done a good job in bringing things under control.

In early 1992 Leeson applied for a post in Singapore to take charge of the back office of the newly established Baring Futures Singapore (BFS), a wholly owned subsidiary of BSL. Partly as a reward for his success in Jakarta, his request was granted and Leeson arrived in Singapore in April that year. By mid 1993 he was appointed general manager of BFS, thus becoming responsible for dealing as well as settlements. His reporting lines were not clearly defined or understood from the start. In effect there were substantial 'holes' in the control structure.

Throughout his career Leeson had entertained ambitions of becoming a dealer, and prior to being posted to Singapore had applied for authorisation in the UK. He had been turned down by the Securities and Futures Authority (SFA) because he had failed to disclose in his application form an outstanding county court judgement against him for personal debt. This rejection did not appear to have caused any problems at BSL. Leeson then applied to the Singapore International Monetary Exchange (SIMEX) for permission to take the necessary examinations, and when these had been successfully completed he applied for a licence as trader.

The basic business of BFS was equity derivatives, trading on behalf of a few clients, including Baring Securities Japan. The main external client was the Banque Nationale de Paris. Trading was in simple derivatives only, no 'rocket science'. All dealings were conducted through recognised, and therefore regulated, exchanges. There was no 'over the counter' dealing. In accordance with BSL's policy, all bargains were to be matched and no open position should be held. The exchanges used were SIMEX, the Osaka Stock Exchange and the Tokyo Stock Exchange. SIMEX worked on 'open outcry', while the Osaka and Tokyo Stock Exchanges were computer-based. This gave some room for arbitrage because of differing market structures, and Leeson began to exploit the opportunities.

Eventually Leeson began 'proprietary trading', that is, trading for the bank's own account rather than for clients, and appeared to make excellent profits from what was believed at headquarters to be a risk-free activity. However Leeson was declaring trading gains and hiding losses. The abnormal profits were not queried by London or investigated during the Deloitte & Touche audits of 1992 and 1993. By this time the concealed losses had reached £23 million (they later escalated to more than £200 million).

After the Kobe earthquake the Nikkei Index collapsed and Leeson doubled up and chased his losses. Huge cash advances were requested from London to meet the SIMEX margin calls. In January and February these rose cumulatively to £700 million, twice Baring's capital base. Headquarters failed to pick up all sorts of warning signs. According to the Board of Banking Supervision Report on the matter, 'No one in management accepts responsibility for Leeson's activities between October 1993 and 1 January 1995 . . . some members of management believed that the responsibility for certain activities (for example, equity derivatives) rested with other managers, who deny they had such responsibility. This resulted in confusion'. Eventually someone was sent to Singapore to investigate. Leeson disappeared, the ominous phone call to Peter Baring in London was made, and the venerable bank collapsed.

Later investigations showed that Leeson had skilfully covered up the huge losses that stemmed from his unauthorised dealings. He was furthermore accused of having forged an audit confirmation letter to conceal part of the losses.

Reading this incredible saga, one immediately asks the obvious question of whether or not there were any internal control systems in place. As the subsequent investigations showed, there were failures at several levels in the organisation, from the board down to the operational level.

There had been an internal audit in Singapore in July 1994 but it had failed to pick up the fraud. Nevertheless recommendations to tighten the control system were made, and if these had been followed the fraud would have been detected. In addition, Deloitte & Touche had reported to Coopers & Lybrand (C&L) in London in connection with the 1993 group audit, that there were no weaknesses in the control systems of sufficient significance to bring to C & L's attention. Regulators had been fed false information and did very little independent investigating.

After a long odyssey following his sudden departure from Singapore, Leeson was caught in Germany and eventually extradited to Singapore.

We have gone into this case in some detail because it is by no means an isolated story. Similar cases occurred at around the same time: Peter Young of Deutsche Morgan Grenfell Asset Management (a key subsidiary of Deutsche Bank), Kyriacos Papouis of NatWest Markets and Toshihide Iguchi of Daiwa's New York branch led their organisations into similar disasters.

## COMMON FEATURES

These cases all seem to have certain features in common. First, *there was a lack of supervision at the operational management level*. The following are some of the testimonials made in response to the cases mentioned above:

- 'We have found a major deficiency in controls', confessed Martin Owen, Chief Executive of NatWest Markets, about Kyriacos Papouis's options mispricing. 'Although it seems to have occurred in an insolated area, it still gives us concerns because these losses remained undiscovered for a significant period.'[3]
- 'No one in management accepts responsibility for Leeson's activities between October 1993 and 1 January 1995' stated the Board of Banking Supervision in their report on Barings, which was presented to the House of Commons in July 1995; the inquiry by the Board had been headed by the Governor of the Bank of England.
- 'there was a breakdown of controls and supervision', admitted Michael Dobson, the CEO of Deutsche Morgan Grenfell on Peter Young's operations.[4]

All this happened in spite of the fact that the Futures and Options Association had strongly recommended that 'senior management should establish clear written procedures for implementing the derivatives policy set by the Board' and that 'senior management should ensure that derivative activities are properly supervised and are subject to an efficient framework of internal controls and audits'.[5]

Second, *there was inadequate board oversight*. Not only did Leeson's immediate supervisors fall down on the job, but also effective oversight was not exercised by the board, as nobody on the Barings board seems to have understood the intricacies of dealing in derivatives. The evidence presented to the House of Commons Treasury Committee is a telling testimony to the Barings case, as this exchange of questions and answers shows:[6]

Q:  'Were there members of the Board of Directors of Barring plc who were knowledgeable about derivatives trading?
A:  (Mr. Norris) No.
Q:  Nobody at all?
A:  No.'

This flies in the face of another clear demand by the Futures and Options Association that 'Directors should establish and approve an effective policy for the use of derivatives which is consistent with the strategy, commercial objectives and risk appetite of the organisation'.[7]

Third, *poor control systems plagued the companies affected by the disasters*. Here are telling statements on two of the cases:

- 'We are deeply embarrassed that our internal controls and procedures were not sufficient to prevent this fraudulent action', said Masahiro Tsuda, General Manager of Daiwa's New York branch about the actions of Toshihide Iguchi.[8]
- 'The Board of Banking Supervision Report makes abundantly clear [that the] blame for the collapse of Barings PLC cannot be pinned solely on a mischievous trader named Nick Leeson . . . . Three months before the bank's collapse, the head of the Barings group treasury complained to his chief executive that it was "a struggle to get hard information" about the bank's control systems, and that "it is becoming much clearer that our systems and control culture are flaky"'.[9]

Fourth, *the auditing and regulations by third parties were inadequate*:

- The abnormal profits of the Singapore branch of Barings were not investigated during the Deloitte & Touche audits for 1992 and 1993.[10]

- The Bank of England never made an inspection visit and also allowed Barings to break the '25 per cent exposure' rule limiting a bank's exposure to any one activity.[11]

As a result of these failings, the Securities and Investments Board of the London Stock Exchange has embarked on an attempt to elaborate industry-wide accountability principles that could apply to general managers as well as to their subordinates in the field.[12]

## CONTRIBUTING FACTORS

At the root of the common features discussed above were several contributory factors. First, *there was widespread complacency and ignorance about the underlying business.* According to the Board of Banking Supervision's report, 'Until the collapse, Barings' management in London believed the trading conducted by Baring Futures Singapore to be essentially risk free and very profitable.'[13]

Second, *enormous performance pressures existed.* Michael Dobson, chief executive of Deutsche Morgan Grenfell, said of Peter Young: 'Ironically, all the pressure on this fund manager came from himself. He had a good track record and made a lot of money for investors. He put a lot of pressure on himself to continue that performance.'[14]

Third, a *'star system'* existed. The Board of Banking Supervision's report stressed the impact of that phenomenon 'Leeson was, in view of his high level reported profitability, considered to be a 'star performer' and that there was concern not to do anything which might upset him'.[15] The supervising echelons in the organisations did not dare to upset these high-level performers.

Fourth, *the effect of remuneration packages.* Remuneration schemes, which are common in the dealer environment and pay enormous rewards for risk-taking behaviour, may put a control system under great stress. 'If remuneration is linked to profitability, it is important that the control environment should be particularly rigorous.'[16]

Make no mistake: the board members and supervisors of all of these companies hit by disaster were normal directors and normal managers who commanded the respect of their peers – as long as things went well. These cases are telling examples of how difficult it can be for a board and top management to control a sprawling, internationally active organisation (and business is not alone in this situation, as the quote from Abraham Lincoln at the beginning of this chapter shows). In our context, the case of Barings plc is of particular importance. The failure to assert effective and efficient control was one of the reasons why a proud family lost a highly respected bank that they had owned and run for more than 200 years.


## A CONCEPTUAL APPROACH TO CONTROLLING

Having looked at some sobering examples of the breakdown of the control function, it is appropriate to look at the control task more systematically and prescriptively.

Let us face it: no control system is absolutely watertight. On the other hand, the widespread occurrence of cases such as the ones described above is not inevitable. During the last decade we have made major progress in formulating control techniques that make the controlling task of the board somewhat easier. This does not, however, mean that they make it easy. Controlling is a formidable task for any board as well as for any family, particularly in the light of the growing diversity in the activities of firms and their increasing geographic spread, both of which tend to lead to a loosening of the board's or a family's grip on the organisation.

As the family is frequently rather remote from the business (particularly if the firm has reached the cousins' confederation stage), the family typically relies on the board when it comes to overseeing management's activities. This is a practical and logical solution, particularly if there are high-calibre family members on the board. This is the reason why in this chapter we place the board at the centre of the discussion. And as we have said all along, a good board will keep the family informed about the control system and performance.

### Insist on a First-Class Control System

In addition to other topics, in his *Letters to a new Chairman* Hugh Parker addresses himself to the management information system a board ought to have at its disposal.[17] Just as war is too important to be left to professional soldiers, he believes that a board cannot leave the design of such a system solely to system analysts. In Parker's opinion the users – starting with the chairman – must be involved in specifying what is required, and thereafter be involved in ensuring that the specifications are met. This means that the information system should be designed from the top downwards and not built from the bottom upwards. The starting point for formulating specifications is to ascertain what data will be needed to allow the board to carry out its dual control task, namely:

- To monitor and judge the performance of management (has management created additional value for owners?)
- To fulfil the board's fiduciary duty *vis-à-vis* the family (for instance by making sure that good systems are in place to prevent the assets of the firm being squandered or even embezzled).

Most people are flattered by an invitation to become a member of a board, but in the words of an experienced chairman: 'When you join a board, you take a lot on trust.' While trust is vital if a board is to function well, a newcomer cannot be expected to provide that trust blindly. It is therefore highly advisable for a board candidate, prior to accepting the invitation, to ask the company whether he or she can see a copy of the external auditors' report for, say, the previous two years[18] (this obviously has to be done on a confidential basis), but it would be even better if the candidate obtained permission to talk to the auditors in person. An informal conversation may reveal finer nuances than are expressed in the report. Such a discussion would also allow the candidate to get a feel for the quality of the reporting system of the firm and whether it is suitable to help the board fulfil its control tasks. If the answers received are not satisfactory, he or she may decide to turn down the invitation to join the board.

**Two Means of Judging**

Let us now turn to a control system proper. Boards can base their control efforts either on measurable outcomes of the management process (so-called *outcome controls*) or on the quality of the management processes in place (*behaviour controls*).

Many outcome controls are analytical and/or financial in nature, which means they can be quantified. In addition they give the impression of being 'exact' (although, unfortunately, they frequently are not). Another strength is that their application has a long tradition (and hence they are understood by many people) and on the whole they are universally accepted. The most prominent outcome controls are measures of profitability (for example return on investment), liquidity (for example cash flow) and growth (for example sales growth). Their biggest drawback is that they are produced after the fact: by the time we get to know of the faults or weaknesses, the child has already fallen into the well, so to speak.

Nothing can be done to change the results. Many managers feel that the results simply arrive too late at their desks. In order to introduce some dynamism, we have extended the list of suitable measures to include future-oriented yardsticks such as order inflow and order backlog as well as market share measures and product- and service-quality assessments (the latter two are frequently considered indicators of future profitability).

While nobody suggests doing away with output controls, many observers believe that they have to be accompanied by assessments of management processes, control systems and managerial behaviour, in short *behaviour controls*. For many practitioners, these are of similar importance to outcome controls. As an experienced manager once put it, 'I may have to settle for bad results (which may be caused by influences management cannot be held responsible for), but I will not tolerate bad processes.'

Behaviour controls have several specific characteristics, some of which are considered to be of enormous importance. First, they look at ongoing processes; this means that, in principle, one can intervene before a major mishap occurs. Second, by their nature they are judgmental, that is, they are based on subjective information. This is not necessarily a handicap. After all, the higher one is in the hierarchy of the firm, the more complex the problems become. This holds true for control issues as well, and as a result they frequently cannot be dealt with by neat analytical tools alone. A case in point is the ultimate judgement of the performance of a CEO and whether he or she should be retained or fired. Such a decision should, of course, be based on as much quantitative data as possible. There are, however, many aspects of the performance of a CEO (such as leadership qualities, entrepreneurship and so on) that can only be judged subjectively by looking at how the CEO carries them out in his or her everyday management of the organisation. The third important characteristic of behaviour controls is that they typically require information that is not produced by conventional reporting systems; some information can actually only be gathered 'by osmosis', for instance absorbed when walking around in the firm or talking to customers and competitors.

**Overall Control Systems – the 'Wheel' with Four 'Spokes'**

Figure 9.1 presents the control issue from a somewhat different angle. It is based on the seminal work of Robert Simons, who sees control systems as a primary means of realising a strategy.[19] In the centre of the wheel in Figure 9.1 are the vision (created by the board, family and top management), the strategies (chosen by management and approved by the board

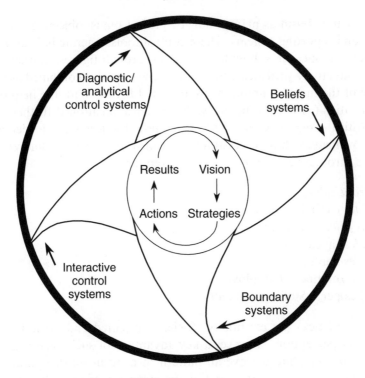

**Source**: Adapted from Simons (1995).[20]

**Figure 9.1** Control systems as wheel and spoke

to implement that vision) and the actions taken to realise the strategy. The four spokes of the wheel represent the means by which the 'virtuous spiral' from vision to strategy to action and results is achieved. The four spokes, which represent the key control mechanisms available to the board and top management, are all composed of outcome *and* process controls, but to varying degrees. Analytical systems (top spoke) are based more on output controls than for instance interactive control systems, (left-hand spoke). We shall discuss this in some detail below.

*Diagnostic/Analytical Control Systems*

A closer look at each of the spokes should probably start with a discussion of *diagnostic or analytical control systems*, as these are the most widely used control mechanisms.[21] These are feedback systems that monitor the outcomes of organisational processes and correct deviations from preset performance standards. They include traditional control tools such as business plans, budgets, project plans, objectives, strategic plans and reporting systems. These control tools generate indicators like: profitability measures, liquidity measures, growth figures, market shares and productivity yardsticks. Frequently, they are also combined as ratios. Some of the more common ratios are listed below. With the help of this set of ratios (as well as the twelve 'trend lines' mentioned further down) the British company General Electric, under the legendary leadership of Lord Weinstock, has successfully controlled around two hundred companies through very rigorous monthly reporting.[22]

- *Profit*/sales
- *Sales*/capital employed
- *Profit*/capital employed
- *Sales*/inventories
- *Sales*/debtors
- *Sales*/number of employees
- Sales per £/$ of emoluments

These yardsticks are essentially efficiency oriented and do not address customer perception. However a key advantage of such measuring tools is that, by revealing the overall pattern of a business, they allow for a systematic supervision of operating management. If one adds the softer measures of customer and staff satisfaction and retention as well as supplier, shareholder and other stakeholder feedback, one can create a strong framework within which the board can regularly review the organisation's total performance. The latter is particularly true if one adds important 'trend lines' such as the ones listed below – these too stem from Lord Weinstock's empire:

- Sales (£/$)
- Export sales
- Orders received
- Orders in hand
- Net profits
- Direct wages
- Overheads
- Capital employed
- Stock levels
- Number of employees

One problem is determining how much analysis-based information should be distributed to the board. During our research we have come across cases where management has virtually snowed the board under with information, thus rendering it ineffective. The opposite can hold true as well: management can starve boards when it comes to information. The only way out is for the board to determine what information they really want to receive and insist on receiving it early enough to allow for reasonable analysis. Every firm should realise that the board members have lent their good name to the firm and have a right to receive news on the performance of the firm as soon as possible – particularly bad news.

In the overwhelming number of firms, diagnostic/analytical control systems dominate the other three spokes of the wheel in Figure 9.1. This is unfortunate as they were originally conceived as top management tools (and less as instruments for use by boards). From the board's perspective, some of the other spokes are probably far more important when it comes to exercising the control function.

*Interactive Control Systems*

These are control systems that board members use to involve themselves regularly and personally in the life of the organisation.[23] They are seen as a means of 'taking the pulse' of the organisation by insisting on a regular dialogue with top management, in management by walking around, in seeking direct access to the line. They represent an age-old tool; even the Scriptures say already that 'the watchful eye of the master makes the cattle fat'.

The German High Court (Bundesgerichtshof) placed particular emphasis on this means of control when it stated in a landmark decision on 25 March 1991 that the supervisory board can only exercise effective control by both having a continuous discussion with and providing ongoing advice to the board of management. Regular advice from the supervisory board is the most prominent instrument of future-directed control of the board of management.'[24] Some German commentators on the decision even call this demand for a regular and ongoing interchange mandatory dialogue (Erläuterungszwang).

(To fully understand this decision one has to keep in mind that the German corporate law has a two-tier board system: the – non-executive – supervisory board on the one hand and the board of management which is charged with the everyday running of the company on the other. Overlapping membership between the two bards is not permitted.)

In many firms the dialogue between board and management leaves a lot to be desired. Our research has revealed that a good number of boards are 'cosy clubs' where the desire for harmony is far greater than the appetite for robust questioning.[25] Unless there exists a board culture that ensures key issues are put on the table and 'thrashed out', the board's functioning is severely impaired. As an Australian chairman aptly put it, 'Our CEO should know that we love him dearly, but this does not prevent us from asking tough questions.' Another successful businessman, Henry J. Bruce, considers that 'the most valuable director of all is the one who can challenge the CEO while at the same time supporting him, a person who has mastered the difficult art of "disagreeing without being disagreeable." '[26]

Familiarity with the different parts of the organisation is of great importance to the board for a number of reasons. For example their usually vast experience means that many board members have developed such extensive 'gut reactions' that they quickly register an intuitive discomfort when they encounter a dubious situation in the organisation: they may not be immediately able to identify the reason for it, but they do know that something 'smells'.

If a board member happens to be visiting a country where an important subsidiary of the firm exists, this provides a good opportunity for him or her to obtain a first-hand impression of that subsidiary. However the board member should let the CEO know that he or she would like to pay a visit to that subsidiary. The CEO will rarely object, particularly if he or she knows that the board member will adhere to an iron-clad rule for such visits: listen carefully, but refrain from making statements. If board members fail to keep their mouths shut they soon find themselves between the millstones of the corporate centre on the one hand and the periphery on the other. Should any written exchange between the board member and the local subsidiary management result from such a visit, obviously the CEO should be given a copy.

### Boundary Systems as a Means of Control

The rapidly changing, complex world in which most family businesses work today requires employees to behave entrepreneurially. While at first sight this demand is acceptable, it is also fraught with risks. How can we make sure that these 'eager beavers' do not take the firm into too many new areas of activity, which in the end will only serve to dissipate the forces of the firm and reduce its 'punch' in the market?

As a means of preserving the positive aspects of entrepreneurship on the one hand and preventing the dissipation of forces on the other, boundary systems have turned out to be an effective tool.[27] They represent formally stated policies, rules, limits and proscriptions tied to defined sanctions and the threat of punishment. Such boundary systems allow individual creativity within defined limits of freedom. For example good pricing policies leave room for discretion and movement by management but prevent extensive, undesirable deviations.

In this context we can even come back to the concept of a vision. As indicated earlier, a vision, by describing a desired future state of the firm, defines the rules of inclusion and exclusion. Measures that are covered by the 'umbrella' of the vision are acceptable, those outside are not. A vision thus allows opportunity-seeking behaviour while at the same time setting meaningful limits to it.

There is a school of thought that believes appropriate policies might have prevented the Nick Leeson case.[28] If Barings had had tough policies on risk management and ensured their strict implementation, Nick Leeson might have thought twice about embarking on his catastrophic pursuit. As a logical follow-on, the same school of thought questions whether the majority of banks would be able to answer the following important questions:

- Are our risk management philosophies and procedures clearly codified and distributed?
- Do employee compensation policies include incentives that skew behaviour towards or away from the appetite to take risks?
- Are the sanctions for violating the controls understood and enforced?
- Do we have educational and training techniques that reinforce the corporate risk management culture?[29]

Boundaries are a subtle but rather powerful control mechanism. It seems to us that family-controlled enterprises could easily make much more use of them, and it is the task of the board to make sure that a carefully selected number of them are in place in the company. One should recognise, however, that their enforcement requires the full attention of management. Insisting on the strict enforcement of such policies may take some courage and call for some backbone.

### Beliefs Systems as a Means of Control

The last of the four spokes, the Beliefs system, is another subtle control instrument, but some observers consider it to be one of the most powerful tools around.[30]

Beliefs systems provide an explicit (or implicit) set of beliefs and convictions that represent or mirror the organisation's basic values.

The atmosphere and work ethics that beliefs systems create in a company tell members of the organisation that 'certain things are not done around here'. They set a particular tone, represent a major element of the culture of the firm, and have an ethical dimension.

Like policies, beliefs are closely related to the vision statement. When we discussed the vision statement we said that, in addition to 'strategic architecture' and big audacious goals, *the core values of a company* are one of the building blocks of a vision statement. We also stressed that the board has a particular responsibility to provide guidance when such a value system is developed.

The power of beliefs systems tends to be particularly strong at the centre of the family business. There the spirit of the founder generation may still linger on and influence codes of behaviour. As members of the organisation move away from the centre – physically and/or emotionally – the power of the belief system may start to fade away. A good example in this context is Daiwa, one of Japan's largest banks. Japanese companies, not unlike many family businesses all over the globe, are largely built on the trust that typically prevails among their managers. Yoshihide Iguchi, a trader in Daiwa's New York office, lost an incredible US$1.1 billion of his bank's money. He was able to conceal his losses for 11 years, but then all hell broke loose and he was hastily removed. In an editorial on the Daiwa scandal the *Financial Times* stated thoughtfully, 'In their home market, internal controls are buttressed by an exceptional esprit de corps which acts as an informal safety mechanism. This is hard to maintain in overseas operations.'[31]

In an essay entitled 'Values Code Gives Control', John Ward brought into sharp focus the issue of beliefs systems and their role in family-controlled enterprises: 'the real accountability of an owner-managed business is to a philosophy or a code. And the role of the inactive family shareholders is to clarify and monitor values and philosophy'.[32] There is hardly a much stronger way of expressing the need for such systems.

### If Controls Fail: Director Liability and Insurance

Matters of board liability and insurance packages to protect board members are vast and highly complex areas. In dealing with them, the owners of a family business need competent professional advice. All we can offer here are some general remarks. Privately owned and small firms often mention the threat of liability and the cost of insurance as obstacles to the creation of forceful boards of directors. In our experience this is not totally unfounded; a towering Swiss entrepreneur who controls a large, internationally active group of firms told us that he is leaving a number of boards (outside his group) because his 'deep pockets' may make him the preferred target of liability lawsuits.

One case where a family-dominated board clearly fell down on their job of controlling is the Guinness saga, which filled the pages of the press in the UK and elsewhere a few years ago. During a major takeover battle the top management of Guinness was caught in a massive share-price manipulation. The board did not prevent this activity – for all sorts of reasons. The Guinness family members on the board of the company were lucky not to be drawn more deeply into the trial of their (non-family) CEO, Ernest Saunders, who was eventually found guilty and sent to prison. The box overleaf is a thumbnail sketch of the story.

The issue of directors' liability has clearly moved to the fore in recent years, even outside the United States, where such lawsuits have been common for quite some time. In the Scandinavian countries, for instance, several law suits against board members are pending, clearly a novel situation for that region. In Germany a public discussion is going on about making it easier for shareholders and other parties to sue board members. Even in Japan, where shareholders have been extraordinarily docile in the past, certain shareholder groups are considering suing their boards.

To sum up: in the future it will be more risky to join a board, regardless of the legal framework under which the company is operating.

The question of director liability must be part of the discussion a family has with those invited to join their board. One way of making that liability more palatable to potential board members would be for the company to insure them against any liability that could be attached to them with respect to any negligence, default, breach of duty or breach of trust of which they may be accused in relation to the company. The extent to which the company would be willing to provide such insurance cover should be made part of the preparatory discussions with a potential board member. Family-controlled businesses are often poorly informed about such insurance; as the matter is complex, they should seek the advice of specialists before reaching a conclusion.

Some interesting facts on insurance for board members have been unearthed by John Ward and James Handy in a survey of 147 privately controlled US companies.[33] Only about one third of the companies surveyed had purchased liability insurance for their directors and officers, although about two thirds of the larger firms in the sample (those with more than 499 employees) were insured. The most common protection was corporate indemnification. Such indemnification promises directors

## Where was the Board?

After joining Guinness as chief executive and board member in 1981, Ernest Saunders successfully turned the troubled family business into an efficient commercial organisation. When Saunders arrived at Guinness the family held the majority of board seats but only 25 per cent of the shares (a percentage that has since reduced further). He quickly decided to dispose of many of the acquisitions the company had made, often under the influence of the family, and started the process of easing out the Guinness family: some retired, some remained on the board. By 1985 Guinness had nearly tripled its earnings and the firm's market capitalisation had grown by a factor of six. Saunders was acclaimed by the family, the company and the media. He was considered to be one of the most successful managers in the UK.

In 1986, however, a scandal arose following the takeover by Guinness of Distillers in what was described as the dirtiest bid in British corporate history. Guinness, the world's most profitable beverage producer, and some of its directors and advisers were accused of illegal share-price maintenance. Clandestine activities boosted the bidder's market price to encourage Distillers' shareholders to accept the takeover. In 1990, after a 107-day trial, Saunders and three codefendants were found guilty of multiple charges of theft, conspiracy, false accounting and breaches of the Companies Acts. How could such a nightmare happen?

Saunders had massive power over the company and reported only to the chairman, Lord Iveagh, a Guinness family member who spent most of his time with his horses in Ireland. His attendance at board meetings was rare and the chairmanship suffered for decades. Other family members, together with shareholders, praised Saunders, who had boosted the value of their shares. It seemed that Saunders could do no wrong.

Before and during the Distillers takeover bid, Saunders handled all the discussions and negotiations. The board was informed of the proposed bid only one day before the official announcement was released, and this was the first that some members had heard of the offer. An executive director noted, 'The non-executives could have said no, but there was great pressure on them not to.' The full Guinness board met three times during the bid process so that Saunders could keep the members informed.

After the takeover Saunders was made chairman and CEO of Guinness, a decision endorsed by an overwhelming majority of the shareholders voting at an extraordinary general meeting. In the eyes of many, Saunders was a hero. 'When you have done very well as a shareholder, you tend to be uncritical', explained a board member.

Later, when an investigation revealed that Saunders had personally arranged for Guinness to give illegal financial support to its own shares during the bid (a $100 million payment to a third party), a family member remarked, 'The board could also have known about the $100 million payment if they had bothered to read their board paper: the details of the payment were buried in the small print of a board document.'

Norman Macfarlane was subsequently appointed to head the company, and thereafter finished the process of removing Guinness family members from the board.

that the company will pay all legal costs if they are named in a work-related lawsuit. Between 20 and 25 per cent of the firms had shareholder indemnification, whereby shareholders (not the firm) promise to pay that cost. Ward and Handy speculate that this special form of protection might be considered more often in the future by family businesses with several shareholders.

Ward and Handy's study also shed some light on the cost of such insurance. It showed that the average cost of insurance in medium-sized firms was about US$25000. This means that insurance costs about the same as board salaries. In other words, insuring a board roughly doubles the cost of having a board. (The cost of insurance among the larger firms in the study was distinctly higher, probably because the shares of several of them were traded on the stock exchange.)

To give companies a better perspective of the weight of these expenses, Ward and Handy suggest an interesting comparison: 'Perhaps the best way of justifying the perceived cost of a board is to say that on the basis of our survey, for instance companies that had insurance, the total cost of having a board was between US$20 and US$25 per employee – probably much less than 0.1 per cent of the company's payroll.'[34] While this sounds reasonable, one should realise that fewer and fewer insurance companies are willing to offer such policies, and the cost of such protection seems to be going up. One of the reasons for the latter seems to be that in some countries more and more courts are inclined to side with the underdog –

presumably the shareholder – particularly if the judge learns that the sued board member is insured (by so doing, the courts drive up the insurance premiums).


## A BRIEF WORD ABOUT REPORTING/ACCOUNTING FOR

When we defined corporate governance, we mentioned that the controlling aspect of governance can also be seen as embracing the task of reporting to parties with a legitimate interest in the firm. A brief word on this board task is therefore in order here.

In a publicly owned company the board has primary responsibility for the accounts of the company (the responsibility of the public accountants for the accounts is only secondary to that of the board). In addition, it is quite clearly set out in various national legal frameworks what reports the board has to furnish to parties with a legitimate interest in the accounts.

The case of a privately owned business is somewhat more complex. Co-owning family members – including inactive ones – are entitled to specific pieces of information that are usually prescribed and periodically disseminated, typically annually. As long as the family is small, throughout the year a large amount information is informally disseminated over the dinner table, so to speak.

When the family becomes larger, for example when it turns into a cousins' confederation, the situation usually becomes more complicated. As soon as family companies have a hundred or more shareholders, for instance, they increasingly resemble a publicly held company, and many of the reporting practices used in public companies are typically applied.

There is, however, an additional aspect that requires particular attention in family businesses. Experience shows that one of the central issues in family-controlled enterprises is perceived fairness *vis-à-vis* all family members. 'At the heart of the management relationships in a family firm lies the concept of fairness', writes Sir Adrian Cadbury. 'Divisions and ructions within the family can be caused only too easily through the suspicion that some family members are benefiting at the expense of others, or that the contribution which some are making to the firm is not being properly recognised.'[35] Related to this phenomenon is the complaint, frequently voiced by non-active family members, that those who are involved in running the business are well informed while remote family members are kept in the dark on the developments in the firm.

One means of counteracting these complaints is to ensure sufficient transparency of the dealings of the business, in particular the dealings of individual family members. A well-designed approach to regular reporting on a broad basis can help here. As well as receiving the annual financial statements, the owners should be kept regularly informed about all important developments in the firm. Family assembly meetings provide a good venue for this to happen. The range of issues discussed there can be rather broad. In our experience, the one subject that always gets the special attention of the family – particularly those whose stocks are not publicly traded – is a regular investment bank report on the development of the overall value of the business, calculated on the basis of the methodology investment banks typically use to assess the value of companies (in merger and acquisition cases for instance). While the validity of the evaluation may be disputed, the trend over time usually gives a good idea of whether or not the family fortune locked up in the business is increasing.

In the context of providing transparency, the family council can play a significant role here. Not only are its members the spokespeople of the family *vis-à-vis* the management and the board (and as such a natural channel of communication), they can also keep the family informed about the goings on in the business through regularly disseminated written communications, in the form of a bulletin for instance. Of course the less active family members must be willing to study this information carefully. They simply cannot have it both ways: demanding to be thoroughly informed while at the same time being unwilling to make the necessary effort to assimilate the information provided to them (we return to this theme in the Epilogue).

Transparency *vis-à-vis* the outside is something that family businesses have even greater difficulty accepting, although this is probably unwise. An interesting case of proactive transparency with regard to the public occurred recently. Campari, a 137-year-old, family-controlled company, publicised its annual accounts without being obliged to do so (see box below). The family obviously felt that the long-term advantages of doing this outweighed the disadvantages.

## CONCLUSION

'Trust is good, control is better.' One does not have to adhere fully to the attitude that seems to underlie this statement (which is attributed to Lenin) to insist on good control systems even in a family enterprise. In this chapter we have sketched a comprehensive but rather subtle system of controls that seem suited to this purpose.

---

**Campari's Accounts Published**

'Campari, the Italian family-controlled drinks group, yesterday broke 137 years of silence on its financial affairs by publishing its annual accounts and reporting first quarter results.

It stressed the move did not imply the company was about to seek stock market listing, although it would not rule that out in the longer term.

According to Mr. Marco Perelli-Cippo, chief executive, the move reflected Campari's efforts to adapt to the financial market demands for transparency.

He acknowledged, however, that the decision was made easier by the company's encouraging results last year and even stronger performance in the first quarter this year.

Although the net revenue fell from L670.5bn in 1995 to L592.8bn ($349m) last year, net income rose from L53.2bn to L123.3bn.

Last year the company also had a positive cash flow of L224.1bn and a net positive financial position of L74.4bn, compared with negative cash flow of L347.3bn and a negative financial position of L153.1bn in the previous year.

In the first quarter of this year, operating income rose 158 per cent to L28bn, while net revenues climbed 18.6 per cent to L158bn.'

(Paul Betts, 'Campari Publishes Accounts for the First Time', *Financial Times*, 18 June 1997.)

---

We have also touched on the role and significance of regular reporting, in particular to the family. The role of comprehensive reporting should not be underestimated in a family business. This is not a new insight. Luca Pacioli (c. 1445–1517), the Italian monk who is credited with having written the first treatise on double-entry accounting, says in his *Particularis de Computis et Scripturis* (1494), 'As the proverb says: "Frequent accounting makes for lasting friendship."'

## NOTES

1. Subsequently confirmed as £860 million.
2. S. Hamilton, 'The Collapse of Barings Bank', IMD Case Study, 1995, p. 1. With the permission of the author, this section draws heavily on the work he has done in this area.

3. J. Gapper, 'NatWest bank suspends four over option losses', *Financial Times*, 14 March 1997.

4. J. Gapper, N. Denton and R. Taylor, 'Deutsche Bank admits to failure of controls', *Financial Times*, 6 September 1996.

5. The Futures and Options Association, *Managing Derivatives Risks – Guidelines for end-users of derivatives*, December 1995, p. 7.

6. *Evidence to the House of Commons Treasury Committee*, Minutes of Evidence, 10 June 1996, p. 42.

7. The Futures and Options Association, *Managing Derivatives Risks*, op. cit., p. 9.

8. *Guardian*, 27 September 1995.

9. C. M. Seeger, 'How to Prevent Future Nick Leesons', *Wall Street Journal*, 7 July 1995.

10. S. Hamilton, 'The Collapse of Barings', op. cit., p. 5.

11. Ibid., p. 6.

12. 'Rogue control', *Financial Times*, 20 March 1997, p. 17.

13. *Board of Banking Supervision: Report of the Board of Banking Supervision Inquiry into the Circumstances of the Collapse of Barings*, London: HMSO, 18 July 1995, p. 7.

14. J. Gapper, N. Denton and R. Taylor, 'Deutsche Bank admits to failure of controls', *Financial Times*, 6 September 1996.

15. *Board of Banking Supervision: Report on Barings*, op cit., p. 121.

16. D. Davies, 'Remuneration and risk', *Bank of England Financial Stability Review*, Spring 1997, pp. 18–22.

17. H. Parker, *Letters to a new Chairman*, London: Director Publications, 1990.

18. We thank our colleague Stewart Hamilton for this valuable suggestion.

19. R. Simons, *Levers of Control*, Boston: Harvard Business School Press, 1995.

20. Ibid., p. 7.

21. For more information on Analytical Control Systems, see ibid., pp. 59–90.

22. B. Garrat, *The Fish Rots From the Top*, London: Harper Collins Business, 1996, pp. 108–10.

23. For more information on Interactive Control Systems, see Simons, *Levers of Control*, op. cit., pp. 91–124.

24. P. Frerk, 'Praktische Gedanken zur Optimierung der Kontrollfunktion des Aufsichtsrates', *Die Aktiengesellschaft*, 1 May 1995, p. 213.

25. A. Demb and F. F. Neubauer, *The Corporate Board,* New York: Oxford University Press, 1992, pp. 131–58.

26. H. J. Bruce, 'Duty, honour, company', *Directors & Boards*, Winter 1997, p. 14.

27. For additional information on boundary systems, see Simons, *Levers of Control*, op. cit., pp. 39–58.

28. *Wall Street Journal*, 21 July 1995.

29. Ibid.

30. For this control tool, see also: Simons, *Levers of Control,* op. cit., pp. 33–58.

31. *Financial Times*, 27 September 1995.

32. *The Family Advisor*, vol. IV, issue 11 (November 1995), p. 5.

33. J. L. Ward and J. L. Handy, 'A Surrey of Board Practices', in C. E. Arnoff, J. H. Astrachan and J. L. Ward (eds), *Family Sourcebook II,* Marietta, Georgia: Business Owner Resources, 1996, p. 265.
34. Ibid., p. 265.
35. A. Cadbury, 'The role of directors in family firms', in *The Director's Manual,* edited by Bernard Taylor and R. I. Tricker, Hemel Hempstead: Director Books, D3, p. 11.

# Part VI
# Putting Governance Insights into Practical Use

## INTRODUCTION

In Chapter 10 we show the reader how to put to work all the concepts and tools studied so far and to develop a corporate governance structure for his or her business.

Finally, the Epilogue looks at what it means to be a responsible and enlightened owner of a family business – particularly one that has existed for several generations and some of whose members want it to be kept in the family for at least the next generation.

# 10 Putting it All to Work: Creating a Governance Structure for a Family Business

Hell begins on the day when God grants us a clear vision of all that we might have achieved, of all the gifts which we have wasted, of all we might have done which we did not do

> (Gian-Carlo Menotti, contemporary Italian composer).

A practitioner is typically looking for a step-by-step process when he or she is asked to apply a conceptual scheme in his or her firm. The same is true of applying a corporate governance scheme in a family business. It is the aim of this chapter to provide such a process.

Before we start, it is appropriate to utter a word or two of caution. First, this process will not produce pat answers to all the firm's governance problems; this would not even be desirable. Rather it provides a platform for a systematic and reasoned argument on the different governance issues, allowing participants to combine the insights offered in this book with their own experience and knowledge base in order to come up with the solution that best suits their company. After all, we believe in the words of the philosopher Martin Buber (1878–1965) 'I have no doctrine, but I lead a conversation.'

Second, rigidly structuring and formalising such a complex process would rob the exercise of its creativity and thus should be avoided. One of the ways to achieve this aim is to perceive the process as a guide to stimulating and focusing the thinking of the 'architect' of the corporate governance system. Every person embarking on our suggested process is therefore invited to modify it as he or she sees fit. Expand it where there is a need for more depth, and drop the parts that do not seem to be relevant at a particular point in time. It should also be realised that the process is never finished; just as a lobster has to replace its shell regularly in order to accommodate its growth, the constitution of a family business has to change as the company evolves.

One thing is critical throughout this voyage: the leaders of the process must be able to nurture the sense that such an undertaking is relevant, particularly in this day and age when corporate governance is one of the key topics of the business world. Creating a governance system involves hard work and persistence. This significant investment in time and emotions is only justified if the outcome helps the family and the top organisation of the firm – the board and top management – to improve the steering and controlling of their enterprise. Family businesses have neither the time nor the means for a *l'art pour l'art* effort.

## SOME ASSUMPTIONS

To keep the task manageable it is necessary to make a few assumptions. (If these assumptions do not correspond with the situation in your business, the scheme can be modified to fit the specific circumstances to which it is to be applied. This is relatively easy to do, as we shall see).

To demonstrate the process, let us create a fictitious company that wants to establish a governance system for itself. For this company a number of assumptions probably hold true.

First, we shall assume (as we have throughout most of this book) that the company in question is a 'cousins' confederation', that is, a relatively large number of family shareholders control the company and the family is split into two or more branches.

Second, in this book so far we have described firms with what we consider to be a classical governance structure. In contrast our fictitious company has no formalised governance system, not even a board of directors. Starting from scratch will give us the freedom to create the most appropriate corporate governance structure for the company in question.

Finally, we assume that the owning family want to be on top of the process (and even spearhead it), even if for practical reasons the 'legwork' may have to be farmed out to small. specifically appointed task forces. A governance system deserving that name cannot be bought ready-made in the market place. It has to fit and reflect the 'personality' of the firm and the family involved. This is not to say that the family and the task forces could not benefit from carefully selected outside help (for instance from external process specialists). These outsiders must, however, be teamed up with high-calibre insiders. Otherwise there is a great danger that the end result will be a 'canned' solution to the problems at hand.

## THE PARTICIPANTS IN THE PROCESS AND THEIR INTERACTION

Typically, several groups of participants are involved in such a process:

- The family (in their role as owners), whose interest in improving the ways and means of steering and controlling the firm is obvious.
- Representatives of the top management of the company, be they family members (this time wearing their managerial hat) or outsiders. They have to carry out a good proportion of the practical steering and controlling.
- Possibly, process consultants.

The role of the family is to initiate and monitor the process and to stamp their imprint on the key outcomes of the deliberations, turning them into 'the law of the land'. At the cousins' confederation stage the family is probably too large to drive the process directly, so they may appoint a small task force (five to seven members) which, in addition to the owners (perhaps through the family council), will typically also include representatives from the upper management echelon of the firm. For all practical purposes, this small group will have to serve as the driving force behind the process. They will explore the issues in depth and make suggestions to the family on how tackle them within a custom-tailored governance system. (The role of outside facilitators is to keep the process on track, to contribute the experiences they may have gained when applying the process in other firms and to play the devil's advocate in the discussions.)

## STAGES OF THE PROCESS

As shown in Figure 10.1, there are typically two stages to the process. At the beginning of the first stage the family members recognise the need for a formal governance system and initiate the process of creating one. The next move is to appoint a corporate governance task force. This working party will prepare suggestions on a formal, integrated, overall governance structure and the contours of its key components. These suggestions will be discussed (and probably modified) by the family and adopted formally. Thus at the end of stage 1 there exists a blueprint of the overall governance structure.

An overall idea of the desired governance structure is an important starting point. The existence of a blueprint can be helpful to the family

238

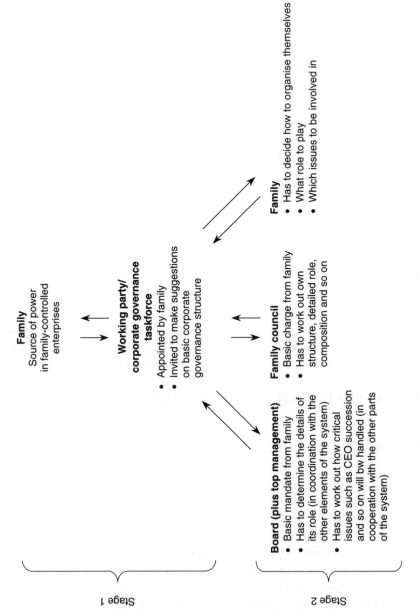

**Family**
Source of power
in family-controlled
enterprises

**Working party/
corporate governance
taskforce**
- Appointed by family
- Invited to make suggestions
  on basic corporate
  governance structure

**Family council**
- Basic charge from family
- Has to work out own
  structure, detailed role,
  composition and so on

**Board (plus top management)**
- Basic mandate from family
- Has to determine the details of
  its role (in coordination with the
  other elements of the system)
- Has to work out how critical
  issues such as CEO succession
  and so on will bw handled (in
  cooperation with the other parts
  of the system)

**Family**
- Has to decide how to organise themselves
- What role to play
- Which issues to be involved in

Stage 1

Stage 2

**Figure 10.1**  Stages in building a governance structure

when setting priorities and answering questions at the second stage, such as what form should the family council take and what type of board do we really want?

This blueprint also allows the work to be spread among more people than those comprising the original task force. To give an example, if in Stage 1 of the discussion the family decides to create a family council and elects a number of family members to it, that small group can take on the development of this component of the governance system. It can design in detail the role and functioning of the new family council, thus freeing the original task force to concentrate on other aspects of the system. (The family assembly typically would have to approve the resulting provisions concerning the family council.)

The lower part of Figure 10.1 shows the elements of a classical governance system in a family business and thus the main options for creating such specialised task forces. The figure obviously assumes for the time being that the overall governance system developed in Stage 1 of the process is similar to that described in the preceding chapter of this book (that is, it will consist of a family assembly, a family council and a board of directors). If this is the case, in addition to having a task force on the family council, there will also be one working on the role, composition and working style of the contemplated board of directors. The original task force will concentrate on how to organise the family proper. For example, should there be a formal family assembly? How should it be organised? What decisions should it reserve for itself?

Let us now look at a practical way of carrying out the work in stages 1 and 2.

**Stage One: Determining the Overall Governance Structure**

Dissatisfaction with the decision-making process in the family, internal friction due to the absence of sophisticated conflict-resolution mechanisms, failure of the family business to handle legitimacy issues in the public arena, sagging economic fortunes – these and similar features usually trigger the process of creating or revamping the governance structure of a family business. In our experience it is usually one of the more active family members who gets the ball rolling. In the case of the Bergman AB family business (where the two authors were invited to help generate an overall governance system), it was the family CEO who took the initiative. The initiator could also be a family member without an official role in the firm, such as a senior family member with a certain standing in the family.

Let us assume that the family is convinced of the value of such an effort. As the next move, the family – as the source of power in the family-controlled enterprise – will create a task force to work out a blueprint of an overall governance system. The group should consist of about five to seven members. The group should be small enough to allow for fruitful work within the group, but large enough to remain functioning when one or two members are unable to attend a meeting. To give the group the necessary clout, it would be prudent to include widely respected family members (with or without an official role in the firm), and one or two key members of the top management or board.

The *modus operandi* of the task force when creating the blueprint of the overall governance system is shown in Figure 10.2. This process was originally developed by the IMD faculty for work with various boards. It has been thoroughly tested in a number of board retreats, and each time it has produced very meaningful results.

We will use this *modus operandi* not only when preparing suggestions to the family with respect to the overall governance system (stage 1 in Figure

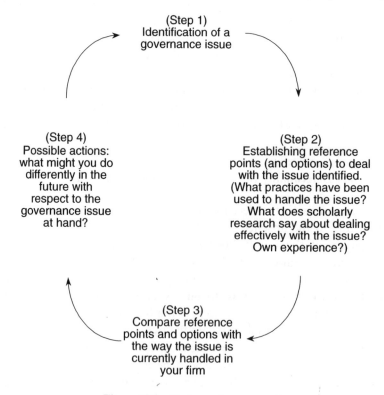

**Figure 10.2**  Basic modus operandi

10.1), but also when investigating what should be done to flesh out the individual components of the system (stage 2 of Figure 10.1).

As shown in Figure 10.2, each round of the process involves four steps. In step 1 the governance issue is identified and formulated. In our case the issues are obvious: how should we structure our overall governance system, and what type of a family constitution do we want? The issue can usually be sharpened by the task force; this typically happens in close cooperation with the family. In the case of the Bergman family enterprise, the final formulation of the issue read as follows: 'The issue at hand is to create a governance system which would preserve the particular culture and values of the corporation, as well as of the influence of the founding family, while at the same time ensuring that the businesses of the group remain forceful entities in their chosen industries.'

To help answer the two questions asked above, the task force will investigate best practices in other companies that can serve as benchmarks (step 2 in Figure 10.2). In establishing these reference points, the various chapters of this book can serve as a good starting point as they provide an overview of the situation in particular areas. If the task force requires more input they can turn to the growing body of family business research and the associated literature. Another source of input could be visits to other family-controlled companies with more experience in the area. In addition the task force could draw on their own experience in other family business settings.

Obviously, numerous options on the configuration of the overall governance system are open to the task force, ranging from a complete (classical) governance structure to simpler solutions where only one or two of the components of the classical structure are used. To allow for a more comprehensive treatment of the process in this chapter, we shall concentrate on the classical solution, but a few remarks will be made on simpler solutions.

As the task force will have to offer the family well-reasoned arguments to support their suggestions, they will have to weigh up the pros and cons of the different components of the proposed governance system and determine how they interact. The following are some of the questions they may want to ask themselves:

- Is there a need to organise the family in order to counter the danger of an erosion of the relationship between the family and its business? As the number of generations grows, this risk increases, threatening the very essence of the family business.

- Has the time come to offer some education in family business matters to the upcoming generation?
- How do we build trust between the members of the extended family, who may not know each other well?
- Does the younger generation know what it means to be a responsible owner in the broad sense?
- How does the company nurture that sense of responsibility? One frequently used approach to deal with these issues is the creation of a formal family assembly.
- What is the experience of other companies in this respect?

One family that has carefully cultivated the relationship between family shareholders are the owners of the German Röchling Group, as the following mini-case shows.

If the family is widely dispersed geographically, and it is therefore not easy to bring them together for family assembly meetings, the task force might consider creating a family council to serve as a bridge between the family and the business throughout the year. If the task force can put together an idea of what the concrete role of the council will be, this will help to sell the idea to the family later on.

One issue the task force cannot avoid addressing is the question of whether or not the company ought to have a board. In order to come to a decision the task force may ask representatives of family businesses that have differing experiences with boards for help with ideas.

Another important question the task force will have to ask itself is what the relationship between the different components of the governance system under consideration might be. How do others relate them to each other? What does the pertinent research in this area say?

At the end of step 2 of the *modus operandi* the task force will prepare a first sketch of the governance blueprint.

In step 3, the task force will compare the results of step 2 with the way the company has so far handled the question of governance. What elements of a governance system are already in place? What is the firm's experience with them? The aim of this step is twofold: it will provide an idea of the gap between the best practices elsewhere and the practices in the company; and it will provide an indication of the amount of effort needed to install a comprehensive, state-of-the-art corporate governance system in the company. If the gap is large, will the family be willing to put in the effort required? Should the company opt for a governance structure that is somewhat simpler than the classical model?

## An Enmeshed Family[1]

The German Röchling Group, founded as a coal trading company in 1822, is owned by a family that tries to work together in close collaboration. Soon after the founding of the firm, the family broadened their interests and played a significant role in the development of the German iron and steel industry. Unlike Thyssen and Mannesman, which originated in the Ruhr area, the Röchling group was based in the Saar, near the German–French border. Röchling became a major political factor when the Saar was claimed by the French after the Second World War. In a plebiscite forty years ago the Saar decided to stay with Germany, and as a consequence the Röchlings regained their property (which had been confiscated).

In the ensuing decades the family changed its fields of interest and its organisational structure was built around two holding companies. The first, KG Gebr. Röchling, controls 81 companies in 16 countries and has sales of US$1.5 billion. The second, Röchling Industrie Verwaltung GmbH (RIV), controls 126 companies in 18 countries and has sales of US$2.2 billion.

The family that controls both groups has 187 members. The head of the family, Wigand Freiherr von Salmuth, sees it as one of his main tasks to bind the family together and prevent a break between the family and the group of firms. To promote this idea the family has created 'meetings for the youth' (*Jugendtagung*), a once a year get-together where the younger-generation Röchlings (18–30 years old), with the help of outside speakers, discuss economic and business issues. Another purpose of the meetings is to give them the opportunity to get to know each other well. Von Salmuth insists that it is vital that they know and trust each other. According to him, there is a need for a strong consensus in the family about strategic direction and the speed at which they should move forward.

This discussion leads to step 4 of the *modus operandi*: what might be done differently in the future with respect to the overall governance structure? In this phase, the task force will present the blueprint to the family. The proposition should be reasonably brief, but the family must be able to understand the salient features of the proposed system, its components and how they interact. Brevity is necessary for two reasons. First, in order to keep interest in the process alive, the results have to be presented relatively soon after the process has been launched; and therefore the task force will not have sufficient time to produce a lengthy document. Second, the family's reastion to the task force's proposition should be obtained before too much time, effort and money are invested.

In order to add clout to their presentation, the task force may invite a representative of one of the benchmark companies to address the family. A thorough discussion ought to follow and the original proposal may well have to be modified.

Stage 4 of the *modus operandi* (Figure 10.2) coincides with the end of stage 1 of the process of building an overall corporate governance system (Figure 10.1). The resulting blueprint is fleshed out during stage 2 of the process.

### Stage Two: Fleshing out the Blueprint

It is conceivable that, at the end of stage 1, quite a number of the proposed components of the family business constitution and individual governance issues will require further investigation. It is important to avoid hectic activism, with a considerable number of task forces working away at numerous problems, so at this point the family should establish a set of priorities. Which of the components of the system are to be fleshed out first? Should the family decide that the family council takes priority, the first job is to appoint a task force to look into the matter, applying exactly the same *modus operandi* as was used when working out the overall blueprint (Figure 10.2). The same applies to organising the family itself more tightly, for instance by instituting a family assembly, but an additional word or two is justified with respect to the creation of a board of directors.

As we have stressed throughout the book, the board typically plays a pivotal role in the corporate governance of a corporation. If the family decides to have a board, particular care should be taken by the family when formulating the mandate of the board, determining its composition, and to working out the relationship between the board and the other parts of the corporate governance system (for example the family). Once the board has been constituted the members have a say in what their future roles will be, and hence a degree of give and take is necessary at this stage.

Special attention has to be given to ensuring that the key governance tasks discussed in Chapters 6, 7, 8 and 9 will be properly addressed, namely:

- Securing CEO succession.
- Creating a vision and a strategy for the enterprise.
- Securing financial resources.
- Ensuring effective and efficient control and accountability.

These tasks are usually spearheaded by the board; but because their overriding significance for the steering and controlling of the enterprise the details should be hammered out between the board and the family in close cooperation. Here again, what has been said in previous chapters of this book on the board and the key governance tasks can serve as a starting point for the discussion.

There is a great danger of being overwhelmed by the number of governance issues to be dealt with, so here again priorities may have to be set by the family and the board. For instance if a new CEO has been appointed and seems to be working out well, there may not be a pressing need to develop an elaborate scheme to secure an appropriate CEO succession (see Chapter 6). Therefore, a more burning issue can be moved up the priority list and the question of succession postponed. As the owners and top management gain experience with the process, the work will become easier and the quality of the output will increase. Aristotle put it well when he said, 'Excellence is an art won by training and habituation. We do not act rightly because we have virtue or excellence, but we rather have those because we have acted rightly. We are what we repeatedly do. Excellence, then, is not an act, but a habit.'

## CONCLUSION

This chapter has outlined a process of developing a governance structure for a family business. It is based on simple logic and has been used successfully in many well-known international companies, both family and non-family. Strengthening the vitality of a family business by creating a meaningful family constitution is a demand of the times. Missing the opportunity to take such a step at the appropriate time may later lead to regrets. Remember the words by Gian-Carlo Menotti at the beginning of this chapter: 'Hell begins on the day when God grants us a clear vision of all that we might . . . have done which we did not do', words that relate well to improving the steering and controlling of a family business at the highest level.


NOTE

1.  This mini-case is taken from F. F. Neubauer and A. G. Lank, 'Appraising and redesigning a governance system for a family business', *The Director's Manual–Supplement 8*, September 1996, p. B12/10.

# Epilogue: Enlightened Ownership of Family Enterprises

> Riches are a good handmaid, but the worst mistress.
>
> (Francis Bacon, 1560–1626)

By now the reader will be aware that both authors are enthusiastic supporters of family enterprises and the role they play in society. This does not mean, however, that we are unaware of their weaknesses – and particularly their poor longevity record, which is in part due to the complexity of managing succession and designing an appropriate governance structure.

Of course the nature of the ownership challenge varies according to the stage of development of the family enterprise. In Stage 1 ('the founder', see Table 2.2) it is assumed that most if not all the shares are in the hands of the owner and that there is no separation of ownership and management. Total control is exercised by the person at the top, who is often the patriarch of the family. This is the typical situation in the founder's generation or where a Stage 2 or Stage 3 company has circled back to Stage 1. Generic ownership challenges at this stage are relatively minor.

If a family firm makes it to Stage 2 ('sibling partnership'), unitary management and ownership control, by definition, no longer exist. The siblings may or may not have an equal number of shares, may or may not be active in the business on a day-to-day basis, may or may not sit on the board of directors. In terms of the 'three circle and tie model' explained in Chapter 1, there not only are more people involved, but also the risk of conflict between the family members increases, simply because their role-based perceptions may be quite different. For example the non-active sibling owner may have views on dividends and remuneration (including perks) that differ from those of his or her brothers and sisters who work in the business and sit on the board of directors.

In the rare instances when the firm makes it to Stage 3 ('cousins' confederation'), the inherent problems of Stage 2 are compounded, especially if there has been no pruning of the family tree. Thus it is not uncommon – particularly in families that have reached the fourth, fifth or later generations since the founding of the enterprise – for literally hundreds of family shareholders to own a very large company. At the annual shareholders' meeting, name tags are *de rigeur* because many are strangers to each other. In all probability only a handful (if any) of the family will be active in the business or sit on the board of directors. Each family shareholder may hold only a tiny fraction of the shares and may feel distant from the enterprise and its objectives. Pressure may, and often does, start to develop to increase the liquidity of the shares or maximise dividend payouts. Centrifugal forces may be almost impossible to thwart, and the sense of family cohesion and identity may start to disintegrate. Conflict cycles may start to emerge, changing what might have been an unusually healthy family into a highly dysfunctional one.

There is nothing inherently bad or wrong in the evolving scenario described above. In fact it is a very probable evolution *unless* there is a manifest desire to take action to keep the family together and retain ownership of the firm. One family that became deeply concerned about the dangers inherent in Stage 3 were the Bergmans of Bergman AB, cited a number of times in this book. The CEO and chairman of the family council (both fourth-generation members of the family) approached the two authors to discuss what, if anything, could be done to keep the 200-plus family shareholders interested in the company (just two of the shareholders were active in the firm). The result was a modular educational programme that came to be called 'The Bergman Family Business Workshop'.[1] The workshop had three objectives:

- To acquaint the participants with the special characteristics of family firms in their global context, thereby allowing benchmarking for the Bergman family and its enterprise.
- To familiarise the participants with the particularities, strengths and weaknesses of Bergman AB, as well as possible threats and opportunities.
- To generate constructive ideas about how the family could best interact with Bergman AB, thereby enhancing its developmental potential.

The workshop faculty comprised the two authors, the CEO, the chairman of the family council, the chairman of the board (also a family member) and senior non-family executives from Bergman AB. Almost all the participants were from the fifth generation. Their subsequent evaluation of the workshop was extremely positive and they confirmed that the three objectives had largely been achieved. In particular, all the participants had strengthened their resolve to keep Bergman AB totally family-controlled and had defined for him- or herself what had to be done to ensure that he or she became an 'enlightened shareholder' working in the best interests of the family and its enterprise.

For the authors, too, it was a highly educational experience that prompted the following reflections. Let us assume that a family enterprise is in Stage 3 (cousins' confederation) and in at least the third generation. Let us also assume that all the shares are held by the family and that no single person holds more than 3 per cent of the equity. In addition, very few of the family work in the firm, although the board of directors mainly consists of family members. The company has sales of well over a billion dollars, is profitable, has several thousand employees, and operates world-wide. Lastly, let us assume that certain centrifugal forces are starting to become manifest, but that key members of the family wish control of the firm to stay in family hands and want the family to remain relatively cohesive. (These assumptions reflect the reality of the Bergman family and its enterprise.) We then ask ourselves, 'What would characterise 'enlightened ownership' in such a situation to enhance the chance of family cohesion and family control continuing into future generations?' Accordingly, we shall now discuss the ten descriptors of 'enlightened or responsible ownership' that our study of various Stage 3 companies has suggested to us.

## APPROPRIATE FAMILY INSTITUTIONS

This book has described various institutions or organs that can play a role in governance, both of the family and its enterprise. Each family must determine the kinds of institutions needed, depending on the value system laid down in the written family constitution, or whatever name is given to the family statement(s). By the time a family enterprise has reached Stage 3, enlightened ownership will necessitate a family assembly, a family council and a family shareholders' committee, at the very least. Additional bodies, such as Bergman AB's family review committee, may also be desirable.

While family institutions play different roles, they are all vital to creating a sense of involvement within the family and between it and its enterprise and as forums for discussion and decision making for the family as a whole or subsets thereof. It is through these bodies that the family's values are made explicit and communicated not only to the family but to the board of directors and top management of the enterprise. But this is not a one-way street. These same bodies are forums at which the board of directors and top management can report to the family on their stewardship of the family's firm.

Quite apart from their role in the interface between the owning family and the enterprise, family institutions, especially the family assembly and family council, are critical in providing the opportunity for family members to socialise simply as members of the same family irrespective of their joint ownership of the business. While these get-togethers provide no guarantee of cohesion, it is hard to imagine that the extended family would remain close-knit without them. As many enmeshed families have discovered, using the existing institutions for 'fun' (as well as business) purposes can bring huge benefits. The meal following the formal family assembly or family council meeting, and the recreational activities held at the family compound or estate can be a much welcomed bridge-builder between family members. Both provide the chance for them to become acquainted at the personal level thereby transcending the purely owner-ship link between them.

## CLEAR DEMARCATION OF ROLES

Just as it is imperative that the roles of each of the family institutions be made clear, so must their roles be clearly differentiated from the roles of the board of directors and top management. As noted in Chapter 4, the Bergman family's 'Values and Policies' statement attempts to do exactly this. After indicating the jobs of the family assembly, family council and family review committee, the statement sets the general boundaries by stating 'that it is the authority and responsibility of the Board and the company management to handle business and company matters while family matters are handled by the family'. Clearly included in 'family matters' is the family's role as owner. Thus guiding parameters are set up for the board and top management, particularly in connection with certain 'financial criteria', including:

- Return on equity targets.
- The need to build up capital.
- Dividend pay-out targets.
- Amount of leverage.
- Portfolio balance.

The statement then specifies the role of the holding/parent company and its board.[2] Certain criteria relating to board membership (for example the 'family shall have the voting majority in the board') are then made explicit. Importantly, the family makes clear the part it will play in the critical strategic decision about CEO succession: 'The CEO of the Holding/Parent company shall be appointed by the Board of Directors after consultation with the Family Council. It is the Chairman of the Board who leads the nomination process of the CEO, but other Board members can also initiate the process if the Chairman does not move or act.'

Whether or not one agrees with the way the Bergman family as owners has delineated the roles of family institutions and those of the board of directors/top management is not the issue. For us, the fact that there has been an honest attempt to do so points to enlightened ownership. The costs of not doing so can be exorbitantly high, including constant bickering between the family and the board of directors/top management. Furthermore, unless the demarcation lines are clear it is extremely difficult, if not impossible, to attract the high-quality, independent board members the authors believe are necessary if the governance role of the board is to be done efficiently and effectively.

## KEEPING INFORMED

There is no enlightened ownership unless the family keeps itself up to date on the progress and strategy of the business. How else can the owners vote responsibly (at the annual general meeting) on matters that, by law or custom, must be approved by the shareholders? How else can they pass judgement on the board's and the CEO's performance, not only in business terms but also in terms of whether or not the family's values are being respected as the board and top management go about their governance tasks?

This information requirement, however, is a two-way street. No board or CEO can operate effectively without input from the owning family. The family has to voice its reactions to information provided by the board and top management and to report any family developments that could impact on the enterprise and its governance. Examples of the latter are significant changes to the family's value statement or a major change in the shareholding distribution, such as one family branch buying out another or the need for the firm to buy back shares. If the family would like to change the firm's basic organisational structure (in Bergman's

case, for example, to move from an operating company to a holding
company structure with subsidiaries that in time could be partially
floated), clearly the board must be involved. Likewise, should the family
want to get out of certain businesses or markets (as happened with many
family companies during the apartheid era in South Africa), this must be
communicated to the board. In other words, any family decision that will
impact on strategic or major operational decisions must be conveyed
immediately to those who are running the enterprise. Failure to do so in a
timely fashion will almost inevitably lead to chaos.


## BECOMING AND/OR STAYING EDUCATED

At the very least enlightened owners have to understand how a business
(and particularly *their* business) operates. This involves knowing the
probable determinants of success and failure and being able to understand company documentation and reports from the board and top
management when delivered at the family assemblies and annual general
meetings.

All this seems self-evident, but can be extremely difficult to realise when
a family is in the fourth or fifth generation and numbers, say, 250
shareholders – few if any of whom work in the family enterprise. In the
Bergman family a large number of professions are represented and the
levels of education vary widely. While many family members have been to
university, their fields of study often had little to do with business, finance
or economics. Some of the women are full-time homemakers; others are
involved in professions far removed from the business in which the
enterprise is involved, such as music or dance teaching. A significant
proportion may not be able to read and understand profit and loss
accounts and balance sheets.

Thus in our view enlightened ownership goes beyond the simple giving
and receiving of information. It involves having enough basic business
education to *understand* what the company is distributing to its owners.
More than one of the Bergman workshop participants vowed to take a
course in 'how to read a financial statement' or basic accounting. Several
family companies facilitate this process by launching quite extensive
educational programmes as remedial measures as well as providing
'stretching' ones for those already cognisant of the basics.[3] The result is
much better informed family discussions on company matters and a
better balance of influence among the shareholders. The MBAs and those
experienced in management have new discussion partners 'who speak

their language', thereby increasing the probability of quality decision making by all the owners.

## UNDERSTANDING LEGAL RIGHTS AND RESPONSIBILITIES

It is striking how many family shareholders in cousins' confederation enterprises do not have the slightest inkling of the rights and duties of ownership. Hence, it is practically impossible for them to vote responsibly as they do not know whether or not what they are doing (not to mention what the board and top management are doing) is legal. With the increasing interest shown by law makers, regulators and other stake-holders of the firm in its governance, it is becoming mandatory for owners to be fully up to date on what the law and other regulations say about their role.

Once again, the family council would be well advised to ensure that the family is apprised of the current status of pertinent laws and regulations. To this end the company lawyer would make an excellent speaker at a family assembly meeting.

## STOCK LIQUIDITY MECHANISMS

A potentially serious cause of family squabbling is that non-active shareholders may feel bound by golden manacles to the family enterprise. Unlike the shareholders in Stage 1 and Stage 2 family companies, many shareholders in cousins' confederations may feel no emotional ties to a company that was founded many decades ago by an unknown ancestor. On paper their net worth may look impressive, but in reality the inherited shares can be seen as an untappable source of money. Family firms tend to reinvest much of their profits in the businesss, causing (usually but not always) non-active shareholders to complain not only about the illiquidity of their shares but also about the 'pittance' they receive in the form of dividends. Negative comparisons are made with what they believe they could have received from the same capital had it been invested in other stocks and/or bonds. For many shareholders in certain families, the dividends received may be the only source of income, or the greatest part thereof. They look with envy at the salary and perks enjoyed by their siblings or cousins who have the luck or privilege to work in the family firm. This is not an uncommon scenario in cousins' confederations and it can spell disaster. The centrifugal forces may become so strong that family cohesion disintegrates and the pressure to go partially or totally public may become irresistible. There is nothing inherently bad about going public (most long-lasting family enterprises consider or actually do so at some point in their history). However, one of the assumptions of this chapter is that key members of the family wish the firm to remain totally private.

The authors believe that enlightened ownership requires the creation of mechanisms that will allow family owners to increase the liquidity of their shares, or at least have access to family or family enterprise resources (for example loans) to meet their liquidity needs. Internal stockmarkets are far from uncommon and usually have tight rules about who can be sold shares, how often and at what (usually discounted) price. Such systems, if well designed and communicated, can act as a significant safety valve to reduce family conflict and increase the possibility of pruning the family tree (which many cousins' confederations find a desirable objective).

We would offer one caveat if the family wants to remain relatively cohesive: do not make being a shareholder a condition for acceptance by the family. This may seem frivolous, but we have encountered several Stage 2 and Stage 3 families who have effectively expelled 'wayward' shareholders, basically finding them guilty of treason. They are no longer invited to Christmas dinners or to the family compound for holidays. Birthday cards are no longer sent. This not only crushes the feelings of those excluded but can also bitterly divide the remaining family share-holders, as they are almost inevitably forced to take a position for or against the departing shareholders. We know of one example where the resulting bitterness led to the decision that the family no longer wanted to be in business together and a very profitable, 100-year-old firm was sold out. This happened several years ago but the recriminations echo to this day.

## REALISTIC BUT DEMANDING EXPECTATIONS

If the above descriptors are in place, the enlightened owner is in a much better position to undertake yet another important task: to convey his or her realistic yet demanding expectations to the board of directors and top management. Enlightened ownership does not mean sitting back and uncritically endorsing whatever positions are taken by the board and top management. Too often this is the case with non-active, ill-informed, family shareholders. There is a need to ensure that the representatives of the owners comply with the spirit and the letter of the family statements as they govern the enterprise. This requires a willingness and ability to ask tough questions and demand clear answers.

However the demands made on the board and top management must be realistic as well as complying with the guidelines on the appropriate roles of the three critical governance institutions: the family, the board of directors and top management (particularly the CEO). Care should be taken not to kill the goose that lays the golden eggs or to create the conditions where competent directors and top management believe that the family is destroying the ability of those active in the business to govern it in the best interests of the owners and the other stakeholders. One common example is dividend policy. While the owners can legally insist on huge pay-out ratios to the short-term advantage of the family, they must take care that these demands do not jeopardise the financial future of the firm if they wish to keep the enterprise viable for future generations.

## SPREAD THE NEWS

This descriptor of enlightened ownership is of a somewhat different nature than its predecessors and potentially very controversial. It relates to what family shareholders can do to enhance the public reputation of private ownership in general and family ownership in particular.

Family owners and their enterprises are notoriously secretive and prize confidentiality. Many, sometimes valid, reasons are given for this tendency to stay out of the public arena, for example the need to protect strategic plans from the prying eyes of competitors, preventing unacceptable wage demands by keeping the books closed to employees, minimising the tax bite and so on.

The countervailing arguments are many. This very secretiveness invites investigative journalists to probe deeply into the affairs of large (and not so large) family enterprises, often resulting in exposés that badly distort the truth. Even if the facts are correct, there is a natural tendency to emphasise the dramatically negative. The social and economic impact of large cousins' confederation companies such as Cargill, to take one example of a multi-billion dollar family firm, is such that it could be argued that the public has the right to know what is going on.

Enlightened owners of particularly large companies have realised that their traditional secrecy is counterproductive in the long term for family firms in general and their own in particular. Hence, they publish annual reports and other documents that are as fully informative as the best of those produced by publicly traded companies, despite the fact that there may be no legal requirement to do so. Relevant data (both good and bad) are available to employees, suppliers, customers and the public in general. Regular updates are given to the business press. The A. Ahlström Corporation of Finland and the Axel Johnson Group of Sweden are two excellent examples to be emulated. With this openness the credibility of family enterprises is increased and a more realistic picture can start to develop in the public's mind of the vital contributions being made by family enterprises to, for example, the economic development of society.

At the micro level, individual enlightened owners can do much more to tell the good news about family enterprises, their own included, in the circles in which they operate. Without boasting or divulging confidential information, they can talk to friends, business colleagues and members of the associations to which they belong about what their firms are doing to market new products, expand geographically, provide better working conditions for their employees, provide new employment, respond to societal problems and so on. There is so much good news to tell, and keeping it hidden under the proverbial blanket often does an enormous disservice to private and family enterprises. Luckily there are signs in various countries that the situation is improving in this regard. The favourable development of family enterprises and the public policy initiatives needed to back it up cannot help, in our view, but be bolstered. Our guess is that the longevity of these firms will tend to increase as a result.

## SHARE THE WEALTH

This penultimate descriptor will find a sympathetic audience in North America, but possibly less so in other parts of the world. Private philanthropy is well established in the United States, and it is estimated that more than US$25 billion will be given away for charitable purposes by individuals, families, family charitable foundations and corporations in the 1990s. In fact charitable foundations have become big business in themselves, to the point where specialised consultants have sprung up and professional associations founded. One important example of the latter is the Council of Foundations, which groups 1200 (of which 40 per cent are family foundations) grant-making organisations in the United States and several other countries.

Charitable foundations, or charitable trusts as they are called in the UK, serve as many purposes as the different founders have been able to imagine. They may have as little as a million US dollars in assets or up to several billion. The grants may be large or small, focused on broad aims, geographically constrained or have world-wide beneficiaries. Most, however, share a common characteristic: they have been funded by wealthy private individuals or families whose assets have derived directly or indirectly from the activities of family enterprises.

The following are some relatively well-known examples of philanthropic donations. Andrew Carnegie funded 1000 public libraries early in this century – not to mention the famous Carnegie Hall in New York. All told, Carnegie gave away an estimated US$3.5 billion in today's dollar value. The chairman of Home Depot, Bernard Marcus, plans to leave all of his US$850 million in Home Depot stock to the Marcus Foundation, which will support education and the handicapped. John Edward Anderson, a California beverage distributor, gave US$15 million to the University of California – Los Angeles business school in 1987. Claude Pennington, a Louisiana oil and gas tycoon, contributed US$125 million towards the construction of a nutrition centre. The Wolfson Foundation, established in 1955 by the owners of Great Universal Stores (UK), in 1993 alone gave £18.6 million in grants to medical, scientific and educational causes. Oxford and Cambridge have colleges named after the family. The box below on the annual Lego prize is another example.

One fascinating example of philanthropy comes from Hong Kong. The Kadoorie family derived their wealth from the China Light & Power Company, a monopoly that supplied electricity to Kowloon and the New Territories. Second-generation brothers Lawrence and Horace Kadoorie rebuilt the company (and diversified into hotels) after the ravages of the Japanese occupation and the upheavals of the communist revolution in China. Both brothers were great believers in self-help and self-sufficiency, and these values motivated a large part of their philanthropic giving. The most dramatic example was their practical response to the influx of an estimated 300 000 refugees fleeing from China to Hong Kong in the mid 1950s. The Kadoorie Agricultural Aid Association was instrumental in resettling this mass of humanity in the New Territories. Each family was given two chickens and a pair of piglets so that a smallholding could be established. Training was provided to them on the Kadoorie farm, located near one of the company's power stations. As a result of this focused philanthropy, a community of poultry farmers, pig breeders and vegetable growers was established, to the benefit not only of the displaced families but all of Hong Kong.

There are many reasons for creating family foundations with philanthropic goals, ranging from the highly pragmatic to the highly

## A Prize for the Children of the World

The Danish toy manufacturer, Lego, was founded in 1932 by Ole Kirk Christiansen. It is now led by Kjeld Kirk Kristiansen, a member of the third generation of the family. In 1985, moved by a deep commitment to children, the Lego group founded an annual international prize of Dkr1 000 000 (some US$180 000). The prize is awarded every year to a person or an institution that has made an extraordinary contribution to the development of children. The symbol of the prize is the *Ygdrasil*, the tree of life in Nordic mythology.

In recent years the Lego prize has been awarded to such institutions as:

- The Saek Dong Organisation in Korea, which helps children discover the wonderful world of stories and fairy tales, theatre and songs.
- The Children's Centre of Sports and Rest in Poland, which provides annual holidays for disadvantaged Polish youngsters aged 6–16. Partly as a result of the award of the Lego Prize, the camp has recently attracted a great deal of attention and the number of children visiting has quadrupled over the past five years.
- The Hole in the Wall Gang Camp in Connecticut, a special summer camp opened in 1988 by Paul Newman and his wife Joanne Woodward. The main aim of the camp is to provide a fun holiday for seriously ill children who would not normally be able to enjoy such a holiday.

Former winners also include a school for the handicapped in Morocco, the Danish Society for Prevention of Child Abuse and Neglect and many other institutions.

The Lego prize has been awarded to a rich diversity of outstanding people, projects and organisations and has helped to put a smile on many a child's face.

philosophical. Clearly in many instances the primary motive is to avoid taxes. Furthermore some founders, such as Bernard Marcus mentioned above, believe that inherited wealth is potentially corruptive and even a curse, and thus insist it must be given away outside the family. David Packard, cofounder of Hewlett-Packard, may have been of this school, as it is said that he made charitable donations of more that US$5 billion before he died.

More common, in our experience, are motives that relate to strongly held family values concerning the responsibility to society of those who have wealth. Benjamin Franklin urged his fellow countrymen to use their wealth for the public good. Many families see philanthropy as the means to perform their duty to be compassionate to those less fortunate than themselves. Others see their charitable foundations as a concrete way of returning to society a portion of the wealth that the community has allowed them to accumulate over generations.

From the standpoint of enlightened ownership, there are strong arguments in favour of devoting some of the family's energy to philanthropy. The foundation can provide meaningful work to members of the family who are not active in the business, thereby reinforcing linkages with the family and its business. The foundation board can be a venue for further strengthening family ties and commitment to its fundamental values, as reflected in the foundation's aims and objectives. Many foundations have created adjunct boards that report to the main board and are composed of younger family members. The junior boards have their own charitable budget and all spending has to be accounted for, thereby giving the members valuable management experience in a highly complex field. Philanthropic work is no sinecure and requires professional skills and governance systems of the highest order.[4] Finally, foundations may provide an ideal answer to the perennial question, 'Is there life after retiring as CEO of the family company?' It is not uncommon for a retired CEO to become the chairperson of the foundation's board and take great pleasure in using his or her skills in this new field.

Beyond the potential benefits discussed above, competently managed family foundations can bring direct and indirect benefits to the family firm itself.[5] In many countries philanthropists are highly revered, and attaching the family's name to 'good works' can enhance the reputation of its firm. This public relations spin-off may be reflected in enhanced customer good-will. Furthermore, donating private money to improve the social infrastructure of the community can lead to enhanced human potential (for example improved education, less poverty, greater self-sufficiency, entrepreneurial spirit), which can create a better climate and resource base not only for the family firm itself but for all of society. From such results, 'win–win' situations can multiply to everyone's benefit.


## CLARITY OF THE FAMILY'S VALUES AS OWNERS

Implicit in all the above descriptors of enlightened ownership is the necessity for the family to make clear what its values are, what it stands for as a family (preferably in written form as already indicated) so that the family, the board and top management can appreciate the 'rules of the game' as it is to be played by the family and the business it owns. We listed the Bergman's family values in Chapter 4.

The Mogi Family constitution also reproduced in Chapter 4, presents a different set of values but similarly serves to make explicit the values by which the family as well as its enterprise will live and be judged. And both families have undertaken the task of ensuring that their values will be respected by all concerned. This, in our view, is a critical determinant of enlightened ownership.


## CONCLUSION

This last chapter has reflected the authors' experience in terms of what cousins' confederations (and by extrapolation, *mutatis mutandis*, even Stage 1 and Stage 2 companies) can do to create the conditions for enlightened ownership to develop. It has broken totally new ground in that little if any work has been done on the very concept of enlightened ownership. At this early stage, the ten propositions can be offered only as hypotheses that will need reformulation and additional research. This said, we strongly believe that enlightened ownership plays a vital role in the governance of family enterprises and can help families to increase not only the robustness of their families but also of the enterprises they own – for as long as the family wishes to stay in business together.


## NOTES

1. For a detailed description of this workshop, see A. G. Lank and F. Neubauer, 'A Cousins' Confederation as Enlightened Owners: A Case Study', *Family Business: Key Challenges II*, Lausanne, IMD, 1996, pp. 26–8.

2. The authors believe that, given the vital importance of the board of directors in the governance process (see Chapter 5), it is imperative that the 'rules of the game' be made clear with regard to its role, composition and so on. It is only the owning family that can and should undertake this task. The issue of family involvement, if any, at the board (and top management) level must be made explicit.

3. Developing and implementing educational programmes for the family is a classical role for family councils. These programmes need not be restricted to subjects closely related to understanding the family's business but could range from art appreciation, to how to invest in the stock market, to career options for the new generation.

4. The governance of family foundations deserves a fully-fledged research project in its own right. Very little is known on the subject.

5. One Greek family we know, which for generations has been involved in the wine trade, has endowed a wine museum. This is greatly appreciated by the local community and visitors alike. While the primary aim was not to sell more wine, it is reasonable to assume that the wine museum might spark a desire to purchase wine, including the family firm's own fine vintages. One could call this enlightened self-interest.

# Index

262